DATE DUE

AP 27 00			

DEMCO 38-296

Dickens and New Historicism

Dickens and New Historicism

William J. Palmer

St. Martin's Press
New York

ISBN 0-312-17427-6

Library of Congress Cataloging-in-Publication Data
Palmer, William J., 1943-
    Dickens and new historicism / by William J. Palmer
        p.   cm.
    Includes bibliographical references and index.
    ISBN 0-312-17427-6
    1. Dickens, Charles, 1812-1870—Knowledge—History. 2. Literature
and history—Great Britain—History—19th century. 3. Literature
and society—Great Britain—History—19th century. 4. Historical
fiction, English—History and criticism. 5. Dickens, Charles,
literature. 8. Historicism. I. Title.
PR4592.H5P35   1997
823′ .8—dc21   97-16019
                                                            CIP

Permission
"The Movement of History in *Our Mutual Friend*" by William J. Palmer,
reprinted by permission of the copyright holder, the Modern Language
Association of America.

Design by Acme Art, Inc.
First edition: December, 1997
10 9 8 7 6 5 4 3 2 1

This book is dedicated to the memory of Professor Joseph M. Duffy
of The University of Notre Dame

Contents

Acknowledgements

An earlier version of Chapter Two, "Dickens and the Eighteenth Century," appeared in *Dickens Studies Annual*.

An earlier version of Chapter Three, "Dickens and Shipwreck," appeared in *Dickens Studies Annual*.

An earlier version of Chapter Five, "The Movement of History in *Our Mutual Friend*," appeared in *PMLA: Publications of the Modern Language Association*. Reprinted by permission of the copyright holder, the Modern Language Association of America.

My appreciation to my translator, Rebecca King, Purdue University.

List of Abbreviations*

Abbreviations for Dickens's works:

BH   *Bleak House*
BR   *Barnaby Rudge*
CC   *The Christmas Carol*
DC   *David Copperfield*
D&S   *Dombey and Son*
GE   *Great Expectations*
HT   *Hard Times*
HW   *Household Words*
LD   *Little Dorrit*
MC   *Martin Chuzzlewit*
NN   *Nicholas Nickleby*
OCS   *The Old Curiosity Shop*
OMF   *Our Mutual Friend*
OT   *Oliver Twist*
PP   *The Pickwick Papers*
TTC   *A Tale of Two Cities*

List of other frequently cited works:

CW   *Caleb Williams*
JA   *Joseph Andrews*
RR   *Roderick Random*
TLM   *The London Merchant*
TS   *Tristram Shandy*

*All in-text citations for Dickens's works and for other frequently cited works will be noted in parentheses following the quotation by a title abbreviation, a book number in roman numerals, and a chapter number in arabic numerals, for example, (*HT*, II, 8). I use the notation style of chapter number rather than page number because it allows the reader to find the cited passage in any edition of the work in question.

Dickens and New Historicism

ONE

Dickens and New Historicism

At a roundtable meeting of the Crummles' acting company, Nicholas Nickleby is graced with the patronizing presence of a "literary gentleman" who "had dramatized in his time two hundred and forty-seven novels, as fast as they had come out—some of them faster than they had come out." The literary gentleman smugly declares, "When I dramatize a book, sir, . . . that's fame for its author" and remains undaunted when Nicholas sarcastically replies "So Richard Turpin, Tom King, and Jerry Abershaw [all highwaymen] have handed down to fame the names of those upon whom they committed their most impudent robberies?" Naturally, their conversation turns to Shakespeare who also "derived some of his plots from old tales and legends." This literary gentleman, who refers fondly to Shakespeare as "Bill" as if they had just eaten breakfast together, mistakenly thinks that Nicholas is making a complimentary comparison when he describes Shakespeare as a writer who "brought within the magic circle of his genius traditions peculiarly adapted for his purpose, and turned familiar things into constellations which should enlighten the world for ages" (*NN*, XL, vii). What this literary gentleman doesn't seem to understand is the difference between an exploitative literary imperialist and an artist like Shakespeare, who could clearly see the evolution of an idea, a story, an influence, an image, within time's empire, the realm of evolving history. This literary gentleman, whom young Nicholas Nickleby exposes, is akin to Joseph Conrad's rapacious "pilgrims" and "flabby devils" in *Heart of Darkness*. But young Nickleby is speaking for Dickens here also and, in doing so, reveals Dickens's overarching sense that past history, in all its events, people, texts, ideas, and images, must necessarily be a part of present action (and literary production) in order for a coherent future to evolve. For Dickens, time exists as an interactive dynamic in which past, present, and future all co-exist and interact equally. Neither the past nor the future can ever be marginalized for the benefit of the present. The present cannot rapaciously exploit the past or short-sightedly ignore the future for the sake of present profit. Young Nickleby and Dickens both see in this straw man—in his hollowly presentist imperialistic literary production—an utter lack of any philosophy of history, of any relation to either the past or the future. Comical and sarcastic as this conversation between young Nicholas Nickleby and the literary gentleman may be, the exchange, nonetheless, does strike at the core of the nature of Dickens's (and Shakespeare's) alchemic imagination; its power to turn "familiar things into constellations," its relation to the past, to history, to "old tales and legends," as well as to the present "familiar things" that bring his fictions to such vibrant life.

Like Shakespeare, Dickens uses everything in his novels. His memory is like a gigantic portmanteau out of which, at the proper time and appropriate place, he can pull anything that he needs and transform it by the alchemy of his imagination into art. The stuff of his own life—the books he has read, the stories he has been told, and the plays he has seen and acted in, the history that preceded his life, the people he meets and the sights he sees on his notorious night walks about the city—fills his curious portmanteau and feeds the fires of his art.

If Wordsworth's belief that by "a certain colouring of imagination . . . ordinary things should be presented to the mind in an unusual aspect"[1] is a Romantic view of the relationship of the artist's imagination to the available world, then Dickens, as well, might be called a Romantic. But Wordsworth's view was the innocent view of an eager poet unaware that he was perched precariously on the brink of a literary revolution. Dickens's relationship to past history and the present revolution gave him the sharper edged, more complex, perhaps more cynical view of the Victorian "social realist" who has no choice but to consider his art as product (in a quite Marxian sense) as well as process. But still it is the process of writing histories that interested Dickens, for in his novels he repeatedly meditates on how the past caused the present and how the future might unfold.

For Dickens, the writing of a novel was the plundering of memory. Like graverobbing, that honorable profession of Jerry Cruncher, the amicable "resurrection man" from A Tale of Two Cities, in his fiction Dickens is constantly exhuming and resurrecting the past in all of its forgotten forms. But there is a reason for Dickens's fascination with both past and future. In a sense, he is like Dr. Frankenstein. He pieces together and resurrects the past in order to make the present and the future viable. Dickens's creations, his novels, his histories, are carefully nurtured to keep them from becoming monstrous. He realizes that the social historian bears a moral responsibility toward his creations that demands that those creations be allowed to act on their own terms and speak in their own diverse voices. Only then can future history be given life. Little wonder that postmodernist critics are almost universally reading Mary Shelley's *Frankenstein* as a "metafiction," a fiction about the writing of fiction, for she develops the creative artist's relation to his creation in these same terms.

The New Historicism

Both Mary Shelley and Dickens are exercising a new sort of historical sense in their novelistic "tropes" (as Hayden White would call them); a sense of history in which the people who never got to speak before or were not fully attended to by the historians are given their day in court. This is a revision of history in which working people and footsoldiers are given the same voice as the Captains of Industry and the military Generals. It is a verticalized history in which the life, art, thought, and work that exist beneath the horizontal line of factual historical events are acknowledged and described rather than ignored. It is a history in which children, women, the destitute, the criminal, the sick, the deformed, and the insane co-exist with the rich, the great, the notorious, and the powerful.

Is Charles Dickens a historical novelist? Sometimes, certainly, in the traditional sense of historical fiction, he is. In *Barnaby Rudge* and *A Tale of Two Cities*, he is, like Sir Walter Scott, most certainly a traditional historical novelist who places his characters in the midst of the horizontal line of events that the official master texts of history describe. In both of these novels, however, he also carefully verticalizes his depiction of history by splitting his time and text between the great men and the great events that drive the horizontal movement of the master text of revolution and the followers and footsoldiers who populate the vertical depths of the revolutions and tend to be run over and forgotten in the forward motion of the juggernaut of history.

Perhaps a familiar episode from *A Tale of Two Cities* best represents Dickens's discomfort with the big event/great man emphasis of traditional history. Early in the novel, Monsieur the Marquis climbs into his coach in Paris and is driven at breakneck speed through the narrow winding streets with "furious recklessness"—according to "the fierce patrician custom of hard driving" (II, 7)—until the inevitable happens: his coach runs over and kills a small child. But, like traditional history itself, Monsieur the Marquis pays little attention to such an insignificant event. He scowls and sneers at the poor people of that Paris slum who gather about the tiny corpse and impede his implacable course. He is more worried about the damage to his horses than about the death of the child. He tosses the poor mourning family a coin and drives on. After all, history moves by horse and children must learn to stay out of the way.

Thus, if Dickens is in some ways a traditional historical novelist, he is also acutely aware that history involves much more than the events and personalities of its master texts; that history cannot just bull its way toward the future, ignorant of the culture, marginalized voices, modes of expression, and subtexts that lie beneath, and contribute to, that master text of history.

Therefore, if Dickens is sometimes a traditional historical novelist, he is almost all of the time a "New Historicist" in his novels, a novelist who "decenters" the portrayal of history in his fiction. Dickens sees history less as a horizontal line of facts and events, and more as a vertical pit within which the disenfranchised masses find themselves trapped, either to perish (and disappear from history altogether) or to fight their way out to make some contributory impression upon what Michel Foucault calls "historical consciousness." Dickens never, out of neglect, rapacious exploitation, or intentional suppression, allows history to become monstrous. Instead, he listens to its many voices (Mikhail Bakhtin's "dialogized heteroglossia")[2] and forms a benevolent philosophy of history that functions as a fulcrum between the past and the future.

For Foucault, it is necessary to stop trying to understand history as "some great evolutionary process,"[3] but rather it should be understood as a web or network of events, peoples, texts, and contexts. In Dickens's *Hard Times*, Stephen Blackpool, a poor textile mill laborer, a man caught in the implacable juggernaut of Utilitarian history, falls into the Old Hell Shaft and disappears from the world for four crucial days, days when he might have influenced its history. In a sense, this is Dickens's metaphor for what happens to the disenfranchised, the "other," of society as horizontal traditional history pushes its implacable linear progress toward the future.

Dickens, then, calls into question, both directly and metaphorically, the very philosophy of history upon which the genre of the historical novel is based. But whether he is a traditional historical novelist or a "New Historicist" novelist participating in a network of literary paradigms—defined in the twentieth century by the likes of Michel Foucault, Mikhail Bakhtin, Hayden White, and Dominick LaCapra—a similar set of questions concerning his writing of and use of history need to be posed:

1. How does he employ history throughout the body of his work? For what purposes? Ideologically? As social commentary? Philosophically, or as a means of defining and exploring philosophical themes?

2. Does Dickens, either in individual novels or consistently throughout his expansive canon, develop a philosophy of history or, to use Foucault's word, does he "situate" himself within any particular set of historical contexts?

These are not, by any means, new questions to be asked either of literature in general or of Dickens's fiction in particular. Historically-focused literary critics have been asking these questions throughout the twentieth century, and, at certain times, as from the 1940s to the late 1960s when New Criticism ruled the roost, they have even been ostracized for asking them. But, more recently, following the lead of social philosophers like Foucault and historiographers like White and LaCapra, literary critics have been answering these questions in more diverse ways, with a more complex vision of society, history, and culture, heeding of the voices that provide a complete new archive of historical documents or "chronicles" (to use White's term) upon which to draw. As a result of this recent, more sophisticated theory's positing a "New Historicism," all manner of new and complex avenues of entry into the Dickens world have been opened.

History as Dialectic

But history, as it participates in and reflects upon the plots, characters, metaphors, themes, and, most of all, worlds of novels does not just involve a "remembrance of things past"; it is not simply a line of "evolution" toward some higher desired future. History is the past and present interacting, establishing a vibrant dialogue, with the future. History, at best, exists only as an idea, a conception not embodied, certainly not born.

Like water forming a wave, history is a phenomenon of flux and motion. It moves in many directions simultaneously, like a wave whose momentum determines its break point. In nineteenth-century England, Dickens, along with philosophers like Marx and Engels, scientists like Charles Darwin, and cultural historians like Richard Francis Burton, found himself riding the crest of that wave, balancing the eighteenth century, the age of Revolution and Romanticism that followed, and his own strange, puzzling, frightening Victorian age against one another in his art—and doing it with what now we can call a rather visionary twentieth-century existential sensibility.

Perhaps the contemporary American historical novelist E. L. Doctorow's view of his own dilemma approximates Dickens's situation in the nineteenth century. In a recent interview, Doctorow insisted:

> The truth is, I don't see my books as historical novels. My interest has more to do with myth than with history. . . . You aspire to writing a book so that the difference between periods—between the author's time and the characters' time—disappears. There is in every age a presumption of modernity. We have computers and CD-ROM and all the rest, but in 1871 they had the rotary press, which gave birth to the modern newspaper, and they sent cables through wires under the ocean. . . . When you write about the past, you are always reflecting on your own age.[4]

Dickens found himself similarly situated historically. Aside from his overtly historical novels, *Barnaby Rudge* and *A Tale of Two Cities*, both set in the late eighteenth century, and his readily datable semi-autobiographical works, *David Copperfield* and *Great Expectations*, Dickens's novels tend to be set rather fuzzily in conveniently unspecific historical time. Some can be dated rather precisely from interior evidence, such as the building of railroads in *Dombey and Son* and the growth of the union movement in *Hard Times*, but most, though clearly Victorian in temporal setting, are not really tied to a particular year. Why did Dickens choose to not set *Bleak House* precisely in 1851 or *Little Dorrit* in 1855? Because as Doctorow wrote and Dickens knew, "when you write about the past, you are always reflecting on your own age."

In an essay titled "History, Totality, Opposition: The New Historicism and *Little Dorrit*," Joseph W. Childers rather clearly offers Dickens (and Doctorow, who, at least in his most recent historical novel, *The Waterworks*, is a late twentieth-century novelist writing a Victorian novel) a path out of the dilemma of just how traditionally historical a novelist must be. Childers writes that the "question of whether to historicize has never been much of a question for critics of nineteenth-century literature." He goes on to argue that the "New Historicist" critics of nineteenth-century literature embark upon "projects [that] attempt in diverse ways to reexamine representations of middle-class or patriarchal Victorian society, to challenge descriptions of the period as one of consensus, and to reconsider accounts of Victorian literature as a product of a shared pool of ideas and goals for society."[5] For Childers, the projects of New Historicist critics, then, are projects of reexamining and challenging the consensus or master-text views of Victorian society. But that is a very limited view of what the historicizing project can potentially do.

History as Archaeology

By coming at the documents—"the chronicles" of history—from a completely different direction, the New Historicist can generate drastically new readings of those documents. Or the New Historicist, examining what Dominick LaCapra calls the "mechanisms of diffusion"[6] of history, may unearth new documents, different sources of history, that may present a history parallel to, convex to, moving in a completely opposite direction from, or lying submerged beneath the long accepted master text of history. The New Historicist project, then, must be revisionist; simultaneously widening and deepening and archaeologically discovering new dimensions of the accepted master text.

Conversely, by either reviewing or archaeologically expanding history, the New Historicist critic of literature, will also discover new ways of reading canonical texts, whose issues may be seen from an at least partially different perspective. Thus, New Historicism is a project that reexamines the extant master texts of history and the documents from which those master texts were composed, but also digs up and translates new documents, artifacts, social attitudes and situations, and, by studying them, adds to the master texts. As a result, the historicist purview is widened by examining new historical sources that were either not found, not considered (ignored as inconsequential), or intentionally never consulted (suppressed) in the composing of the original historical master text. More often than not, the newly unearthed sources are comprised of the documents, voices, and cultures, of the disenfranchised, marginalized, and unempowered members of society from the time and place of the master text's composition.

An elaborate metaphor for the New Historicist project is the Argentinian film *The Official Story* (1985). *The Official Story* is a film about a family coming apart at the seams, but it is also a film about the corruption of the official story of history, the conscious manipulation of history under fascist rule. The film relates a bourgeois woman's political awakening to the plight of the *"desparicidos"* (the disappeared) under evil death squad terrorism—state terrorism. It is also, however, about the awakening of the woman, who is a high school history teacher, to the layered "truth" of history as opposed to the "official story" of history. As a result of this subtext, it may be the most direct New Historicist film project yet undertaken, Oliver Stone notwithstanding. It is a truly "metahistorical" film—a historical film about history itself. Early in the film, the woman proclaims to her students that "history is the memory of the people," but one of the students challenges her and charges that "history is written by assassins." By the film's end, the woman has learned to reject the false, one-dimensionality of the official story of history and to explore the wider, deeper levels of true, new historicism. [7]

History as Popular Culture

In a less sinister vein, newly sought-out sources of history may simply have seemed too ordinary, too mundane, for the composers of the master text of history to consider, especially if they were academics operating prior to the eras of popular culture and cultural studies. Susan R. Horton writes that "for the New Historicist critic, cultural practices and attitudes are most happily studied in the everyday practices of life: how we file wills, do laundry, keep pets."[8] Certainly in the Dickens world, the logistics of everyday life, such as the filing of wills in *Bleak House* or the keeping of pets in *Oliver Twist* and *Barnaby Rudge*, under the alchemy of the novelist's imagination become symbolic representations of moments in history when the disempowered members of society found expression in cultural acts available only to them. Krook's certainty, though he cannot decipher it, that an important historical document is filed somewhere in the anarchic confusion of his rag and bottle shop is symbolic of the certainty of the lower, illiterate classes that their voices are not being heard because they have not been provided with the tools whereby they can enter into the master text of history's project. Every time Bill Sykes kicks his dog he represents the underclass' frustration with its disempowerment—its inability to express itself in terms other than violence to itself.

Rereading history from new perspectives, archaeologically discovering new voices, widening and deepening our view of history by examining more closely the historical everyday, are all aspects of the New Historicist project. As John Kronik writes,

> Once upon a time history was an innocent word in an innocent world. In that time, long ago, professors and people lived happily. They didn't know there was an old history and a new one. . . . They went about their daily labors in the simple belief that history was facts, occurrences, story, unsuspecting that it was, instead, discourse and narrative. . . . Times have changed. History, whether national or literary, isn't what it used to be. Stripped of its luster, history, when not berated or ignored, is now the site of anxiety and wrangling. . . . History's duality as event and account of that event, word and word of that word (I borrow the phrase from Barthes), is the substance of its condition.[9]

But as Kronik emphasizes, equal to the repositioning of the historian, the archaeologicalizing of the research, the refocusing upon the popular culture, is the deciphering of the extant master texts; what Hayden White calls learning to read by "emplotment."

History as Many Voices

Deciphering the "emplotted" discourses of history is the first step in the project of creating new counter discourses to old history. New Historicists, having read the master texts of history with a skeptical, revisionist eye tend to inquire into what was swept under the carpet by the mythic readings of history that developed in late nineteenth-century England and Western Europe.[10] Michel Foucault argues, and Dickens certainly exemplifies, that "nineteenth-century man did not simply discover history: he needed to discover history, or, as it were, to remake history on his own terms."[11] For Foucault, nineteenth-century man took on "the task of re-discovering in the depths of himself . . . a historicity which was linked to him essentially."[12] For a Victorian like Dickens, this historicist task, which he embraced as a central facet of his fiction, was a very personal, existential act occasioned, certainly, by the uneasiness of his age. Part of the uneasiness that Dickens felt was with the surface consensus of Victorian life, which one of Dickens's strenuous night walks through the city—with all of its poverty, crime, and confrontation—would immediately dispel. But the uneasiness that Dickens felt was also occasioned by a personal need to understand, from the bottom up, the truth of his times as expressed in the voices of the streets.

Those voices—of the poor, the powerless, the marginalized—dispel a traditional trust in the supposed "objectivity" of the master text of history. That long-standing inclination to accept the illusion of factuality of the big event/great man "story" of traditional history without exploring the various agendas emplotted in that history is a symptom of what T. S. Eliot labeled "Bovarysme, 'the human will to see things as they are not.'" Eliot's Bovarysme is that inclination toward self-deluded historicizing that so fascinates critics of traditional Romantic history.

In his *History and Criticism*, LaCapra diagnoses the ailments of documentary history and prescribes the New Historicist cure: "all forms of historiography might benefit from modes of critical reading premised on the conviction that documents are texts that supplement or rework 'reality' and not mere sources that divulge facts about 'reality.'"[13] Robert Newson, writing about Dickens, discusses a similar sort of Bovarysme that at times afflicts the reader of the fiction of social realism. Readers must be aware, Newson writes, of "how documents which purport to represent reality are misleading and even false" to the point that what the reader thought was familiar seems instead the very opposite of the 'familiar,' the 'romantic.'"[14]

Jonathan Arac reiterates both LaCapra and Newson as he analyzes how one should read realistic fiction with a healthy dose of skepticism. He writes "neither Dickens nor Twain is absolutely, objectively critical, complacent, subversive, or anything else. If we accept [Walter] Benjamin's claim that 'there is no document of civilization which is not at the same time a document of barbarism,' then it will depend upon circumstances which aspect we emphasize. There are different ways of using cultural objects."[15] Whether historian or novelist (or New Historicist critic), the choices of the many ways to use cultural objects in the creation of a story of history, of emplotting agendas within the chosen rhetoric of a text, of seeing the world through the self-deluded eyes of Bovarysme, are discourse choices that need to be decoded and understood if the often competitive discourses of both historical and literary texts are ever to approach some dialectical synthesis. As Arac ends his argument concerning the way that texts redeploy cultural objects, quoting George Orwell, "'All art is propaganda.'"[16]

If Arac and Orwell are right, can we not apply the same principle to the discourses of history, philosophy, and economics? "When we try to make sense of such problematic topics as human nature, culture, society, and history, we never say precisely what we wish to say or mean precisely what we say," Hayden White writes in *Tropics of Discourse: Essays in Cultural Criticism.* "Our discourse always tends to slip away from our data towards the structures of consciousness with which we are trying to grasp them; or, what amounts to the same thing, the data always resist the coherency of the image which we are trying to fashion of them."[17] White defines the central problem of the composition of history. It is a discourse problem. Each historian tends to bring his or her own particular discourse agenda to the writing of history.

This resistance to the ordering process of language is the dialectic opposition that the New Historicist endeavors to synthesize. For White, that synthesis lies dormant within the already extant historical texts that need to be read with new eyes, analyzed with the new tools of literary criticism and philosophical and cultural studies, and seen as much more complex documents than they have been thought to be before. Thus, the New Historicist critic tries to find the point of synthesis between the master text of history and the new voices, documents and critical approaches that he/she applies to the rereading of that master text.

For a literary critic of Charles Dickens's novels, this rereading, rein-terpreting, and revising of the Romantic tradition of history serves as a model for critical reentry into the complexly historicized world of Dickens's fiction. Perhaps more importantly, however, although still certainly in a Romantic tradition, the New Historicist critic can define history as the main catalytic agent in the alchemical process of Dickens's imagination, which consistently transubstantiated "familiar" things into the stuff that historical stories are made of. In other words, like the New Historicist critic, Dickens tends to work from the bottom up in creating his world, his themes, his characters.

A New Historicist reading is clearly a dialectical critical act. As Marlon Ross argues, "In the last decade, an increasing number of literary scholars have refocused their attention on the problem of history, a trend that has resparked ongoing controversies over such matters as the relation between literature and history." Ross sees the New Historicism as a bridge between literature and history which does not give priority to either. He does not suggest, however, that history is just another kind of fiction.[18]

The New Historicist project, then, is an act of literary criticism verging upon detective work. As Ross puts it, "in New Historicism . . . the anecdote joins the eventuality of the historical structure (what happened when) to the structure of the historical event (why did it happen in this way) so that structure and event can reflexively explain each other without being inter-rogated by each other."[19] In his definition of the New Historicist project, Ross agrees with both Michel Foucault and Theodore B. Leinwand that this dialectic is "centered on the operations of power."[20] It is this focus upon the voices of power and on those without power that drives Dickens's alchemical transubstantiation of the anecdotes of Victorian political, social, economic, and aesthetic history into his own particular concept of the historical novel.

Especially in his panoramic anatomies of the social history of the disenfranchised, such as *Oliver Twist, Dombey and Son, Bleak House, Hard Times, Little Dorrit,* and *Our Mutual Friend,* Dickens consistently examined the struc-tural question of "why." Like his own Inspector Bucket, Dickens relentlessly pursues the "why" of historical anecdote or eventuality by restaging it in the same manner that a detective revisits the scene of a crime and minutely reconstructs the crucial act—rereads the text of that crime—as a means of understanding it and, perhaps, even solving its inherent mystery. History is always a mystery, and the historian is always a detective. The New Histor-icist reader is a detective returning to the scene in the attempt to see it anew and, thus, more clearly.

However, the first step of any New Historicist foray into the Dickens world must always be the factual reconstruction of anecdotal eventuality, the pinning down of the sources, the events, the circumstances that Dickens observed, experienced, read of and encountered on his night walks. In fact, this cautionary historicist strategy was present, albeit in a marginalized way, in Dickens criticism as early as the 1960s, well before New Historicism had become a rallying cry of postmodernist critical theory.

In *The Dickens Theatre*, which was appropriately, and possibly prophetically, subtitled "A Reassessment of the Novels," Robert Garis complained that in the critical reading of Dickens's fiction

> one might indeed go further, go anywhere, because the fact is that in all these "readings" we are on our own, making up our own novel, the kind we may like to read but not the kind Dickens wrote. Modern Dickens criticism has spawned many such "free" readings, for the discovery that he is a symbolic novelist has apparently exempted his critics from even the most elementary standards of relevance.[21]

Robert B. Partlow Jr. seconded Garis, writing that the researching of the "factual backgrounds of Dickens' novels" is a necessary first step:

> We have long known that Dickens "borrowed" people, scenes, and events from other books, his own experiences, newspaper articles, and the like, but the task of securely and finally identifying them—and, more importantly, assessing their significance in the total achievement—is hardly begun.[22]

In other words, a revisionist Dickensian project cannot just blithely embark upon "free" readings of Dickens's novels without first anchoring those readings within their historical, philosophical, economic, cultural, or literary context. For instance, a study of Dickens's fascination in his fiction with shipwreck metaphors or an analysis of his recurring character of the troubled apprentice as a marginalized "other" can be much more clearly explained by means of a verticalized historicist analysis of the many socioeconomic factors that thrust those images and those characters to the forefront of Dickens's imagination.

Many other Dickens critics, principally Richard Altick, Trevor Blount, John Butt, and Kathleen Tillotson, Peter Coveney and Ellen Moers, Phillip Collins, K. J. Fielding, Humphrey House, R. D. McMaster, John Manning, Ada Nisbet, Harry Stone, Alexander Welsh, have undertaken similar historicizings of the anecdotal phase of the New Historicist Dickensian project. They have taken particular characters, themes, social and cultural objects, and historicized them—traced their origins and identities. Their work is essential to the dialectical conversation of the structural phase that asks why particular people, events, and modes of thought were catalysts for Dickens's imagination and how, then, did he structure his fictions around them. In what Marlon Ross calls this structural phase of the New Historicist project, pertinent questions are asked of a literary work's anecdotal/historical background. This is where, in fact, history is, in the best tradition of Inspector Bucket, interrogated by art. The concern of this structural phase is, first, defining the rhetorical "emplotments" of history (the agendas embedded in both language and argument), and second, critiquing—from the perspective of power relationships—the version of history presented in the text, and, third, examining the text's own philosophy of history as expressed in its various voices (which could belong to its author, its narrator, its characters, or its language constructs). In the text's own interrogation of history, the new voices of the marginalized, the dehistoricized, tend to surface to express their hitherto neglected versions of history, and, pushing the power relationships of history one step further, try to find in their new versions some relevance to their present and future histories.

Dickens's Philosophy of History

Writing about the "deceleration and decay" of history, in Dickens's *Bleak House*, J. Hillis Miller argues that "it is impossible to stop the forward movement of things in time. Both an attempt to freeze the present as a repetition of a past time and the eternally repeated moment of expectation which awaits some definitive event in the future are essentially a denial of the proper human relation to time and to the objective world."[23] In other words, history does not stand still; it always moves forward, and man must constantly redefine his relationship to it. In this vein, a persistent thematic strain in Dickens's novelistic project is the articulation of a characteristically Victorian philosophy of history along side the interrogation of history by a whole new set of previously neglected voices (principally those of the marginalized poor).

Consistently, in every one of his novels, Dickens questions the accuracy of history, redefines history from new perspectives, and critiques from below the accepted power relationships of the master texts of history. The New Historicist approach to Dickens's fiction locates him, historicizes him, at the fulcrum of a history of ideas that balances the eighteenth-century philosophical view of man and society with the social history of the Victorian age; a balance that is meant to give the Victorians some direction for the future.

As a novelist Dickens was striving for a historical vision, attempting to ride along with the movement of history, straining to see the past more clearly in order to envision the future. Except perhaps in the first half of *The Pickwick Papers*, for Dickens, history is never nostalgic, is always revisionist, but above all it is visionary; more concerned with the future than with the past.

The title of this study of Dickens's imagination designates it as an analysis of Dickens's criticism of history, participation in history, and development of a philosophy of history that hopes to open new gates of entry into Dickens's novels. By reexamining Dickens's handling of the anecdotal possibilities of the historical entities in his fiction—characters, settings, events, cultural objects, ideas, even occupations—new readings emerge that show Dickens to be a social historian who is constantly moving between master text, parallel text, and subtext in an attempt to arrive at illuminating truths that can provide a lighthouse for the future.

For example, the most common gate of entry into *David Copperfield* is by land, the key to that gate being the early psychological trauma of Dickens's own blacking factory anecdote of social humiliation. If this gate of entry is taken, then *David Copperfield* indeed appears to be an autobiographical apologia, as critics of the 1940s and 1950s, such as George Orwell or Edmund Wilson in "The Two Scrooges," termed it. But what happens if a reader chooses to enter *David Copperfield* by sea? What happens if one reads that novel in terms of one of its most prominent and controlling metaphors, that of shipwreck. The result is a much more expansive, sociohistorical reading in which psychological struggles become secondary to a historical commentary on the loss of faith and heroism in the face of the "Condition of England" in the 1840s. Thus *David Copperfield* can be seen as part of the historical project that Carlyle undertook in both *Sartor Resartus* and *Past and Present* and that Tennyson represented not only in *In Memoriam*, but also in *The Idylls of the King* and "Locksley Hall." All of these writers were warning the Victorians of the dangers their society, driven by the philosophical principles of a heartless Utilitarianism and the economic principles of a ruthless Social Darwinism, was blindly sailing toward. In their works, these writers attempted to build lighthouses to warn the Victorians off of the dangerous reefs upon which they would most certainly run aground.

Abundant evidence exists that shows Dickens was very aware of his own philosophical participation in the writing of a new "Realist" history to replace the old "Romantic" conception of history. In his preface to *Oliver Twist* (written for the 1838 first edition's three volume publication), Dickens writes in answer to the critics who had objected to his novel on "high moral grounds":

> It was, it seemed, a coarse and shocking circumstance, that some of the characters in these pages are chosen from the most criminal and degraded in London's population; that Sikes is a thief and Fagin a receiver of stolen goods; that the boys are pickpockets, and the girl is a prostitute. . . .
>
> But I had never met (except in Hogarth) with the miserable reality. It appeared to me that to draw a knot of such associates in crime as really did exist; to paint them in all their deformity, in all their wretchedness, in all the squalid misery of their lives; to show them as they really are . . . would be to attempt something which was needed, and which would be a service to society. . . .
>
> In every book I know, where such characters are treated of, allurements and fascinations are thrown around them. Even in *The Beggar's Opera*, the thieves are represented as leading a life which is rather to be envied than otherwise. (*OT*, 1838)

In this apologia, Dickens is quite aware that his new sociohistorical fiction must reject the Romantic "allurements and fascinations" of previous historical representations (principally of Sir Walter Scott's sort) for a more Realist approach that paints the dispossessed "in all their deformity . . . as they really are." Dickens clearly sees himself as residing at a fulcrum point of sociohistorical representation and views himself as a stylistic revisionist of that particular field of social representation. His is a rejection of a Romanticized master text of social history in favor of a counter text of Social Realism that cuts sharply against the grain of the historical illusions of order, reform, and institutional benevolence that the Victorian age (and its Utilitarian historians) was constantly nurturing and proselytizing. Dickens's philosophy of history, then, is one that listens to the many voices of the disaffected and marginalized lower classes who are being run over by a steam-driven, Industrial Revolution society. Dickens was one of the few who was able to hear the pain, the despair, the anger, and the threat of violence that was rising in those voices. In Dickens's view, the real history of the Victorian age was one veering precariously toward an escalating confusion that would culminate in a thoroughly historical chaos.

History as Chaos

In a 1989 interview, the actor Robert DeNiro, discussing his shockingly realistic acting method, said: "If it's really important, you'll remember it. You see someone on the street and they have a certain walk, and you pick that up and say, 'Remember that walk,' and you'll just apply it automatically when you're doing a character. Sometimes you write it down, but I try to rely on my memory, and somewhere it's stored in the computer and comes out when it's needed."[24] That is exactly, uncannily, Dickens's method, the manner in which his imagination worked. He saw, heard, or sensed something on the streets and was able to incorporate it as event or character, quirk, image, or idea, into the fabric of his fiction. Taking his cue from the work of Steven Marcus, H. M. Daleski describes Dickens as having an "analogical imagination" and believes that "the rich resourcefulness of Dickens's art" and "the swarming multifariousness of the worlds Dickens creates"[25] were dependent upon Dickens's constant construction of analogies out of realities, of the alchemical transforming of almost everything he encountered in his Victorian society.

But Dickens's sources were not just the people he met on the streets in the course of his notorious nightly walks. Rather, they were also comprised of the texts of his world, which he read on the cluttered pages of London, from Fleet Street to the City to the East India Company docks on the Thames to the stages at Drury Lane and Covent Garden. No one read the sociohistorical texts of the age better or more perceptively than Dickens, and no historian was able to transform those texts more accurately or imaginatively into a history of the times. From the night streets to the great merchant houses to the bleak houses of Parliament to the opera houses to the toppling houses of the poor in London's industrial slums, Dickens tracked the history of his age in the lives of its people, whom he transformed into his characters, who became the voices of Victorian society's disenfranchised and their oppressors.

But in attempting to construct this new version of history Dickens realized that the sort of history he was trying to construct was consistently resistant to that very act of construction. Writing about the relationship between "Historicism and Fiction," Mario Vargas Llosa describes Dickens's dilemma in attempting to refigure the historicist project. "History has no order, logic, sense," Vargas Llosa writes, "much less a rational direction that sociologists, economists, or ideologues can detect in advance 'scientifically.' History is organized by historians; they are the ones who make it coherent and intelligible, through the use of points of view and interpretations." But as Vargas Llosa (and Dickens, especially in a multiple-narrative, dual-narrator novel like *Bleak House*) realizes, history is a "constant multiple improvisation, a lively chaos to which historians give an appearance of order, an almost infinite contradictory multiplication of events." In other words, the attempted construction of an ordered history is always a deconstruction; the historical project doesn't realize that it is resistant to "the real history of the vertiginous totality of human activity that always overflows rational and intellectual attempts at apprehension," that "all written histories are partial and arbitrary."[26]

Conversely, the New Historicist project is at ease amidst the decentered "vertiginous" multiple "improvisations" of history. Like Dickens, the New Historicist comes to view history as an asynchronic symphony of constantly competing voices, layers of sound, levels of expression. For Dickens, the world, or "reality," or attempted history, can only be portrayed as a dialectical failure in terms of binary counter histories that fail to create the Romantic order of synthesis. Dickens, in writing his histories of "lively chaos," articulated and embodied one hundred years before the fact, the governing principles of the New Historicist project. That is why, as J. Hillis Miller so eloquently argued in the 1950s, the Dickens world evolves (especially in the novels written after *Barnaby Rudge*) into a world of disintegration, isolation, and chaos; a world in which the historical project, when undertaken by a character like Inspector Bucket in *Bleak House*, Sidney Carton in *A Tale of Two Cities*, or Noddy Boffin in *Our Mutual Friend*, is doomed to the failure inherent in the attempt to bring order to something as fluid as history.

History as Deconstruction

The chapters that follow analyze Dickens's work in terms of New Historicism, as it contributes to his philosophy of history (in chapters 2 and 5), in terms of his use of economic history to define a major metaphor for Victorian social chaos (in chapter 3), and in terms of literary history as a major influence upon his characterization of the historical dilemma of the Victorian underclass (in chapter 4). New Historicism provides a collection of discourse maps that Dickens was already intuitively following in the chaotic landscape of Victorian society and literature. Though, to echo Vargas Llosa, these following chapters must by nature be "improvisations" and journeys into a "lively chaos," they do revision the historical project of Dickens's fiction by heeding the disempowered voices of Victorian culture. Those voices participate in the philosophical debates, economic confrontations, and subversive social commentaries of Victorian popular culture. Those voices contribute to the formation of a new version of history that draws its material from the disintegration of the eighteenth century's obsessively ordered view of the world and its history and breaks the bondage of the great chain of being once and for all.

For Dickens, the result is what Joseph Conrad would later term an immersion into the "destructive element"[27] of a new historical reading. In trying to read the texts of time's empire, to listen to the marginalized voices of the Utilitarian Victorian society, Dickens is, like Marlow in Conrad's *Heart of Darkness* and like the title character of *Lord Jim*, immersing himself in the "destructive element" of his contemporary social history. For Dickens, this results, as best seen in his last completed novel *Our Mutual Friend*, in a philosophy of history based upon flux, progress, and an ability to deal with the chaos of the Victorian world.

The furnishings of Dickens's mid-nineteenth-century historical consciousness are almost all provided by his connection to the past; the philosophical, economic, and literary culture of the eighteenth century. Each of the succeeding chapters explores those particular emplotted connections. Just as in *David Copperfield* where he writes of all the associations that emanated from that "blessed little room" where he would retreat from his wretched Murdstone life into the past worlds where "Roderick Random, Peregrine Pickle, Humphrey Clinker, Tom Jones, the Vicar of Wakefield, Don Quixote, Gil Blas, and Robinson Crusoe, came out, a glorious host, to keep me company. . . . I have been Tom Jones (a child's Tom Jones, a harmless creature) for a week together. . . . I had a greedy relish for a few volumes of *Voyages and Travels*" (*DC*, Ch. 4), Dickens pushes off for his voyage into mid-nineteenth-century history from points of embarkation in the eighteenth century.

Dickens was intent on exploring the movement of history from those eighteenth-century ports of order into the chaos of a new postindustrial world. For Dickens, the culture of the eighteenth century became a strange curiosity shop of antiquated artifacts that represented an old illusion of order that had broken down in the confusing new Victorian world. Repeatedly, Dickens, in the tone of his novels, through the voices of his narrators and his disempowered characters, expressed his historicist's awareness of the daunting challenge of his contemporary project of representing England and its people as they really are. He was like those explorers in his beloved "few volumes of *Voyages and Travels*" setting off to map a new world of savagery and chaos where eighteenth-century conceptions of order simply have no relevance.

That need for a clear, decentered consciousness of history is perhaps best expressed in the 1867 revision of the Preface to *Oliver Twist* that I quoted earlier. "As I saw no reason when I wrote this book," Dickens declared,

> why the dregs of life (so long as their speech did not offend the ear) should not serve the purpose of a moral, as well as its froth and cream, I made bold to believe that this same Once upon a time would not be All-time or even a long time. I saw many strong reasons for pursuing my course. (1867)

Dickens's strong reasons for engaging time—past, present, and future—through the medium of the phrase "Once upon a time" reveals, even as late in his career as 1867, a surviving hope that his descent into the chaos of his Victorian world might still serve as a way of pointing toward some new order amidst the disorder, some new sense of history within the terrible disintegration of nineteenth-century life.

TWO

Dickens and the Eighteenth Century

"A novel is never anything but a philosophy expressed in images," so Albert Camus began his review of Jean-Paul Sartre's *La Nausee* in the *Alger republicain* [1] No one would question the philosophicalness of Sartre's novels since Sartre was a renowned philosopher, but Dickens's novels are something quite different. Dickens has been stereotypically portrayed as a novelistic mind rich with comic sense and satiric power, with imagery, with grotesque, psychological and stereotypical characterization, and with growing social consciousness. Less frequently, however, do critics write of Dickens's basic philosophical beliefs and the philosophy of history that he developed in his novels.

If one of Dickens's major concerns in his fiction was to develop a philosophy of history, it seems only appropriate that somewhere in his background Dickens should have encountered a history of philosophy that would qualify him to become a philosopher of history. Dickens's historical project was his attempt to "situate" himself and his art in relation not simply to the history of his contemporary time, but much more complexly to the web of historical interconnections between past, present, and future that defined his position as a Victorian philosopher of history. Thus, defining the philosophical idea stream within which Dickens, in the mid-nineteenth century, found himself "situated" is the starting point for confronting the two major questions posed in chapter 1: how did Dickens employ history in his fiction and did he develop a philosophy of history in his fiction? In order to answer these questions, then, Dickens would have had to been anchored in the philosophical stream of ideas; an eminent Victorian firmly tethered to the principles and theorems of his age. But that is not the case at all. If anything, Dickens's philosophical discourse is both "heteroglossic" in Mikhail Bakhtin's sense of being based on many voices, and progressive in its sense of historical time as a stream that flows from past to future on the current of present discourse. In other words, Dickens was a novelist of historical flux and social chaos, and, in some rather roundabout ways, he acquired the philosophical anchors to which he tied his historical views. In those instances when Dickens has been considered philosophically, he has been characterized as a radical Marxist,[2] as a radical Christian,[3] and in the 1950s and 1960s as an existential writer.[4] However, while Dickens's philosophical sympathies may warm toward a Marxist polemic or an existential concern at different times in individual novels, he never consistently affirms any one of those philosophical positions throughout all of his novels. What he does construct, however, is a basic philosophy that combines all of the above into a philosophical vision that can be defined through its origins, its beliefs and ideas, and its consistent expression in images.

Other modern critics, while not labeling Dickens either a radical or an existentialist, have used general descriptors to characterize his world view. These critics (principally Edmund Wilson and Lionel Stevenson in the early 1940s)[5] defined the Dickens canon as made up of "light" and "dark" novels with the sun sinking at Bleak House and never rising again. This division in terms of tonal metamorphosis has been rather docilely accepted throughout the last four decades of Dickens criticism. In the 1950s, Edgar Johnson's fine biography of Dickens fully endorsed the "dark" novel descriptor.[6] In Volume II of the biography, Johnson's critical essays on Bleak House, Hard Times, Little Dorrit, and Our Mutual Friend repeatedly emphasize the negative, pessimistic imagery as opposed to the positive images of light, imagination, and love.[7] Otherwise one of the most intriguing and innovative Dickens studies of the 1960s, Taylor Stoehr's The Dreamer's Stance reiterates the "dark" novel theory by underlining the importance of the blacking factory experience that Edmund Wilson had first emphasized two decades earlier.[8] No Dickens critic should minimize the shattering effect of the blacking factory experience upon the young Dickens, but it is entirely possible that Dickens sufficiently exorcised that particular devil in David Copperfield, before the so-called "dark" novels even began with Bleak House.

The most obvious facts that the simplistic "light/dark" descriptors overlook are that Dickens's early novels, especially The Pickwick Papers, are not unregenerately optimistic, and the later novels are hardly as pessimistic as they have been painted to be. In the later novels, Dickens's interest in the urban crisis in Victorian England certainly has matured. Tom-All-Alone's, the festering slum of Bleak House, is much more vivid and infecting than the slums in Oliver Twist, and the manufacturing city in The Old Curiosity Shop is but a shadow of Coketown in Hard Times. But though Dickens's novelistic world changes, his world view does not. Though his social consciousness matures, he still finds his eighteenth-century philosophy of "natural benevolence" and the "perfectibility of man" applicable to the changing Victorian world. J. Hillis Miller analyzes at length the heightened sense of the existential "absurd" in Dickens's later novels. However, he recognizes that these novels are not about the implacable pall that absurdity casts over the world, but about the positive and imaginative ways that the characters cope and find order and happiness in spite of the absurdity of existence.[9] Perhaps Dickens realized what Camus later realized with regard to Sisyphus: man can exist, be happy, alive, human, even in a darkly absurd world. Thus, one aspect of the New Historicist project is to challenge the dark novels descriptor by examining the consistent operation in both early and late novels of Dickens's optimistic philosophical vision. The Dickens canon, studied whole and chronologically, demonstrates that no drastic change from picaresque carefreedom and benevolence to dark "bitterness and frustration"[10] really occurred in Dickens's vision.

Every New Historicist project, however, involves the interdisciplinary analysis of its subject's (in this case, Dickens's novels') modes of discourse. My approach combines Bakhtin's "dialogical heteroglossia" theory of many voices with White's theory of unearthing the emplotted narratives to present decentered readings of the historical texts. This combines social and personal history, the history of philosophy, and applied literary criticism. After describing the optimistic eighteenth-century cast of Dickens's mind——its origins, its moral values and beliefs, its ways of solving human and social problems—the focus must naturally turn to an analysis of the consistently optimistic vision present in both early and late novels (I will look at *The Pickwick Papers, The Old Curiosity Shop,* and *Little Dorrit*). Each of these novels invites comparative study of specific eighteenth-century influences (particularly *Joseph Andrews, The Vicar of Wakefield, Tristram Shandy,* and *Caleb Williams*). By means of his reading of these major works of the previous century, Dickens developed the eighteenth-century attitudes and beliefs that later formed the philosophical base for his own characters' actions.

Thus, the application of this New Historicist model to Dickens's philosophical position emphasizes three things. First, it attempts to describe what J. Hillis Miller would call the "consciousness of [the] consciousness"[11] of the artist. Second, it defines the origins of one initial aspect (the philosophical) of Dickens's alchemic vision. Other aspects, specifically those of economic history and social history, will be considered in later chapters. The philosophical aspect involves the eighteenth-century philosophic and novelistic influences upon his art. And third, it analyzes those influences at work in individual Dickens novels, both early and late novels, both supposedly bright, comic novels and seemingly "dark," pessimistic novels, therefore showing that the vision is consistent throughout. Dickens, then, emerges as the fulcrum of a history of ideas. The Dickensian vision becomes a connecting link between eighteenth-century and twentieth-century philosophical views of human existence. Defining this vision and analyzing individual novels reveals the way Dickens tended to act (and to write) based on emotion rather than practicality, on belief rather than rational analysis, on often unrewarded faith rather than the empirical evidence of ugly fact. Thomas Hobbes, the author of *Leviathan*, and Lord Shaftesbury, the philosopher of perfectibility, fought this same war in the eighteenth century, the Romantics sustained a rearguard action, and Dickens, an isolated guerilla, was merely carrying on the fight a century later. Dickens's "vision" derived from an eighteenth-century philosophical view that all his life he tried to apply to an unaccommodating Victorian world. He would have felt quite comfortable in the company of Camus's Sisyphus.

Dickens the Philosopher

The Dickens vision begins with Mr. Pickwick, Dickens's first major character, who is introduced to the world almost as if he were an ambulatory philosophical abstraction. "The praise of mankind was his Swing; philanthropy was his insurance office," the esteemed Secretary of the Pickwick Club first introduces the venerable Tittlebatian to the accompaniment of "(Vehement cheering)." Later, the narrator describes how Pickwick's "countenance glowed with an expression of universal philanthropy" and how "general benevolence was one of the leading features of the Pickwickian theory"(*PP*, 1). This opening of Dickens's first novel shows Pickwick to be a firm believer in benevolence as a viable mode of social action. And Dickens, at the very outset of his writing career, is bodying forth his own central beliefs in his first major character. However, unlike a Sartre, for instance, who creates and synthesizes a philosophy for his own times, Dickens is not defining a unique, self-engendered world view, a philosophical vision strictly his own. Rather, he is entering a stream of ideas that had been flowing from a source one hundred and fifty years in the past, meandering tortuously from Hobbes and Shaftesbury through most of the novelists of the eighteenth century to the philosopher-novelist William Godwin and the Romantics and then, its current dwindling, on into the nineteenth century to Dickens. Therein, bending back into the past, are the origins of Dickens's vision, a Dickensian headwater that has never adequately been explored.

Two eminent Dickensians, Humphry House and Louis Cazamian, have touched the surface of the theme of benevolence in Dickens's novels. House defines the "main symptoms of Dickens's benevolence" as

1. Generosity, in money and kindness that costs nothing. Both kinds of generosity are chiefly shown by the poor towards each other or by the benevolent well-to-do towards the poor.
2. An acute feeling of suffering in all forms, whether caused by poverty, sickness, cruelty (mental or physical) or injustice. The feeling becomes most acute when all these causes of suffering are combined in the sufferer, and there is somebody who has the power to relieve them all.
3. Righteous, if ineffectual, indignation against all anomalies, abuses, and inefficiency in social organizations or government which cause suffering of any kind. This is the Benthamite strain, found more in Dickens' own words than in the words of his characters.
4. An equable and benign temper in the benevolent person, which is on the whole immune from the changing moods which make human beings interesting in themselves.[12]

This definition briefly mentions the benevolence of the poor, but concentrates upon what House sees as the major Dickensian emphasis: the charitable motives of the rich. Throughout his book, House, when discussing the Dickensian concept of benevolence, considers only that of the rich arbitrarily giving to the randomly selected poor.

Cazamian, writing long before House, first placed this emphasis upon Dickens's benevolence as being the sole property of the open-handed rich when he defined Dickens's *"Philosophie de Noel"* (Christmas Philosophy).

C'est une forme vague et sentimental du socialism Chretien. Timide dans sa partie positive, plus hardie dans ses critiques, elle preche l'interventionisme au nom d'un idealisme religieux."[13]

"Avec les chefs de la philanthropie nouvelle, Dickens reconnait le droit a l'assistance. Les classes dirigeants sont responsables du mal social; elles ont sur les ignorants et les faibles l'autorité naturelle du pere sur ses enfants. Il faut que l'individu et l'Etat interviennent dans la vie des classes inferieures; la charite privee ou publique, l'action devouee, sincere, patiente, doivent sans relache soulager et guerir."[14]

[It is a vague and sentimental form of Christian socialism. Timid in its positive parts, stronger in its critiques, this form preaches intervention in the name of religious idealism. With the chiefs of the new philanthropy, Dickens recognizes the right to assist. The guiding classes are responsible for social evil; they have over the ignorant ones and the feeble the natural authority of the father over the children. It is imperative that the individual and the state intervene in the lives of the inferior classes. Private or public charity, devoted action, sincere and patient must, without relenting, soothe and heal.]

Certainly, flowing from the benevolent Pickwick and coursing through the Cheeryble brothers and Scrooge, John Jarndyce and Noddy Boffin, the Father Christmas figures who need only reach into their pockets to bring relief are prominent. If benevolence were the sole property of the rich in the Dickens world, then that world would be truly dark. There would be no opportunity for moral decision-making among the wide range of characters and no genuine human involvement on the most basic personal level, that of survival. The Dickens world would be a randomly patriarchal welfare system. The only welfare recipients would be those lucky enough to be blundered upon by rich benefactors like Brownlow or Jarndyce.

But in the Dickens world the poor as benevolists far outnumber the rich. Dickens repeatedly affirms the moral value of the act of benevolence in which the giver is an active participant, in which the gift is not just an effortless dole, and in which an equal flow of love is generated between giver and receiver as each participates in the other's misery or meager abundance. Cazamian does not recognize the benevolence of the poor in the novels of Dickens at all, and, while House briefly recognizes this phenomenon in his definition, he subsequently ignores it while proceeding to discuss the Dickensian rich man as a stereotyped caricature. Both of these studies of benevolence in Dickens's novels neglect more than half of the subject. Dickens's philosophy of benevolence, which begins with that embodied abstraction Pickwick, effectively and consistently represents one of the major trends of thought of the eighteenth-century view of man.

In the first decade of the eighteenth century Shaftesbury began this trend toward personal benevolence. His was a reaction against the rationalism of Hobbes, who had posited in *Leviathan* that all human action was "self-regarding." For Shaftesbury, Hobbes's empirical, unsentimental view of the world was antithetical to the real nature of man. Hobbes, writes Shaftesbury, dwells only on fear and "forgot to mention Kindness, Friendship, Sociable-

ness, love of Company, and Converse, Natural Affection."[15] Thus, Shaftesbury started the eighteenth-century rebellion against the Puritan ethic that
defined man as naturally sinful and life in the world as a constantly self-
centered struggle for salvation. He did not deny the idea of personal
salvation; he simply changed the emphasis from the struggle of the isolated,
self-centered man as the only means to salvation to the concept of universal
benevolence as the more natural means to salvation. In 1711, Shaftesbury
wrote of that marvelous clockwork orange, eighteenth-century man:

> A thousand other Springs, which are counter to "Self-Interest", have as
> considerable a part in the Movements of this Machine. . . . The Students
> of this Mechanism must have a very partial Eye, to overlook all other
> Motions besides those of the lowest and narrowest compass. 'Tis hard,
> that in the Plan or Description of this Clockwork, no Wheel or Ballance
> shou'd be allow'd on the side of the better and more enlarged Affections:
> that nothing shou'd be understood to be done in Kindness or Gener-
> osity; nothing in pure Good-Nature or Friendship, or thro any social
> or natural Affection of any kind: when, perhaps, the main Springs of
> this Machine will be found to be either these very natural Affections
> themselves, or a compound kind deriv'd from them.[16]

Thus, Shaftesbury saw men as naturally benevolent and he began a
philosophical movement against Hobbesian empiricism that would be sustained throughout the rest of the eighteenth century.

Shaftesbury and those moral philosophers of the eighteenth century
who followed his lead, principally Frances Hutcheson and Bishop Joseph
Butler, articulated for their age the concepts of innate moral sense and natural
benevolence. But only near the very end of the century, with the writings
of William Godwin in the 1790s, did this optimistic philosophy of man begin
to take on political implications. What Jean Jacques Rousseau had preached
in France, Godwin was arguing in England: if man is naturally good, then
the evils of the world must be attributable to a flawed society.

Not only does Godwin specifically align his thought with the tradition
of Shaftesbury and Butler, he goes one step further than his predecessors by
discussing the natural goodness of man in relation to society: "Neither
philosophy, nor morality, nor politics, will ever show like itself, till man shall
be acknowledged for what he really is, a being capable of rectitude, virtue
and benevolence, and who needs not always to be led to actions of general
utility, by foreign and frivolous considerations."[17] This statement by Godwin opposes Utilitarianism, "general utility," by name before the dominant

socioeconomic philosophy of the nineteenth century had even been articulated. For Godwin, society's recognition of man's innate moral sense, and
the movement thereafter of the habit of benevolence toward universality,
would make possible the establishment of an egalitarian society in which
repressive institutions would be unnecessary.

In *The Pickwick Papers*, the natural benevolence of man is stressed, in the
character of Pickwick, throughout the first half of the novel. However, the
confrontation with society appears in the form of Dodson and Fogg and the
Fleet. By the end of *The Pickwick Papers*, universal benevolence has not perme-
ated the Dickens world, though Pickwick's benevolence has drawn a number
of converts—principally Sam Weller, Mr. Jingle, and Job Trotter—to the
realization of the essential nature of man and the impact that benevolence can
have on a repressive world. Pickwick descends into the underground of the
Fleet, no longer just an openhanded gentleman slumming among the poor,
but an actual prisoner putting on the shoes of the oppressed. Though Pickwick
eventually retreats from the realities of personally involved benevolence, a
casualty of the heart-to-heart combat of personal involvement in the battle
for survival, he emerges a wiser man and no longer a simplistic Father
Christmas. Therefore, in his first novel, Dickens reveals an ambivalence
toward the reality and efficacy of the Father Christmas figure. The thematic
movement of *The Pickwick Papers*, from a group of episodes that emphasize the
natural benevolence of man embodied in Pickwick alone to a group of episodes
emphasizing Pickwick's benevolence in confrontation with society, underlines
Pickwick's deepening understanding of the nature of benevolence. His
progress from an embodied philosophical abstraction to a sobered prisoner
practicing and receiving personal benevolence among the poor represents
Dickens's already maturing conception of the nature of true benevolence. The
realization that true benevolence results only from close personal involvement
mirrors the central conception that developed out of the eighteenth-century
philosophy of perfectibility.

However, one problem exists. Unlike his contemporary George Eliot,
Dickens was virtually unacquainted with and uninterested in philosophy.[18]
George Eliot's companion, George Henry Lewes, after having been shocked
at the emptiness of Dickens's bookshelves, wrote, "Compared with that of
Fielding or Thackeray, his was merely an animal intelligence. . . . He never
was and never would have been a student."[19] Almost certainly, Dickens never
read Shaftesbury's *Characteristics* or Bishop Butler's *Sermons* or even Godwin's
Enquiry Concerning Political Justice. But Dickens did read the novels of Henry
Fielding, Laurence Sterne, and Oliver Goldsmith, and the novels of Godwin,
and these works all stand as firmly built bridges between the dominant

philosophical tradition of the eighteenth century and the Dickensian philosophical vision.[20]

In the preface to *Joseph Andrews* and the dedication and introductory
chapters to the books of *Tom Jones*, Fielding intentionally speaks as a philosopher
of natural benevolence and invokes Shaftesbury's name as a supportive authority. Sterne was a preacher as well as a novelist. His sermons, like those of Bishop
Butler, emphasized that "a charitable and benevolent disposition is so principal
and ruling a part of man's character, as to be a considerable test by itself of the
whole frame and temper of his mind, with which all other virtues and vices
respectively rise and fall, and will almost necessarily be connected."[21]

But Godwin is perhaps the strongest bridge, especially to the later, "dark"
Dickens. Godwin intentionally uses the novel form as a vehicle for the presentation of his own philosophy. For example, in *Caleb Williams*, Falkland fluctuates
between two poles of moral value. The natural qualities that Falkland esteems
most highly, his humanity and benevolence, are always at war with the artificial,
society-imposed value of which he is so constantly aware, his honor. Falkland's
characterization displays the conflict that Shaftesbury, Bishop Butler, and then
Godwin himself (in *Enquiry Concerning Political Justice*) saw as the basic tension
within the nature of man: self-love as opposed to benevolence.

Fielding, Sterne, and Godwin, as well as other important novelists—
Tobias Smollett, Goldsmith, Henry Mackenzie—all represent in the characters
and themes of their fiction the eighteenth-century philosophical view of man.
Dickens may not have been directly acquainted with the original philosophical
treatises, yet that eighteenth-century vision is repeatedly affirmed in all of his
novels. He was closely acquainted with the novels of the middle and late
eighteenth century, and their created worlds directly influenced the birth and
development of the Dickens world. Because of this chain of influence, Mr.
Pickwick appears as a philosophical abstraction at the beginning of *The Pickwick
Papers* and at the very beginning of Dickens's novelistic career. Also, because
of this chain of influence, the theme of the natural goodness of man as
objectified in benevolence appears in all of Dickens's works, from *The Pickwick
Papers* to the alleged "dark" novels, and remains essentially the same throughout.

The Pickwick Papers

The characters and scenes of *The Pickwick Papers* are a striking example of the
eighteenth-century's strong influence on Dickens's vision. Pickwick's characterization and the plot movement of *The Pickwick Papers* are dependent on
the composite influence of three characters from eighteenth-century novels:

Parson Abraham Adams of Fielding's *Joseph Andrews*, Uncle Toby of Sterne's *Tristram Shandy*, and Dr. Primrose of Goldsmith's *The Vicar of Wakefield*. Along with Pickwick, these eighteenth-century characters possess the same Shaftesburian natural goodness and feel the need to practice perpetual benevolence toward their fellow man. Like each of his three predecessors, Pickwick's inclination to benevolence often draws him into situations in which he becomes a comic dupe before the ultimate triumph of his good heart is accomplished. Luckily for Pickwick, these many episodes usually leave him with only the glow of embarrassment on his cheek, rather than with the contents of a chamber pot dripping from his beard, the typical fate of Parson Adams.

Early in *The Pickwick Papers*, Dickens refers to Fielding as an authority (104) and many of the episodes that involve Pickwick in the early parts of the novel are directly reminiscent of the misadventures of Parson Adams. At his first introduction, Adams is described as "a man of good sense, good parts, and good nature; but at the same time as entirely ignorant of the ways of this world as an infant just entered into it could possibly be."[22] Like Pickwick, Adams has "benevolence visible in his countenance" (*JA*, II, 10) and, similar to the way Pickwick Club members feel toward Pickwick, Adams's parishioners know "that he had their good entirely at heart, so they consulted him on every occasion" (*JA*, I, 11).

Pickwick and Adams are alike both in innocence and benevolent countenance. They are also very alike in action. The comic finale of *Joseph Andrews* is the game of mistaken bedrooms that Adams finds himself playing during the night in the confusing rooms and passageways of Booby Hall. At the Great White Horse Inn at Ipswich, Pickwick undergoes a variation of this same experience in his nighttime encounter with the lady in the yellow curlpapers. Dickens, however, because he was writing for an audience that was much different from Fielding's, was greatly restrained in handling the sexual overtones of his comic situation. He could not reproduce the tactile methods of recognition that Adams experiences with Madam Slipslop and then Fanny experiences with Adams, but both scenes are based on the same general premise. Each of the innocents becomes confused as to the whereabouts of his own room in the middle of the night in a strange building; each enters a room that is very similar to his own, undresses, and lies down to sleep in a woman's bed; and each is discovered by the lady (or ladies). Subsequently, each must face the wrath of the lady's suitor. Adams is discovered in bed with Fanny by Joseph, who is momentarily enraged, and Pickwick must face the jealousy of the formidable Peter Magnus in the morning. Finally, both episodes end when the two confused innocents are led back to their rooms by their two comparatively worldly wise companions, Joseph and Sam Weller. Sam's comment to Pickwick on the situation would serve equally well for Parson Adams: "You rayther want somebody to look arter you, sir, wen your judgement goes out a wisitin'" (PP, 22). Thus Dickens used one of *Joseph Andrews's* outstanding comic events as a prototype for Pickwick's misadventures, and he does the same thing with Sterne's *Tristram Shandy*. However, the influence of Sterne's novel upon *The Pickwick Papers* is much greater. Instead of imitating just a comic episode from the earlier work, Dickens chooses an episode from Tristram Shandy to serve as the basis for the whole plot movement of *The Pickwick Papers*.

The character of Pickwick is modeled more closely upon Sterne's Uncle Toby Shandy than upon any other literary character, except Don Quixote. The central focus of Toby's characterization is on the operation of his mind; and Toby's mind is emotionally and intellectually very close to Pickwick's. Tristram pays tribute to Toby's nature in these terms: "Thou envied'st no man's comforts—insulted'st no man's opinions,—Thou blackened'st no man's character,—devoured'st no man's bread: gently with faithful Trim behind thee, didst thou amble round the little circle of thy pleasures, jostling no creature in thy way;—for each one's sorrows, thou hadst a tear,—for each man's need thou hadst a shilling."[23] Both Pickwick and Toby Shandy are emotionally dedicated to helping others who are less fortunate than themselves, while at the same time they are intellectually dedicated to the spreading of "hobbyhorsical" confusion. Riding one's hobbyhorse is the act of describing something that is absurdly simple in the most complex and circumspect terms. Mr. Pickwick's speculations on the inscription,

+

BILST

UM

PSHI

S.M.

ARK

which he finds on a rock in an innyard (PP, 11), are certainly of a hobbyhorsical nature. The inscription is only the name and mark of a rural stonecutter who, due to the shape of the rock, was forced to break up the normal configuration of letters and to omit the spaces between words. Pickwick, however, feels that he has found an ancient rune, a tablet that holds the key to knowledge of early British civilization.

Both *Tristram Shandy* and *The Pickwick Papers* focus on the theme of "meaning," which is both symbolic and ironic in each novel. Symbolically, the comedy of meaning becomes an analogue for human inadequacy, man's inability ever to find real certainty, true meaning, in his world, in his life. In both novels, characters, especially Toby and Pickwick, attempt to invest the world with meaning, but invariably, because of their own hobbyhorsical minds and the elusiveness of the world itself, they fail. Their perceptions never correspond with those of others who similarly look for meaning in objects; their meanings, though well meant, are always erroneous. Ironically, both Toby and Pickwick violate meaning in their attempts to communicate it. When they talk or speculate, no one ever understands what they mean. Their words are ill chosen; their lives are plagued by ambiguity. Their words become weapons that others, twisting the words' meanings, use against them.

The most pronounced similarity between *Tristram Shandy* and *The Pickwick Papers* lies in Toby Shandy's and Pickwick's amorous adventures. And these scenes are also the best illustrations of the identical themes of "meaning" that operate in both novels. Uncle Toby Shandy's affair with the Widow Wadman is the prototype for Mr. Pickwick's unlucky misunderstanding with Mrs. Bardell. Mrs. Wadman first fell in love with Uncle Toby when that gentleman "was constrained to accept a bed at Mrs. Wadman's, for a night or two" (*TS*, VIII, 8) while Corporal Trim was building a bed for Toby. Pickwick also is a gentleman lodger at Mrs. Bardell's when their unfortunate misunderstanding takes place. Like Mr. Pickwick, Uncle Toby stands in complete "ignorance of the plies and foldings of the heart of woman" (*TS*, VI, 29). Both Widow Wadman and Mrs. Bardell are in love with their gentleman boarders and are thus open to the power of the slightest suggestion; Mrs. Bardell "had long worshipped Mr. Pickwick from a distance, but here she was, all at once, raised to a pinnacle to which her wildest and most extravagant hopes had never dared to aspire" (*PP*, 12). Thus, the circumstances and characters in both scenes are essentially the same, and the premise for the comic misunderstandings—the male talking about a harmless subject and the female interpreting his words, relative to her own amorous inclinations, as meaning something completely different from what is intended—is developed in exactly the same manner. The Widow Wadman mistakes Toby's maps for his groin, and the Widow Bardell mistakes Pickwick's benevolent proposal toward her son for an amorous proposal toward herself. As in his handling of the episode modeled on *Joseph Andrews*, Dickens could not present this scene with all of the sexual implications present in Sterne's version. He had to make the basic misunderstanding more general and less physical in order to make the joke acceptable to his audience.

The misunderstanding between Pickwick and Mrs. Bardell in *The Pickwick Papers* serves as the cornerstone for the novel's plot structure, and, significantly, the novel's whole plot from this scene on is based upon a simple act of benevolence that Pickwick wished to undertake. But benevolence in the Dickens world is not always as easy as it was for Sterne's Uncle Toby, who could provide for Le Fever's son without any complications. The influence of the Widow Wadman episode from *Tristram Shandy* upon the conception of the Pickwick-Bardell misunderstanding also points to Dickens's use of *The Vicar of Wakefield* as the inspiration for the plot movement and theme of the second half of *The Pickwick Papers*.

The influence of *The Vicar of Wakefield's* prison episodes has been described by Steven Marcus as the main reason for the tonal change that takes place in the second half of *The Pickwick Papers*. But Dickens had a better reason for turning to Goldsmith than Marcus's theory postulates: that any novelist would naturally turn from Smollett and Fielding to Goldsmith when he feels like "becoming self-consciously serious."[24] Dickens turned to Goldsmith because he had gone as far as he could go with Sterne's Widow Wadman episode. Imitation of the prison scenes from *The Vicar of Wakefield* offered a fitting resolution to the theme of benevolence, which had been the cause of all of Pickwick's trouble with Mrs. Bardell, and would show the power of the good heart in the hardest possible circumstances.

Since *Tristram Shandy* ends abruptly in the midst of the Widow Wadman episode, Dickens was forced to look for a means of resolving what he had begun. The central character of *The Vicar of Wakefield* stands directly in the tradition of the sort of natural benevolence that had inspired the conception of Pickwick, and thus the work was an appropriate choice. One other important reason might well have figured in Dickens's turning to *The Vicar of Wakefield*. Mr. Jingle and Job Trotter, the highly entertaining swindlers of the first half of *The Pickwick Papers*, had been absent from the scene since Pickwick's encounter with them at Squire Nupkin's. The prison scenes in *The Vicar of Wakefield* gave Dickens a means of reintroducing these established characters and of giving Pickwick the opportunity for accomplishing his greatest act of benevolence.

Throughout the novel, whenever outsmarted by his arch enemy, Jingle, Pickwick publicly levels dire threats of revenge against him:

"Whenever I meet that Jingle again, wherever it is, . . . I'll inflict personal chastisement on him, in addition to the exposure he so richly merits. I will or my name is not Pickwick" (26). These threats, however, seem artificial even as they are being shouted. To take physical revenge on anyone or even to nurture the seeds of hatred within himself for longer than the briefest moment of anger would be an abrupt movement out of character for Pickwick. The utter inconsistency of the threats is evident as soon as Pickwick is given the opportunity to carry them out. Pickwick's definitive "wherever it is" evidently does not include the degradation of the Fleet and instead of publicly vilifying Jingle and Job, he "was affected . . . and said: 'I would like to speak to you in private'" (42). Thus, as Dr. Primrose had done to Ephraim Jenkinson, Pickwick forgives, forgets, and redeems himself and others through selfless benevolence.

The actions of Jenkinson in *The Vicar of Wakefield* also can be seen to serve as the inspiration for another and greater act of benevolence in *The Pickwick Papers*. Goldsmith's Jenkinson is split in two by Dickens. One half informs the repentant character of Jingle, but the other half motivates the benevolent action of Sam Weller. A perceptive inmate in the Fleet recognizes Pickwick's naïveté immediately: "If I knew as little of life as that, I'd eat my hat and swallow the buckle whole" (*PP*, 42). And Tony Weller confidently and graphically imagines what Pickwick's relation to the new environment will be: "Why, they'll eat him up alive, Sammy" (*PP*, 43). These assessments of Pickwick are important because these are the voices of reality speaking. If anything, Pickwick is a transparent character, and these men can see immediately that he has never really felt the heat of the world, passed through the fiery furnace of reality. Pickwick is clearly too naïve to survive in a world in which men are scratching and clawing for existence. Sam and Tony Weller and the inmates know the territory and they also know Pickwick even better than he knows himself. In *The Vicar of Wakefield*, Primrose, just as naïve as Pickwick, had a ready-made protector in the repentant Jenkinson, but Dickens, who has created a much more realistic prison world than Goldsmith could ever conceive of, realized the absurdity of suddenly changing a disheartened Jingle into a strong protector who could stand between Pickwick and the hostile world. So Dickens turned to his already established strength, the one immovable force in the novel, Sam. Hope dies for the Pickwickian world if Sam is unwilling to give up all the prospects of his life for love of Pickwick. The Dickensian philosophy of benevolence and perfectibility is never more evident than when Sam does make this sacrifice joyfully and comically with no false emotion.

The Pickwick Papers is Sam Weller's novel. He was the savior when lack of interest threatened to end the adventures of the club, and he was the prime mover behind Dickens's rise to fame. The theme of benevolence finds its most telling expression in the benevolence of Sam Weller. He doesn't fling coins randomly about like Father Christmas; his action involves no sort of monetary giving at all. He simply commits his life to another human being and, in the process, to a way of life that, despite his solidly pragmatic nature, he has come to believe in.

Benevolence on the Road: The Old Curiosity Shop

In The Pickwick Papers Dickens's imitation of specific characters and situations from eighteenth-century novels highlights the affirmation of the eighteenth-century philosophy of benevolence that is his major theme. In another early novel, The Old Curiosity Shop, Dickens carries even further this philosophical theme. At the end of The Pickwick Papers, Dickensian benevolence is not the giving of money to the poor but rather the benevolence of the poor themselves, a Sam Weller sacrificing his own freedom to help Pickwick. The benevolence of the poor, especially in Fielding and Smollett, was a consistent occurrence in the plots of eighteenth-century picaresque or "road" novels, and is still a factor in twentieth-century British picaresque. Listen to Joyce Cary's Gulley Jimson just out of jail and looking for a loan: "I was in trouble and people in trouble, they say, are more likely to give help to each other than those who aren't. After all, it's not surprising, for people who help other people in trouble are likely soon to be in trouble themselves."[25] No matter whether the unfortunate traveler is in a Smollett, Fielding, Dickens, or Joyce Cary novel, the benevolent world he traverses always takes the same form: the rich are, more often than not, hypocritical and penurious; the poor are naturally benevolent and openhanded.

In the British picaresque or "road" fiction, the survival of the hero is always reliant upon someone's benevolent nature. When a young traveler such as Smollett's Roderick Random or Fielding's Joseph Andrews sets out on his journey toward fortune and love, he is invariably penniless. At appropriate times in the story, just when the hero is in a situation of the highest peril or the lowest degradation, a benevolent character appears and saves him. However, the operation of this convention is not always so trite. More often than not the benevolent character who rescues the hero is almost as destitute as the hero himself. Usually, the benevolent character cannot afford to rescue anyone, and after the act is accomplished, the rescued character is left better provided for than his rescuer. Frequently, the benevolent transaction has either nothing to do with money or involves an amount so small that before another day passes the hero is again in need of benevolent assistance. *Joseph Andrews* and *Roderick Random* both demonstrate the operation of this theme of the benevolence of the poor, and both directly contribute to Dickens's verticalized philosophy of benevolence. In the world of the eighteenth-century novel and in the Dickens world, benevolence like history is participated in by all class levels, is invoked by all the voices of society both rich and poor.

In *Joseph Andrews*, Parson Adams is a poor man, yet upon finding Joseph ill at Mrs. Tow-wouse's inn he immediately places at Joseph's disposal all his money, "nine shillings and three pence" (15). As the novel progresses Adams displays his natural goodness many times, but his are not the only acts of benevolence. With Joseph's departure from Lady Booby's London home, Fielding departs from his original plan to parody Richardson's *Pamela* and begins to write his own novel of the road. Repeatedly, he depends on the concept of the benevolence of the poor (as opposed to the unnatural class-consciousness and penury of the rich) for many of his finest satiric effects. Just outside of London, Joseph is beaten, stripped, and left in a ditch to die. A coach stops but a shocked lady, a well-dressed gentleman, and a lawyer refuse poor, naked Joseph admittance. The whole episode becomes a satiric travesty of the parable of the Good Samaritan. Ironically, the Good Samaritan who materializes is the poorest of all the occupants of the coach: "The postilion (a lad who has since been transported for robbing a hen roost) voluntarily stripped off a great coat, his only garment, at the same time swearing a great oath (for which he was rebuked by the passengers) 'that he would rather ride in his shirt all his life than suffer a fellow creature to lie in so miserable a condition'" (12). This is the first example of the benevolence of the poor that sustains Joseph, Fanny, and Adams on their journey. Later, after Trulliber refuses them, a "poor pedlar" (15) pays their bill, and after a seemingly benevolent gentleman refuses Adams a loan, an honest innkeeper trusts them for his bill. In each case the ability of the poor to feel and act is opposed to the hypocrisy and selfish irresponsibility of the rich. Fielding certainly is indulging in class antagonism and creating stereotypes of hypocrisy in *Joseph Andrews;* indulgences that Dickens, who creates both good and bad rich people and good and bad poor people, will avoid. Fielding also will balance his view by creating Squire Allworthy in *Tom Jones.*

Similar characters and events influence the plot movement of *Roderick Random.* Roderick is much more a real picaro than Joseph Andrews. Roderick is disreputable, lecherous, and, worst of all, he makes a habit of exploiting the good natures of the benevolent characters in the novel. The one character most exploited by Roderick Random is the ever faithful Strap, who at one juncture gives Roderick all of his savings and says: "I'll beg for you, steal for you, go through the wide world with you, and starve with you: for though I be a poor cobbler's son, I am no scout."[26] Also, as in *Joseph Andrews*, the rich are portrayed as unfeeling and unnatural (the most unnatural of all is Lord Strutwell, who treats Roderick benevolently in order to attempt a homosexual seduction).

The parable of the Good Samaritan also appears in *Roderick Random* as Roderick, after a shipwreck, is set upon, robbed, and left to die by the crew members and the sadistic Captain Crampley. After being found alive by some country people who refuse to help him, he is taken to the parson, who not only refuses to help him but threatens to excommunicate him as well. Finally, the only person who will give him refuge is a poor old woman "who was suspected of witchcraft by the neighborhood" (38). In the world of the eighteenth-century novel, natural benevolence seems to be much more accessible to the "unenlightened" and financially deprived lower classes. However, one does not have to be poor to be good. The well-established character type of the benevolent squire—Squire Allworthy, Matthew Bramble in *Humphrey Clinker*, and Toby Shandy—demonstrates that the rich also can be benevolent. The benevolent squire, however, does not appear so frequently as the figure of the good-hearted poor person. If the history of eighteenth-century philosophy is marked by an antithetical dialogue between Thomas Hobbes (self-interest) and Lord Shaftesbury (natural benevolence), then the novel genre seems to serve as a mediator between these two opposed views of the nature of man as well as between the discourse of philosophy and the English common reader. Perhaps that is why William Godwin, after articulating his egalitarian philosophy of perfectibility, which turned upon the Shaftesburian concept of natural benevolence, chose to embody that philosophy in the characters of a novel, *Caleb Williams*.

Dickens wrote *The Old Curiosity Shop* in this eighteenth-century mode and with this view of what constitutes real benevolence. Nell starts her journey to the supposedly green and pastoral north almost penniless and utterly defenseless. As she and her hapless grandfather travel, however, they are protected and sustained by a succession of good-hearted people along the way. Outside of London a poor woman notices that one of Nell's feet is "blistered and sore, and being a woman and a mother too she would not suffer her to go until she had washed the place and applied some simple remedy" (*OCS*, 15). The travelers are next befriended by the poor schoolmaster and

the lady proprietor of Jarley's waxworks, neither of whom can properly afford
to be charitable.

After leaving Mrs. Jarley's, penniless because grandfather has lost all
the money at cards, the travelers find themselves isolated and destitute
among the heartless crowds of a large manufacturing city. An underground
man, the tender of one of the huge fires that generate power in the city,
rescues them and leads them to shelter in his miniature inferno. The scene
and the character are ironically symbolic and underline the dialogical quality
of Dickens's theme of benevolence. The fireman is a devil yet his heart is
benevolent. He comes out of an underground hell into the daylight world
of the living to find Nell and save her; ironically, that daylight world contains
only a drifting, faceless crowd of people whose hearts are dead and eyes
blind to Nell's plight, while in the dark inferno men can still feel and give.
As Nell and her grandfather leave, the fireman says, "I wish I could do more"
and presses "two old, battered, smoke-encrusted penny pieces" into her
hand. The narrator cannot help saying, "Who knows but they shone as
brightly in the eyes of angels, as the golden gifts that have been chronicled
on tombs?" (OCS, 44). The pennies symbolically represent an important
quality of the novel's theme of benevolence, a quality that was repeatedly
stressed in the novels of Dickens's eighteenth-century predecessors. Appear-
ances often belie the reality that lies beneath the surface, and, in this episode,
love comes more quickly out of hell to redeem than it ever can come from
the rich who, like Quilp (or Ralph Nickleby in Nicholas Nickleby, Jonas
Chuzzlewit in Martin Chuzzlewit, Bounderby in Hard Times, or Casby and
Fledgeby in Little Dorrit), corrupted by a money lust that corrodes all natural
instincts, often seek only to destroy.

Finally, as in the eighteenth-century road novels, the old schoolmaster
appears just at that moment when Nell has reached the very limit of her
endurance and has fainted from exhaustion. Like the Good Samaritan, he
takes her up from the side of the road where she has fallen, carries her to an
inn where she is restored, and makes it clear "that I am the paymaster for the
three" (OCS, 46).

All of these episodes reiterate confidence in the essential goodness of
man, which Dickens absorbed in his reading of the eighteenth-century road
novels. The very existence of the benevolence of the poor in the industrialized nineteenth-century world of The Old Curiosity Shop is, in itself, a forceful
statement of the enduring power of man's intrinsically good nature. The
industrial world, to which Dickens will later return in Hard Times, attempts
to grind men into being parts of the machines they operate, yet some of
them have not allowed their ability to feel to be burned away by the blazing

fires of the industrial metropolis. In other words, Dickens is arguing (as did the eighteenth-century philosophers of natural benevolence and perfectibility) that man's better nature has the power not only to resist the juggernaut of centered, empowered history, but also is able to actively assert itself against the dehumanizing idea streams of the Industrial Revolution.

This same emphasis on the greater ability of the poor to feel and act also occurs in *Dombey and Son*, where the poverty-stricken crew of the Wooden Midshipman does not hesitate a moment at taking in Florence Dombey, who has been rejected by her rich, unfeeling father, and in *Bleak House*, where Mr. George, financially bankrupt but morally rich, becomes the protector of Gridley, poor Jo, and finally Sir Leicester (in this last case the benevolence of the poor is actually directed toward the rich). In the Dickens world the poor are the real benevolists. The narrator of *Bleak House* realizes this as he describes two St. Albans brickmakers' wives: "These two women, coarse and shabby and beaten, so united; to see what they could be to one another; to see how they felt for one another, how the heart of each to each was softened by the hard trials of their lives. I think the best side of such people is almost hidden from us. What the poor are to the poor is little known, excepting to themselves and GOD" (8).

The poor commit themselves, not just their meager material goods, to those who are even worse off than they. The omniscient narrator of *The Old Curiosity Shop* finds it necessary to intrude in order to place particular emphasis on the theme of benevolence: "Let me linger in this place, for an instant, to remark that if ever household affections and loves are graceful things, they are graceful in the poor. The ties that bind the wealthy and the proud to home may be forged on earth, but those which link the poor man to his humble hearth are of the truer metal and bear the stamp of Heaven. . . . His household gods are of flesh and blood, with no alloy of silver, gold, or precious stone; he has no property but in the affections of his own heart" (26). The benevolence of the poor is more difficult and, perhaps, less materially powerful than the benevolence of the rich, but, it exists in the Dickens world on a much larger scale than the Father Christmas mode of uninvolved benevolence as exhibited by Abel Garland in *The Old Curiosity Shop* and the Cheeryble brothers in *Nicholas Nickleby*.

Little Dorrit, "Dark" Novel?

In *The Pickwick Papers*, *Oliver Twist*, and *Nicholas Nickleby*, the naturally benevolent man, be he rich or poor, displays that power for improving the world and defeating selfishness and hypocrisy that was so strongly emphasized in the novels of Fielding, Sterne, and Goldsmith. But, hardly indulging themselves in any *"Philosophie de Noel,"* the poor in the Dickens world—Sam Weller, Newman Noggs in *Nicholas Nickleby,* a succession of "road" characters in *The Old Curiosity Shop,* Mark Tapley in *Martin Chuzzlewit,* the Wooden Midshipman's family in *Dombey and Son*—best embody the Shaftesburian philosophy of natural benevolence. However, does Dickens suddenly, beginning with *Bleak House,* reject his optimistic eighteenth-century view of man in the world and take on a dark, pessimistic, Hobbesian view of man? Does he deny the concept of natural goodness and emphasize only the oppressiveness of a world that frustrates the individual's powers for good?

Certainly, the settings have changed. The reader no longer is in the open air on the top of a coach with Pickwick and Sam, but is sitting in the Marshalsea with William Dorrit or floating down the stinking Thames fishing for corpses with Gaffer Hexam. The settings have changed, but Dickens's world view, his philosophy of man, is consistent and still remains optimistic. His philosophy of benevolence as found in the novels of the eighteenth century is still at work in these later novels. *Little Dorrit,* for example, is reputedly Dickens's darkest novel, yet in it he articulates and affirms his most sophisticated version of the eighteenth-century philosophy of natural benevolence. William Godwin's *Caleb Williams* and Dickens's *Little Dorrit* possess similar characters and are concerned with similar themes and events, but their greatest similarity lies in Dickens's affirmation of Godwin's view of the individual man's relationship to the world.

In his *Enquiry Concerning Political Justice,* Godwin states that the most important concerns of men must be "the question concerning free will and necessity, and the question respecting self-love and benevolence" (362). Godwin's doctrine of Necessity maintains that man is qualified to predict the future according to his own experience of the past. Thus, history can offer instruction to man because "certain temptations and inducements . . . in all ages and climates, introduce a certain series of actions" (369). For Godwin, the only freedom of the human will consists in the fact

> [t]hat every choice we make, has been chosen by us, and every act of the mind, been proceeded and produced by an act of the mind. This is so true, that, in reality, the ultimate act is not styled free, from any quality of its own, but because the mind, in adopting it, was self-determined, that is, because it was preceded by another act. The ultimate act resulted completely from the determination that was its precursor. . . . All the acts, except the first, were necessary, and followed

each other, as inevitably as the links of a chain do, when the first link is drawn forward." (378)

Thus, in Shaftesbury's view, man is not the originator "of any event or series of events that take place in the universe"(385), but is only the vehicle through which certain events occur, or, if man did not exist, would not occur. Because of the laws of Necessity that rule the material universe, man has no need for the powers of choice. His path in life, the chain of events of his existence, is already determined for him. Man does, however, still exercise some control over the emotional events of his life, though this control is itself dependent on past moral experience and past moral action. Godwin emphasizes that "the doctrine of necessity does not overturn the nature of things. Happiness and misery, wisdom and error will still be distinct from each other, and there will still be a correspondence between them. Wherever there is that which may be the means of pleasure or pain to a sensitive being, there is a ground for preference and desire, or on the contrary for neglect and aversion. Benevolence and wisdom will be objects worthy to be desired, selfishness and error worthy to be disliked" (386). Thus, a man can exercise preference in regard to his moral action because he has acted in a similar way, according to similar feelings, many times before. Also, events in the world occur according to the moral feelings and actions of men. Therefore, man's power of emotional preference, which is ruled completely by past experience, influences the movement of historical events.

One application of Godwin's doctrine of Necessity and his concept of the power of personal preference was to political institutions. If an institution is corrupt and oppressive, the nature of man can recognize the necessity of destroying it; and, by opposing institutions, individuals can become the instruments of Necessity. Thus, the doctrine of Necessity addresses individual action as much as institutional or political change.

Godwin intended his novels to be vehicles for his major philosophical concepts. Therefore, his most famous novel, *Caleb Williams*, which demonstrates the doctrine of Necessity functioning among men, is an event, a moment of translation, in a relentless history of ideas moving toward Dickens. *Caleb Williams* translates dry philosophy into vibrant fiction, thus making philosophical doctrine available to readers who would never pick up Godwin's *Enquiry Concerning Political Justice. Caleb Williams*, with its emphasis on Necessity's operation through the actions of individuals, foreshadows the spontaneous combustion of Krook in *Bleak House*, the fall of the house of Clennam in *Little Dorrit*, the need for Necessitarian apocalypse in the corrupt nineteenth-century world.

In both Godwin's *Caleb Williams* and Dickens's *Little Dorrit*, Godwin's theories of individual man's relationship to his social world are embodied in similar characters, scenes, and situations. In *Caleb Williams*, Godwin presents the doctrine of Necessity in a negative and destructive context. The single word most often used to describe Falkland in *Caleb Williams* is "benevolence." The basic conflict of the novel, however, is between benevolence and selfish pride. Falkland, because he has murdered Tyrrel (his first nonbenevolent act), must express a preference between the rule of justice and the social ideal of honor. Justice in this case would be synonymous with benevolence in that Falkland, by confessing to the crime, would save Mr. Hawkins and his son from the gallows. However, in all of his past life Falkland has dedicated himself to the ideal of nobility, and thus he really has no choice in the matter at all. He must preserve his honor.

Caleb, in his relationship with Falkland, also finds himself caught between the rule of justice and the rule of honor. However, because of his low social class, justice is out of reach for Caleb. Finally, at the end of the novel, Caleb refuses to try any longer to carry out justice upon Falkland, who is a broken man, but instead gives in to emotional preference for pity and benevolence: "Shall I trample on a man thus dreadfully reduced? Shall I point my animosity against one whom the system of nature has brought down to the grave? It is impossible. There must have been some dreadful mistake in the train of argument that persuaded me to be the author of this hateful scene."[27] Ironically for Caleb, honor is synonymous with benevolence as he simply realizes that he has violated the feudal relationship of love between master and servant on which his whole life has been based. Thus, Caleb fulfills a natural and necessary benevolence by wishing to protect his lord in the end. Better late than never, Caleb bows to the same feelings of benevolent loyalty that later motivate Sam Weller to follow Pickwick into the debtor's prison.

The great irony of *Caleb Williams* is that both Falkland and Caleb act according to the dictates of the same set of environmental antecedents. Because of their individual conceptions of the idea of honor, conceptions developed throughout all of their past experiences, Falkland acts selfishly to destroy Caleb while Caleb acts selflessly to protect Falkland. Caleb's natural impulse to benevolence conquers the artificial nobility of Falkland. In Dickens's *Little Dorrit* the same tensions are present and the same higher values affirmed.

The central action of *Caleb Williams* consists of the mental and physical persecution of the innocent by the guilty. In *Little Dorrit*, as Clennam leaves the Circumlocution Office after his first encounter with the administrators of that institution, he meets his former traveling companion, Mr. Meagles, who introduces him to Daniel Doyce: "Mr. Clennam, will you do me the favour to look at this man? . . . You wouldn't suppose this man to be a notorious rascal; would you? . . . You wouldn't suppose him to be a public offender; would you? . . . No, but he is. He is a public offender. What has he been guilty of? Murder, manslaughter, arson, forgery, swindling, house-breaking, highway robbery, larceny, conspiracy, fraud? . . . He has been ingenious, and he has been trying to turn his ingenuity to his country's service. That makes him a public offender directly, sir" (*LD*, 10). As Meagles's rhetoric emphasizes, the Circumlocution Office has turned Daniel Doyce into a criminal guilty of trying to help others. Just as Falkland persecutes Caleb, the Circumlocution Office takes away Doyce's livelihood and drives him out of society, which he is only trying to improve, to the obscurity of Bleeding Heart Yard. Similarly, other innocents—Mr. Dorrit by Mrs. Clennam, Tattycoram by the spiteful Miss Wade, Pet Meagles by Henry Gowan, and the inmates of Bleeding Heart Yard by Casby—are oppressed by the guilty in *Little Dorrit*.

Another striking similarity between these two novels involves the central characters. Initially both Caleb Williams and Arthur Clennam are motivated by relentless curiosity. In surrendering to his curiosity Clennam, though he is forty years old, is just as naïve as the young Caleb Williams, who surrenders to the same impulse and begins to stalk Falkland's secret. Like Caleb Williams, and like so many other Dickens heroes (Richard Carstone in *Bleak House*, Harthouse in *Hard Times*, Sydney Carton, Pip, Harmon/Rokesmith in *Our Mutual Friend*), Clennam becomes both the pursuer and the pursued, driven by some secret wrong that engenders in him an irrational sense of guilt: "The shadow of a supposed act of injustice, which had hung over him since his father's death, was so vague and formless that it might be the result of a reality widely remote from his idea of it" (*LD*, 27). Both Caleb and Clennam share in the guilt even as they are struggling to expose the crime. But, most important, both characters, though innocent, are made to suffer because they have the temerity to say, as Clennam does, "'I want to know.'" Both must give up their work because of their knowledge or suspicion of the guilt of their employers. Both must constantly live with the shadow of the prison upon them. And both, because of their benevolent natures, must always exist in a state of indecision, because they both will to protect their persecutors even as they are being persecuted.

Both Caleb's and Clennam's lives are a constant search for the moment when the benevolence of their natures can rise out of potentiality and by necessity cure the disease that haunts their past. The only way they can attain this moment is through self-abnegation, and both are willing to pay the price. Clennam desires his imprisonment, as does Caleb Williams who goes to jail rather than say "'one word of resolute accusation against my patron'"(*CW*, Postscript). Perhaps the best explanation of the common predicament of Caleb and Clennam is that of Mr. Pancks in *Little Dorrit*: "'I don't say anything of your making yourself poor to repair a wrong you never committed. That's you. A man must be himself'"(II, 8). The similar actions of these two characters are their means of fulfilling their own naturally benevolent natures.

Many points of comparison between the plots and characters of *Caleb Williams* and *Little Dorrit* exist, but the greatest similarity between the two novels lies in their similar affirmation of the philosophy of benevolence that reveals itself by means of the doctrine of Necessity. For Godwin, Necessity is a cosmic power for good that operates through individual men in the world. Dickens's social consciousness in *Little Dorrit* displays the manner in which Necessity can operate in the Victorian world if there are people who care enough to allow the natural benevolence of human nature to express itself. Every institution in *Little Dorrit* is subject to Necessity, which operates through the natural benevolence of man.

One of the great characters in *Little Dorrit* is Mr. Merdle. He is a nondescript, ratlike man, but he is described by Mr. Dorrit as a national institution: "Mr. Merdle's is a name of—ha—world wide repute. Mr. Merdle's undertakings are immense. They bring him such vast sums of money, that they are regarded as—hum—national benefits. Mr. Merdle is a man of his time. The name of Merdle is the name of the age" (II, 5). Mr. Dorrit does not realize just how perceptive his words are. Mr. Merdle is only a name. There is nothing of substance in the man or in any of his enterprises. The narrator, through the use of historical imagery, further hints at the ambiguous difference between the force of Mr. Merdle's name and the substance of the man himself: "He looked far more like a man in possession of his house under a distraint, than a commercial Colossus bestriding his own hearthrug, while the little ships were sailing in to dinner" (II, 12). The Colossus image embodies the far reaching and ruling power of Merdle's commercial enterprises, but it also suggests his transitory existence. Like the great Colossus of Rhodes, which sailors mistakenly thought was a beacon on so sound a base it would exist forever, Merdle and his commercial empire will certainly fall. This image also suggests that Merdle is but an idol with feet of common clay; and when the Colossus falls, its feet are found to be of the commonest clay indeed (or perhaps of an even more vulgar material of French derivation). In death his name no longer has any meaning, and he is only "a heavily-made man, with an obtuse head, and coarse, mean common features." With Merdle's death the great commercial empire that had "set him on his pedestal" comes crashing down because it was based only on "carrion at the bottom of a bath" and "the greatest Forger and the greatest Thief that ever cheated the gallows" (*LD*, II, 25). Later, in *Our Mutual Friend*, Dickens uses the same historical imagery to describe Mr. Podsnap—he stands before the fire "executing a statuette of the Colossus at Rhodes" (*OMF*, I, 10)—who also is a fragile and superficial national institution.

Dickens also deals symbolically with religious institutions in *Little Dorrit*. Mrs. Clennam's house represents the religion operating in the novel and is the tabernacle of that religion. The dilapidated physical condition of the Clennam house presents clearly Dickens's view of such a religion's condition in the Victorian world. From the beginning of the novel the imagery of the house dictates that this repressive religion must fall. In 1860, three years after *Little Dorrit* was published, George Eliot's *The Mill on the Floss* appeared in print. Both of these novels have been accused of using a flagrantly melodramatic *deus ex machina* event as an expedient means of resolving their respective plots. The flood in *The Mill on the Floss* and the fall of the Clennam house in *Little Dorrit* are cataclysmic events surely, but both are meticulously prepared for and both perform a distinct symbolic function. The fall of the Clennam house is prefigured in the very first description of the house: "Many years ago it had had it in its mind to slide down sideways; it had been propped up, however, and was leaning on some half-dozen gigantic crutches: which gymnasium for the neighboring cats, weather-stained, smoke-blackened, and overgrown with weeds, appeared in these latter days to be no very sure reliance" (*LD*, I, 3).

This description clearly indicates that the house could fall for physical reasons. It will fall, however, due to moral reasons as well; reasons made evident by the definition of the house as religious symbol. The religion that is consecrated in this decrepit tabernacle is embodied in Mrs. Clennam as she reads aloud her favorite passages from the Bible: "Sternly, fiercely, wrathfully—praying that her enemies (she made them by her tone and manner expressly hers) might be put to the edge of the sword, consumed by fire, smitten by plagues and leprosy, that their bones might be ground to dust, and that they might be utterly exterminated" (I, 3). Mrs. Clennam's Old Testament-based religion is only destructive, and its tone is only wrathful, with absolutely no trace of benevolence or love. Significantly, the religion of the Clennam house allies itself with intrinsic evil in the world, while simultaneously rejecting all that is good. The second prefiguration of the fall of the Clennam house occurs when Rigaud is accepted into the house for the first time. At the moment of his entrance Affery hears "the strangest of sounds. Evidently close at hand from the peculiar shock it communicates to the air, yet subdued as if it were far off. A tremble, a rumble, and a fall of some light, dry matter" (I, 29). The sound is the voice of Necessity communicating, through the rotted timbers of the tabernacle, the warning that any religion that accepts what is intrinsically evil is itself undermining any spiritual foundation that it may have and will eventually fall.

Mrs. Clennam's religion, which accepts the diabolical Rigaud and emphasizes the "corruption of our hearts, the evil of our ways, the curse that is upon us, the terrors that surround us" (II, 30), is directly opposed to the eighteenth-century philosophical (and religious) ideal of the natural goodness of man with which both Godwin and Dickens were so vitally concerned. Thus, Necessity demands that this religion must fall and fall it does; but at the very moment that the tabernacle of the old religion crumbles into dust and ashes, a new religion, that of Little Dorrit and Arthur Clennam, rises in its place: "From a radiant centre over the whole length and breadth of the tranquil firmament, great shoots of light streamed among the early stars, like signs of the blessed later covenant of peace and hope that changed the crown of thorns into a glory" (II, 31).

In replacing the destructive religion of the Clennam house with this vision of religious hope and joy, Dickens shows that the concept of Godwinian Necessity, when applied to a Victorian religious institution, becomes consonant with the image of Christ as paradigm of benevolence. As the house is falling, Little Dorrit emphasizes that the paraclete of this new religion of man is universal benevolence: "Be guided only by the healer of the sick, the raiser of the dead, the friend of all who were afflicted and forlorn, the patient Master who shed tears of compassion for our infirmities. We cannot but be right if we put all the rest away, and do everything in remembrance of Him. There is no vengeance and no infliction of suffering in his life" (II, 31). Little Dorrit is simpleminded and this act of faith is in character, but for Dickens the importance of this statement lies in the fact that Christ was the paradigm of man, and in his historical existence he affirmed the fundamentally benevolent nature of man. On this point, Godwin and Dickens's atheistic and theistic views of life can easily merge. Thus, like Mr. Merdle's commercial institution, Mrs. Clennam's religious institution falls and destroys Rigaud (as Fagin in *Oliver Twist*, Quilp in *The Old Curiosity Shop*, Carker in *Dombey and Son*, Tulkinghorn and Krook in *Bleak House* were destroyed in earlier novels), the Hobbesian man, the extreme opposite of the Shaftesburian/Godwinian conception of human nature. Necessity simultaneously destroys both the house and Rigaud because of the antibenevolent spirit that both embodied.

The necessitous fall of the other great parasitic institution in *Little Dorrit* also is explicitly prefigured. The Circumlocution Office, Dickens's ganglionic symbol of the bureaucratic corruption of government, must fall because England, as the erstwhile Daniel Doyce puts it, is "a country suffering under the affliction of a great amount of earnestness," in which "in an exceeding short space of time" there will not be "a single Barnacle left sticking to a post" (II, 8). In Godwin's and Dickens's vision, the forces of Necessity are aligned with people like Daniel Doyce and Arthur Clennam. Perhaps Mr. Plornish, in his simple way, best defines the Godwinian ideal of Necessity that is at work in *Little Dorrit*: "Mr. Plornish amicably growled, in his philosophical but not lucid manner, that there was ups you see, and there was downs; . . . there they was, you know. He had heerd it given for a truth that accordin' as the world went round, which round it did rewolve undoubted, even the best of gentlemen must take his turn of standing with his ed upside down and all his air a-flying the wrong way into what you might call Space. Wery well then. . . . That gentleman's ed would come up'ards when his turn come, that gentleman's air would be a pleasure to look upon being all smooth again, and wery well then!" (II, 27).

Because the powers of natural benevolence are triumphant in *Little Dorrit*, just as they were in *Caleb Williams*, the novel cannot validly be called "dark." The Dickensian vision articulated in *Little Dorrit* is one of hope and faith, not in a world hereafter, but in this world, where the power of Necessity works for the good of men. The Dickens vision is based on the optimistic philosophy of man articulated in the novels of the eighteenth century, and Dickens consistently affirmed this attitude toward life in the face of the many changing viewpoints and conditions of his own contemporary world.

That is not to say, however, that Dickens was a Pollyanna in terms of his social history or that, to use Robert Browning's ironic phrase from *Pippa Passes*, he believed that "all's right with the world." Within Victorian English society, certain things were obviously wrong, reforms needed to be undertaken. If Dickens's philosophy embraced Godwinian principles of perfectibility, he was also a quite clear-eyed social realist. In his fiction, he clearly identified the problems present in his society and warned against them. In fact, one of the most powerful, historically-based, recurring images that appears in every Dickens novel, that of shipwreck, serves as an ongoing warning to the Victorians to locate their threatening social problems and avoid running the ship of society aground on them. But, if Dickens was a social realist carefully navigating the shoals of Victorian social problems, he was also a positive and confident social reformer who never for one moment

THREE

Dickens and Shipwreck

If Dickens evolved a clearly defined eighteenth-century philosophical vision of nineteenth-century society, that philosophy of man had to stand up to the historical realities of Victorian life and Industrial Revolution economics. What was the "condition of England" in the mid-nineteenth century, and how was Dickens to portray it? Dickens's mentor as a social historian was, of course, his close friend Thomas Carlyle. Carlyle's *The French Revolution* gave Dickens inspiration and tonal direction for the writing of his overtly historical novels, *Barnaby Rudge* and *A Tale of Two Cities,* but Carlyle's fictional meditation on Victorian social history, specifically *Past and Present,* taught Dickens a valuable lesson about how to portray social history to the masses. To use Carlyle's own term, the realities of social history could not be presented in the form of "dryasdust" philosophical and historical lectures nor in the form of oppressively pessimistic description. Carlyle taught Dickens that the realities of social history must be presented metaphorically.

What Dickens needed to find, then, was a metaphor for the mid-nineteenth-century "condition of England" that would compliment the optimistic philosophy of natural benevolence that he had embraced as his vision for the Victorian age. He found his metaphor in one of the most commonplace events of English social history, in the recurring event that exerted continual influence on Industrial Revolution economics. Throughout his fiction, he envisioned Victorian society as a historical epoch on the verge of shipwreck.

England and Shipwreck

In 1805 the East Indiaman Earl of Abergavenny, under the command of Captain John Wordsworth, wrecked on the rocks off Portland Bill. Two hundred fifty lives were lost to the sea. Immediately, news reports and interviews with at least two of the survivors appeared in the London papers. Only eight days after the shipwreck, a forty-nine-page pamphlet account of the Earl of Abergavenny's demise was published. The next year another chapbook on this particular wreck was published and the story was also included in an important anthology of shipwreck narratives.[1] All of this appeared, as well as three poems about the wreck written by Captain Wordsworth's brother

In 1826 the Frances Mary, sailing out of New Brunswick for Liverpool, ran into fierce storms, became a dismasted hulk, and drifted helplessly in the North Atlantic because her cargo of lumber would not sink. The passengers and crew, starving, took to cannibalism to survive:

> James Frier was working his passage home, under a promise of marriage
> to Ann Saunders, the female passenger . . . who, when she heard of
> Frier's death, shrieked a loud yell, then snatching a cup from . . . the
> mate, cut her late intended husband's throat and drank his blood
> insisting that she had the greatest right to it.[2]

Between 1793 and 1849, the Royal Navy lost 417 vessels not including vessels lost during the Napoleonic wars. Seventy-one of these 417 Royal Navy shipwrecks cost the lives of all on board; for example, 590 lives were lost when the Hero sank off Jutland in 1811.[3]

In 1838, the following title was published in London: Shipwreck of the Stirling Castle, containing a Faithful Narrative of the Dreadful Sufferings of the Crew, and the Cruel Murder of Captain Fraser by the Savages. Also the Horrible Barbarity of the Cannibals inflicted upon the Captain's Widow, whose Unparalleled Sufferings are stated by herself, and corroborated by the Other Survivors.[4]

In 1847, the Son and Heir bound for Barbadoes sank in the pages of Dickens's novel Dombey and Son, triggering the domino effect which would result in the eventful failure of the great London trading house of that book's title. And, in 1850, "a schooner from Spain or Portugal, laden with fruit and wine" (55) broke up and sank close to shore just off Yarmouth in the pages of David Copperfield claiming the lives of all on board and at least one rescuer. These are just some of the more famous shipwrecks of the Victorian age and indications of the whole society's fascination, both morbid and pragmatic, with the most frequent and frequently reported type of disaster of the time.

There were excellent reasons why, during the Victorian age, ship-wrecks were a subject of such intense national interest, of such conscientious reportage and literary exploitation. The most obvious reason was their frequency as a natural and man-made disaster. Earthquakes, volcanic eruptions, floods, wars, revolutions, and plagues only happened in England or the Empire once or twice per century, but violent storms at sea and the shipwrecks they caused occurred almost every day, claimed large numbers of lives, and inflicted huge losses of property. One statistic can be projected out to indicate just how elemental a fact of English life shipwrecks were. In the short period of five years between 1864 and 1869, the Lloyd's registers counted a world loss of 10,000 sailing ships: "In 1856 alone 1153 ships were lost round the British coast. . . . In one day of a great gale in 1859, 195 ships foundered; another 298 ships were lost in the terrible November of 1893."[5]

Even more shocking, however, are the statistics that chronicled the loss of life attributable to shipwrecks in that age. In 1800 the *Queen Charlotte* went down with a loss of 673 of 859 passengers and crew. Four hundred of 500 died in the wreck of the *Invincible* in 1801; 731 died on the *St. George* in 1803; and 587 of 593 on the *Defence* in 1811. In the 1860s, *The Book of the Ocean*, which compiled statistics of shipwrecks, stated: "In England, it is calculated that about five thousand natives of the British Isles yearly perish at sea."[6]

Why did so many ships sink and why were so many lives lost? In his book, *British Shipping*, R. H. Thornton, after enumerating at length all the things that can go wrong with a ship at sea, flatly states: "In short the fast-sailing, full-rigged ship remains about the most dangerous vehicle ever invented by man."[7] But sailing ships were not just inherently dangerous by species; too often they were dangerous due to inadequacy, neglect, and even criminal intent. John Fowles, in his essay *Shipwrecks*, argues that "[b]efore Samuel Plimsoll's Merchant Shipping Act of 1876 [ships] were often sent out criminally overladen, undermanned, and rotten-timbered. Sailors had a name for these: coffin-ships. On a lee-shore or in heavy seas that was only too often precisely what they were——and also precisely what their astutely over-insured owners hoped they would be."[8]

However, such staggering numbers of British ships sank not only because they were defective. They also sank due to the ineptitude of their captains, the inexperience of their crews, and the underdevelopment of their navigational equipment and knowledge. In the course of the debate over the repeal of the protectionist Navigation Laws in 1849, the following analysis of the state of the British shipping industry surfaced:

> For the truth is that since the end of the Napoleonic Wars, British ship-owners had done little or nothing to advance their industry. . . . With the

one exception of. . . . the East India Company . . . the industry had failed to develop any general standard of professional competence or amour-propre. . . . With roads and railways underdeveloped, our coastal traffic was enormous. No finer seamen could be found, nor more jealous of their craft, than the sturdy illiterates who fought their little brigs in all weathers between London and the Tyne. But the supply was not inexhaustible.

An 1843 survey conducted by the Foreign office concluded that "British shipmasters are frequently entrusted with commands or voyages requiring more knowledge of the scientific department of navigation than they possess" and "the persons placed in charge of British ships were too frequently unfit for their duties, and while many of them were so habitually addicted to drunkenness as to be altogether incompetent, not a few were almost without education."[9]

In his history of *British Shipping*, Thornton characterized Victorian seamen as "the rum-soaked illiterates of 1843 . . . the so-called master mariners, who could not read a chart."[10] Not only were there bad ships and overmatched, undertrained seamen, but there also weren't enough lighthouses. Before 1800, along the whole Cornwall coast, one the most dangerous reef configurations in the world, there were only four lighthouses, and two of those—the Lizard and St. Agnes in the Scillies—were undependable, coal-cresset beacons. The most important lighthouse on the south coast of England, the Bishop's Rock, did not go into operation until 1858.[11]

The inherent danger of sailing ships and seafaring—bad boats, bad seamen, poor navigational equipment, especially lighthouses, lack of real education in navigational skills—were all reasons for the astounding frequency of shipwrecks and their prominence in Victorian life. But another factor also contributed to the large numbers that appear in those statistics. The loss of ships and the loss of life was shockingly high simply because of a significant increase in sea-going volume in the late eighteenth and the nineteenth centuries. More ships sailed out more often carrying more cargo and more passengers than ever before, hence more sank and more lives were lost than ever before. The main reasons for this large and sudden increase in volume were emigration to America and the rapid growth of America as a purchaser of British manufactured goods. By 1835, "Europe was sending 50,000 emigrants per year to America and, yearly, the Irish sailed by the thousands from Liverpool to New York."[12] Further, "in the decade following 1845 over two and one half million persons sailed from British ports alone, a vast increase on the annual average of about 70,000 from the whole of Europe in the decade before."[13] From 1787 to 1860 there was tremendous expansion of the import-export figures out of the port of Liverpool. By 1852, for example, Liverpool was exporting 452,000 tons of coal overseas, 116,000 tons coastwise and to Ireland, and 1,000 million yards of piece-goods to all parts of the world.[14] Emigration and trade fed the maw of shipwreck frequency that, in turn, fed the maw of Victorian curiosity, sensationalism, and imagination.

In a certain cold way, all of those aforementioned statistics explain the Victorian preoccupation with shipwrecks, but, in a more human way, that Victorian fascination for shipwreck news and shipwreck myth was also fed by the very real and personal effects that this staggering number of shipwrecks had upon the Victorian population and the society itself. When a shipwreck occurred, the ship was lost, the cargo lost, lives lost, profits lost, jobs lost, mail lost, investment capital lost, and insurance lost. Albeit there might have been some positive effects for salvage wreckers, shipbuilding outfitters, and smart insurers, in no way could the positive ever outweigh the negative effects of a shipwreck. In other words, a shipwreck set off a ripple effect that spread throughout all levels of Victorian society and touched the lives of countless people in large and small, economic and human, ways.

Of course, the major human loss was the lives of loved ones or the instant extermination of whole families emigrating to the New World. The sea and the ships that sailed her were England's life blood, and the history of the sea was part of everyone's personal history. Thus, every time there was a shipwreck, its impact was felt in the hearts of the people as well as in the pocketbooks of the merchants and insurance underwriters, but it was also felt in the basic day-to-day survival of the nation.

In the nineteenth century the British economy was totally dependent upon the British shipping industry, and the British shipping industry was dependent upon three basic strengths:

1. The strong industrial position of the United Kingdom itself, based on free access to the markets of the world for foodstuffs and raw materials;
2. a world-wide Empire with well-distributed coaling stations and ports of call;
3. a large coal export trade that provided ships with outward freights that would otherwise be lacking.[15]

In the mid-nineteenth century, England's life blood flowed in a vein-artery closed system. Coal pumping out; foodstuffs and raw materials (such as cotton) constantly flowing in. Shipwrecks were the clots that slowed the pulse of the nation, clogged the economy and the production capability of the most industrialized nation in the world.

England's shipping had to be a two-way flow system in order for any national benefit or personal profit to occur. It worked in this way: the "majority of ships taking coal from England and Wales . . . bring back to England . . . lumber from the White Sea or Scandinavia, grain from the Black Sea, cotton from Egypt, ore from Spain. Coal, in other words, holds the balance against a variety of imports, thereby giving the carrying trade if not all-around employment, at least much better employment than would be the case in the absence of coal."[16] In 1850, more than 3.2 million tons of coal left the ports of the United Kingdom[17] and that coal was all there was, for the most part, to subsidize the return freight service, especially from distant ports, which was where all the profits and national benefits accrued. As an unknown writer of the seventeenth century wrote: "The coal trade is indeed the refuge and mother of our entire shipping industry."[18] Thus, another major ripple from a shipwreck was the temporary loss of either export profits or import materials to be used within the British capital and industrial system.

A third major ripple-effect ran through the London financial community. When a shipwreck occurred, the ones most quickly affected after the crew, the ship-owner, and the families of the crew were the maritime insurance underwriters. In the aftermath of any shipwreck, the insurers were immediately notified and their investigations of the wreck's cause, the action of captain and crew, and the value of the lost property and cargo were set in motion. The underwriting of marine insurance in the nineteenth century worked rather differently from the sort of insurance experience most people take for granted in the late twentieth century. A policy for a certain amount was not simply taken out with a single company or agent. When a ship went to sea, it could be underwritten by as many as 100 to 200 different marine insurance underwriters, who were quartered under the umbrella of the Lloyd's of London marine insurance exchange.

The history of Lloyd's of London is well known but deserves brief recounting. In the seventeenth century, because of the uncertainty of the mail system and the nonexistence of newspapers, almost all shipping news and intelligence had to be disseminated by word of mouth. Owners of vessels, sea captains, merchants, and anyone else interested in shipping intelligence gathered at certain coffee shops to exchange news and gather information on current events affecting their interests. In the 1680s and 1690s the coffee house of one Edward Lloyd became the most important centre for gaining information concerning shipping matters. By the 1730s the concept of professional shipping underwriting had come into existence and Lloyd's Coffee House was London's major marine insurance center. In 1734 the then proprietor of Lloyd's Coffee House established and published a newspaper, *Lloyd's List*, which was devoted exclusively to shipping intelligence. By 1760 the first *Register of Shipping* was published by the "Society of Underwriters" at Lloyd's Coffee House, who had, in a sense, incorporated themselves. In 1779, seventy merchants, underwriters, and brokers at Lloyd's banded together at a hundred pounds a head to build an exchange where they could conduct the marine intelligence and insurance business. By the turn of the nineteenth century the shipping insurance industry had fully outgrown its coffee house beginnings and was a rather streamlined financial institution in London.[19]

A Captain Robert Dollar, whose ship was wrecked at sea, describes how his Lloyd's policy was set up:

> The ship was insured for One Hundred Eighty Thousand Pounds. I had a Lloyd's policy for it, and on the back of it there were 103 different signatures for various amounts. Some for a hundred pounds, some fifty pounds, some five hundred pounds, and so on. Lloyd's had taken their insurance and then re-issued it and marked it all on the back; so each paid the amount that was on it in his name.[20]

The importance of marine insurance to the British shipping industry and the British economy in the last three centuries is staggering. Without marine insurance,

> only the wealthiest individuals and corporations could afford to risk their vessels on the high seas; without it only such commodities as afford a wide margin of profit could enter into world trade; without it many lands, which today are the homes of millions, would be deserted. Industries would be lacking raw materials; and raw materials would rot for want of transportation. Marine insurance is the basis of credit, without which commercial loans to importers and exporters would be impossible. Marine insurance bears to commerce the relation of bodyguard rather than senile attendant.[21]

It stands to reason, then, that the underwriters on the Lloyd's exchange had to have the best information concerning ships that were sound, not "coffin ships" ("ships overloaded and overinsured, the destruction of which meant more to their owners than their safe arrival");[22] captains who were competent; and the circumstances of any shipwreck that did occur. When a ship was wrecked and the insurance had to be paid, the rule of Lloyd's was very clearly defined: "every Member independently of his actual underwriting funds at Lloyd's is liable up to the last penny of his entire personal fortune outside Lloyd's for the due fulfillment of his underwriting obligations and thereafter his Policyholders have first call on his deposit."[23]

Early in *Our Mutual Friend*, Veneering "institutes an original comparison between the country and a ship, pointedly calling the ship the Vessel of State, and the Minister the Man at the Helm. . . . 'And, gentlemen, when the timbers of the Vessel of the State are unsound and the Man at the Helm is unskillful, would these great Marine Insurers, who rank among our world-famed merchant-princes—would they insure her, gentlemen? Would they underwrite her? Would they incur risk in her? . . . No!" (II, 3).

A fourth major ripple-effect in English society was the effect that a shipwreck would have on employment. At the turn of the nineteenth century, under government subsidization (principally the East India Dock Acts of 1799, 1800, 1802), the West India and East India dock systems turned London into the greatest of all European ports and stimulated the drastic expansion of the British cargo fleets. The Port of London's elaborate dock system as we know it today was fully in place by 1830.[24] Simultaneously, the Liverpool dock system was being similarly expanded.[25] Ironically, the larger, more complex docking systems of these two major English ports not only increased British shipping, but also increased the number of shipwrecks. Collisions, explosions, fires, and small boat injuries were not uncommon in these new, crowded dock areas. In-port accidents were, in fact, so commonplace that laws were written to deal with this particular type of shipwreck. The regulations for the West India docks in the Port of London read:

> Vessels were not to navigate the docks under sail. . . . Vessels were to unload immediately on entrance into the docks. Explosives were not allowed in the docks, and combustible materials were only allowed twelve hours on the quays . . . penalties incurred by seamen or lightermen were recoverable from the masters or owners.[26]

Yet, with the expansion of the London and Liverpool dock system came a parallel expansion of the work force that supported the huge British shipping industry. When a British ship, or any ship that frequented British ports, wrecked or sank, the impact of that disaster was felt not only by those involved directly with that particular ship, but also by an army of support personnel involved in the docking, loading, unloading, outfitting, maintenance, and provisioning of that ship. The in-port workforce began with the pilots, watermen, and lightermen, who guided the ships into the docks and did small transport work, and progressed to the dockside personnel. These included the wharfingers (clerks responsible for the consignment documents), the superintendent, the stevedores, and as one depiction stated, the

> dockers [who] work in gangs of seventeen men of whom some are on the quay, trucking cargo to the ship's side and slipping under it the stout rope slings in readiness to be picked up by the hook of the ship's fall. On deck there will be a winchman . . . and down in the hold will be the remainder of the gang who receive the cargo and stow it. A gang, then, is a self-contained unit and, given time enough, could load a whole ship. Our ship, however, has six hatches and could probably work twelve gangs simultaneously without danger or confusion . . . a half-day is the minimum period of engagement for a docker.[27]

A shipwreck would have the effect of depriving this whole support structure of a significant portion of their employment.

The Shipwreck Literature

In *Dombey and Son*, Dickens is quite aware, in both financial and human terms, of the ripple-effect set off by the shipwreck of the *Son and Heir*. Carker, the novel's villain, shows little concern for the effect of that shipwreck on the House of Dombey and Son when he remarks, "The underwriters suffer a considerable loss. We are very sorry. No Help! Such is life!" (45). But later in the novel the wreck of the *Son and Heir* becomes a metaphor for the fall of the House of Dombey itself:

> Through a whole year, the famous House of Dombey and Son had fought . . . against the infatuation of its head, who would not contract its enterprises by a hair's breadth and would not listen to a word of warning that the ship he strained so hard against the storm, was weak and could not bear it. The year was out, and the great House was down. (58)

The ineptitude of the captain, the complexity of the financial storm, and finally the breaking down of the ship all cause the wreck of the House of Dombey and affect all who are concerned with that house. As evidenced later by the all-encompassing fog in *Bleak House*, Dickens chooses metaphors that can set in motion exactly these kinds of cross-cultural ripple-effects. Shipwrecks are ideal for his purposes.

The Victorian fascination with shipwrecks and the lore that surrounds them can be explained by their statistical frequency and the social ripple-effects they had; but the fascination was also fueled by the Victorian media. Within the limited context of shipwreck media dissemination, there were, in the nineteenth century, two major outlets. First, newspapers: the major newspapers of the day all had shipping intelligence sections while some special interest newspapers were devoted solely either to shipping intelligence or to the reporting of shipping disasters. Second, shipwreck narratives: these were generally first-person accounts of shipwrecks and of the survivors' ensuing trials and tribulations. They appeared under a number of different formats: individual books, chapbooks, broadsides devoted to a single shipwreck, anthologies of shipwreck narratives, and shipwreck novels.

By Dickens's time, newspaper reportage of shipping intelligence and shipwreck coverage was a long-standing staple of most newspapers. *The London Times, The Daily News* (in which Dickens held a proprietary interest, in expectation at least, and for which he wielded editorial power), and Dickens's own tabloid, *The Household Narrative,* had regular sections devoted solely to shipping intelligence and disaster reports. Also, smaller periodicals existed that were devoted solely to shipping news and shipwreck coverage. For example, *Lloyd's List,* begun in 1734, and "published without interruption ever since . . .[was], apart from the official *London Gazette* published by the government, the oldest surviving newspaper in London."[28] In Dickens's time, while the major newspapers had regular sections of "criminal intelligence" and shipping intelligence that included shipwreck reportage, "the comprehensive reporting of recent crimes and disasters . . . became a staple of the cheap newspaper. The waywardness of man and Providence was a double blessing to early Victorian popular journalism, for not only was the supply of such material inexhaustible; so too was the common man's appetite for it."[29] These specialized periodicals were: "*The Naval Chronicle* (1799-1818) [which] included narratives of shipwrecks and disasters . . . [and] *Chronicles of the Sea* (London, 1838-40) [which] consisted of 119 weekly numbers . . . apparently devoted exclusively to maritime disasters."[30]

While there was certainly no shortage of up-to-the-minute news reports of shipwrecks in Victorian England, one of the two most popular genres of nonfiction prose was the shipwreck narrative, published in either single publication or anthology form. Since the beginnings of print, shipwreck narratives have been prominent in the demands of the English common reader. This was especially true in the nineteenth century. Hakluyt's *Voyages,* for example, one of the top ten best sellers of Shakespeare's age,[31] was still being reprinted and selling strongly in Dickens's

age. By the mid-nineteenth century, Hakluyt's *Voyages* had been super-
ceded by more modern, more sensational anthologies of shipwreck narratives such as Archibald Duncan's six-volume *The Mariner's Chronicle*.
Published in 1804, *The Mariner's Chronicle* became the basic source for many
of the other shipwreck narrative anthologies of the nineteenth century,[32]
including Cook's *Voyages*[33] and Hall's *Voyages*.[34] In fact, throughout his
English Common Reader, Richard Altick consistently refers to the popularity
of voyage and shipwreck non-fiction. For example, in 1826 the whole
printing business of Archibald Constable was rescued from bankruptcy by
the success of a reprint of Basil Hall's *Voyages*.[35] Similarly, whenever Altick
offers his different versions of Victorian best-seller lists, shipwreck narratives are always well represented. In 1849, a Buckinghamshire clergyman
described the most popular books in his local lending library: "we require
duplicates over and over again of such works as Bunyan's *Pilgrim's Progress*,
Defoe's *Robinson Crusoe*, Cook's *Voyages*, and works of that description."[36]
In 1838 the London Statistical Society tabulated the holdings of ten
Westminister lending libraries. Shipwreck narratives, "voyages" as they
were most often called, were the second highest in number of holdings.
"Sir Walter Scott and his imitators" compiled a total of 166 volumes and
"Voyages" was second with 136 volumes.[37] In 1883, school children were
still required by public school inspectors such as Matthew Arnold to read
"extracts from standard authors, or from 'such works as *Robinson Crusoe*,
Voyages . . . or Biographies of eminent men.'"[38]

Among Dickens's own characters, shipwreck narratives were also very
popular. In *Dombey and Son*, Solomon Gills and his nephew, Walter Gay, are
well versed in the shipwreck narratives of their day. On a snug night in the
Wooden Midshipman, old Sol and young Walter sit before the fire and talk
of the sea and of famous shipwrecks as if reciting some familiar litany:

> . . . why when the *Charming Sally* went down in the—"In the Baltic Sea,
> in the dead of the night, five and twenty minutes past twelve when the
> captain's watch stopped in his pocket; he lying dead against the main
> mast—on the fourteenth of February, seventeen forty-nine!" cried
> Walter with great animation.
>
> "Aye, to be sure!" cried old Sol, "quite right! Then, there were
> five hundred casks of such wine aboard; and all hands (except the first
> mate, first lieutenant, two seamen, and a lady in a leaky boat) going to
> work to save the casks, got drunk and died drunk, singing 'Rule
> Brittannia,' when she settled and went down, and ending in one awful
> scream in chorus."

"But when the *George the Second* drove ashore, Uncle, on the coast of Cornwall, in a dismal gale, two hours before daybreak, on the fourth of March, 'seventy one, she had near two hundred horses aboard; and the horses breaking loose down below, early in the gale, and tearing to and fro, and trampling each other to death, made such noises, and set up such human cries, that the crew believing the ship to be full of devils, some of the best men, losing heart and head, went overboard in despair, and only two were left alive, at last, to tell the tale."

"And when," said old Sol, "when the *Polyphemus* . . ."

"Private West India Trader, burden three hundred and fifty tons, Captain John Brown of Deptford. Owners, Wiggs and Co.," cried Walter. (4)

Dickens goes on for almost two full pages in this vein with old Sol and Walter reciting the names of the wrecked ships, the circumstances of the disasters, even the cargoes and officers and owners. The shipwrecks that old Sol and Walter so animatedly remember, of the *Charming Sally*, the *George the Second* and the *Polyphemus,* are all shipwrecks of the late eighteenth century that they could only have learned about from reading the shipwreck anthologies of the day. For young Walter, these shipwrecks are romantic events in history and he knows his history of the sea quite well.

Thus, the shipwreck narratives, either in the Victorian media or in the many anthologies of such narratives, were readily available and enthusiastically read and studied, especially by young Englishmen who fancied themselves one day going to sea in ships as so many of their ancestors and countrymen had always done. However, by far the most popular shipwreck narrative among the English common readers and among Dickens's own characters as well was not a work of nonfiction prose found in a newspaper, a shipping intelligencer, or a shipwreck narrative anthology. Rather, it was Daniel Defoe's classic work of shipwreck fiction, *Robinson Crusoe:*

The common reader has always relished a good story, and nowhere has the taste been more pronounced than on the very fringes of the literate public, to which no other form of reading has an equal appeal. Small shopkeepers, artisans and domestic servants—people who had gone to school for only two or three years—at the beginning of the century had devoured *Robinson Crusoe* and the narratives that imitated it, notably *The Adventures of Phillip Quarll.*[39]

All through the Victorian age the popularity of *Robinson Crusoe* held up; "cottages had their little shelf of worn and precious books, family possessions passed down through a century or more—the *Bible*, *Robinson Crusoe*, . . ."[40] In 1867, *Robinson Crusoe* was still mandatory reading for any Victorian school child. One commentator remarked quite negatively, "It is as if we were to begin the teaching of our children with Milton's *Paradise Lost*, and then advance them to *Robinson Crusoe*."[41] In fact, in the 1850s, "penny books about Jack the Giantkiller, and . . . Robinson Crusoe"[42] were the scorn of schoolteachers. Thus, the shipwreck narrative of *Robinson Crusoe* was a sort of universal furnishing of the Victorian consciousness, like ornamental table legs and lace antimacassars.

Allusions to *Robinson Crusoe* are also everywhere in the canon of Charles Dickens. Of all the well known shipwreck narratives, it is by far his favorite. Early in *The Pickwick Papers*, Mr. Pickwick embarks on an ill fated bird shoot with his host who "carrying both guns like a second Robinson Crusoe, led the way" (7). In *The Old Curiosity Shop*, after his return from the dead and his return to being a "devil-may-care bachelor," when he judges his wife's mourning of his supposed death not up to his standards, Quilp sets up housekeeping in his counting house at the wharf, which he characterizes as "a country-house like Robinson Crusoe['s]" (50).

Defoe's novel is, perhaps, the strongest literary influence on Dickens's *Martin Chuzzlewit*. Early in the novel, as Tom Pinch explores the city of Salisbury, he is drawn to a shop "where children's books were sold and where poor Robinson Crusoe stood alone in his might, with dog and hatchet, goatskin cap and fowling-piece, calmly surveying Philip Quarll and the host of imitators round him and calling Mr. Pinch to witness that he of all the crowd impressed one solitary footprint on the shore of boyish memory" (*MC*, 5). Not only does this passage confirm Richard Altick's assertions concerning the prominence of shipwreck narratives, specifically *Robinson Crusoe*, in Victorian bookstores and libraries (both lending and private), but it also prefigures the ironic shipwreck narrative that will serve as the experimental fulcrum of this text, the bitter and debilitating shipwreck of young Martin and Mark in the fallen Eden of America. Later in *Martin Chuzzlewit*, like Crusoe and his man Friday, Martin and Mark Tapley look for the first time upon Eden; it was a "flat morass, bestrewn with fallen timber; a marsh on which the good growth of the earth seemed to have been wrecked and cast away" (23). Other characters in *Martin Chuzzlewit* frequently refer to their favorite works of shipwreck narrative. In his bombastic speech, General Choke refers to "the naked visitors to Crusoe's island" (21) and, when John Westlock seeks to calm

Tom Pinch's fears of imposing, he refers to his rooms as "nothing but a few little bachelor contrivances! The sort of impromptu arrangements that might have suggested themselves to Phillip Quarll or Robinson Crusoe" (36).

Finally, near the end of the first half of the Dickens canon, old Sol Gills decries to his nephew, Walter Gay, the manner in which the new technological world is passing by the sheltered but isolated world of the Wooden Midshipman: "not being like the Savages who came to Robinson Crusoe's Island, we can't live on a man who asks for change for a sovereign" (*D&S*, 4). The footprints of Defoe's *Robinson Crusoe* appear in almost every Dickens novel just as they appear all across the consciousness of Victorian society. The Victorians, Dickens included, inhabited a society in which shipwrecks were not only one of the major concerns of their economic history, but were one of the major fascinations of their cultural history as well.

John Fowles offers a romantic psychological speculation as to why the English love their shipwrecks, their shipwreck narratives, and their shipwreck lore so much:

> There is, from dry land, great poetry and drama about the shipwreck; but no sailor would let me suggest that the amusement of an audience is the heart of the matter. That heart lies, as it always has and always will, in the terror and despair, in the drowned, in the appalling suffering of the survived, the bravery of the rescuers. We should never forget that; and yet . . . I should like to go now into the calmer, though deeper and darker, waters of why the spectacle of the shipwreck is so pleasing—why, in short, there is a kind of Cornish wrecker in every single one of us. . . .
>
> I'm not sure the most important reaction is not the instinctive: thank God this did not happen to me. In other words, we derive from the spectacle of calamity a sense of personal survival—as also, however tenuously, intimations of the metaphysical sea of hazard on which we all sail.[43]

Keith Huntress explains the Victorian fascination for shipwrecks and shipwreck narratives in much less psychological and much more popular and practical terms:

> The primary appeal was, and is, that of adventure and suspense in narrative. The years 1650-1860 made up the peak period for the wooden sailing ship in commerce and in war. . . . Sailors made up a significant portion of the labor force in both England and America, and

ship owners and ship captains were important people of the times. Major sea battles decided the destinies of nations; major explorations had the same fascination as the moon flights of our own times with the same sudden extensions of the boundaries of knowledge; and the sea was dangerous and therefore always interesting.[44]

Thus, for all of these reasons—the statistical frequency of shipwrecks, the wide ripple-effect of shipwrecks through Victorian society, the extensive shipwreck reports in the popular press, the availability and great popularity of true shipwreck narratives as well as shipwreck fiction—the shipwreck had become for the late eighteenth and the whole nineteenth century a fascination bordering upon a cultural preoccupation. Therefore, it should not be the least bit surprising that the most popular and widely read novelist of the Victorian age, the one Victorian novelist who most conscientiously monitored the temper of his times and employed that Victorian temper in his art, should have shared and repeatedly exploited this fascination for shipwreck history.

Dickens's consistent and imaginative use of shipwrecks in all manner of metaphorical constructs from *Barnaby Rudge* on clearly attests to the power of his facility for searching out, recording, and remembering in detail the most commonplace events, people, verbal exchanges, and cultural phenomena. And, like the mythical alchemist, he transformed all of that data garnered in the course of his daily life, harvested out of his frenzied night prowling of the city's streets, into the imaginative stuff of his fiction. To steal an apt phrase from Murial Spark's *The Prime of Miss Jean Brodie*, in his canon Dickens progressively became an expert practitioner in "The Transfiguration of the Commonplace."[45] By the late 1840s, Dickens had gathered a wealth of fact and lore about shipwrecks and had begun to transfigure that material into the images, sustained metaphors, myths, and apocalyptic events of his fiction.[46]

Evidence of what would later become Dickens's shipwreck fascination surfaced slowly in his early works. It appears infrequently as little more than an isolated simile in these early novels, yet it is there. For instance, in *Oliver Twist* as little Oliver, having escaped from Sowerberry and the Bumbles, walks toward London, he receives aid from an "old lady, who had a shipwrecked grandson wandering barefoot in some distant part of the earth" (7). In *Nicholas Nickleby*, as Ralph Nickleby moves relentlessly toward suicide in his garret room, his turbulent emotional state is described in terms of a shipwreck seascape. He is tossed in a psychological "whirlwind of passion and regret" and his mind is like "a stormy maddened sea" (62).

Though there are but a few shipwreck images in *The Old Curiosity Shop*, too few for them to be considered a thematic motif, Dickens's language of shipwreck is becoming more elaborate, his shipwreck similes more direct and extended. Sampson Brass's frowning face, for example, becomes "one of nature's beacons, warning of those who navigated the shoals of the World, or of that dangerous strait the Law, and admonishing them to seek less treacherous harbours and try their fortune elsewhere" (35). Later, as Nell and her grandfather wander destitute in the mean streets of a fiery industrial city, Dickens describes them as "feeling amidst the crowd a solitude which has no parallel but in the thirst of the shipwrecked mariner, who, tossed to and fro upon the billows of a mighty ocean, his red eyes blinded by looking on the water which hems him in on every side, has not one drop to cool his burning tongue" (44). Thus, in the early canon, though the shipwreck images are isolated and infrequent, they are nonetheless developing from mere offhand analogies to more elaborate similes to eloquent extended analogies.

By the early 1840s, Dickens began to use the concept of shipwreck as metaphor and motif in much more substantial ways in *Barnaby Rudge, Martin Chuzzlewit,* and the aforementioned *Dombey and Son.* In *Barnaby Rudge,* the controlling analogy that Dickens chose to describe the religious and political upheaval of the Gordon Riots was that of a violent storm, of nature gone mad. With the same kind of romantic linking of violent man and violent nature that Emily Bronte accomplished in *Wuthering Heights,* Dickens fore-shadowed the riots that were to come:

> There are times when, the elements being in unusual commotion, those who are bent on daring enterprises, or agitated by great thoughts, whether of good or evil, feel a mysterious sympathy with the tumult of nature, and are roused into corresponding violence. In the midst of thunder, lightning, and storm, many tremendous deeds have been committed; men, self-possessed before, have given sudden loose to passions they could no longer control. (*BR*, 2)

This passage from *Barnaby Rudge* serves not only as a prefiguration of the language used to describe the Gordon Riots later in that novel, but also as a preview of the much more mythic and sophisticated storm and ship-wreck metaphors that Dickens will later create to embody the French Revolution in *A Tale of Two Cities.*

Later in *Barnaby Rudge,* the Gordon Riots are repeatedly described as a violent storm, but a motif of shipwreck images is intermixed with and secondary to this storm analogy. Just prior to the outbreak of the Gordon Riots, the city of London is buffeted by a winter storm: "Each humble tavern by the waterside, had its group of uncouth figures round the hearth, who talked of vessels foundering at sea, and all hands lost; related many a dismal tale of shipwreck and drowned men" (33). When the riots begin, the crowd, armed with all manner of household weapons, follows their mad leaders, "roaring and chafing like an angry sea" (63).

Similarly, at the center of *Martin Chuzzlewit* lies the broad satire of American life and the shipwreck of Martin and Mark in the pestilent American Eden. Dickens employs the following ironic "coffin ship" image to portray the voracious greed that he sees as a main cause of the shipwreck of American society: "The more of that worthless ballast, honour and fair-dealing, which any man cast overboard from the ship of his Good Name and Good Intent, the more ample storage room he had for dollars" (*MC*, 16).

In *Barnaby Rudge* and *Martin Chuzzlewit*, the use of shipwreck similes increased in volume, but it is in *Dombey and Son* that Dickens first employed the metaphor of shipwreck as a controlling motif. Beyond the copious knowledge of shipwreck fact and lore that Old Sol Gills and his nephew Walter Gay so gleefully bandy about in the snug parlor of the Wooden Midshipman, the whole language of the novel recurringly depends on the imagery of shipwreck for the presentation of its social and moral commentary. As will be the case in *Bleak House* two novels later, two houses, the great merchant House of Dombey and the small commercial chandlery of the Wooden Midshipman, provide the two poles of action in the novel. Both of *Dombey and Son*'s houses are portrayed as ships wrecked on the shoals of materialistic Victorian society. At the end of *Dombey and Son*'s first chapter, Mrs. Dombey dies in the act of insuring the continuity of family ownership of her husband's great merchant house, and, "clinging fast to that slight spar within her arms, the mother drifted out upon the dark and unknown sea that rolls round all the world" (*D&S*, 1). In the course of the novel, both houses are shipwrecked, with their captains suffering grave personal losses, their surviving crews, Walter Gay and Florence Dombey, being set adrift and marooned in isolation until the respective captains find and rescue them from their respective estrangements from the safe harbor of Victorian family life.

The shipwreck metaphor and its function in *Dombey and Son* is quite obvious in its implication, much more obvious and less interesting than its use in Dickens's later novels. The motif's whole meaning turns on the obvious word play of the name of the House of Dombey's merchant ship, the *Son and Heir*. Leaving the port of London, "upon her voyage went the *Son and Heir*, as hopefully and trippingly as many another son and heir, gone down, had started on his way before her" (*D&S*, 20). When Sol Gills and Florence Dombey are told that "they have never had a ship on that voyage so long unheard of" (23) and begin to worry about Walter, the whole inanimate skyline of the city of London comes alive to the terrible fear of shipwreck: "The weathercocks on spires and housetops were mysterious with hints of stormy wind and pointed, like so many ghostly fingers, out to dangerous seas, where fragments of great wrecks were drifting, perhaps, and helpless men were rocked upon them into a sleep as deep as the unfathomable waters" (23). Houses and ships and people all must undergo shipwreck and rescue in this novel. As Captain Cuttle puts it: "there's been uncommon bad weather in them latitudes, there's no denyin', and they have drove and drove and been beat off, may be t'other side of the world. But the ship's a good ship, and the lad's a good lad, and it ain't easy, thank the Lord . . . to break up hearts of oak, whether they're in brigs or buzzums" (D&S, 23). Finally, when the "Shipping Intelligence" (22) of every newspaper in London reports the sinking of the Son and Heir, "the whole world of Captain Cuttle had been drowned" (D&S, 23).

In Dombey and Son the shipwreck of the Son and Heir is but the objective correlative for the ongoing shipwrecks of the emotional worlds of the novel's central characters. Captain Cuttle is like some Shakespearean fool who babbles on about the perils of the sea yet whose words, within the context of the novel's action, predict human outcomes. Though but another Dickensian grotesque, Captain Cuttle gives good advice to Florence, who has been cast adrift by everyone whom she ever loved. He advises her to ride out the storm and "stand by" (D&S, 49) on her desert island until the wind changes and she is rescued. By the end of the novel, this is exactly what happens. As will be the case for Esther Summerson in Bleak House, for little Dorrit and for Lizzie Hexam in Our Mutual Friend, later cast adrift, Florence Dombey's patience is rewarded and she is rescued from her shipwrecked state by reawakened love.

Though violent storms at sea and shipwrecks are employed as analogs to the situations, both physical and emotional, of the characters in Dombey and Son, it is with the ultimate shipwreck of the House of Dombey that this motif passes out of the descriptive realm of imagery and into the thematic realm of controlling metaphor. By the end of Dombey and Son, the language of shipwreck is no longer just a verbal tool or a plotting device; Dickens has transfigured it into a prophetic metaphor for what can happen in an age ruled by pride and materialism: "the ship he strained so hard against the storm was weak and could not bear it. The year was out and the great House was down" (58).

There is a clear and definite reason why the imagery of shipwreck in the Dickens canon begins to prove more substantial at about the time of Barnaby Rudge and Dombey and Son and continuing consistently on in different forms through the novels of the 1850s. That reason lies in the fact that shipwrecks had become significantly more prominent in his everyday life. This can be found in Dickens's strong editorial commitment to his newspaper work during that time. Since there are relatively few sea-going or shipwreck images and metaphors in Dickens's novels prior to *Barnaby Rudge* and *Dombey and Son*, the quickening of his interest in this particular metaphorical construct can be dated accurately to the mid-1840s, the time of his journalistic prime.

Dickens was founding editor of the *Daily News*. He became a contributor to Forster's editorship of the *Daily News* after 1846. By 1850, he was the founding editor of *Household Words*, soon accompanied by the monthly supplement and news magazine *The Household Narrative of Current Events*. Dickens was, therefore, more familiar with the "shipping intelligence," which was a staple of every London newspaper and most periodicals, than he had been prior to that time.

In the early numbers of *Household Words*, Dickens included numerous feature articles on shipwrecks, shipwreck issues, and the ripple-effects of shipwrecks on English life. In an article titled "A Sea-Side Churchyard,"[47] the writer contemplates the gravestones of all of the residents of a coastal town who have died by shipwreck. In "Lighthouses and Lightboats" (*HW*, 11 Jan. 1851), the writer states, "the sudden withdrawal of a single 'light' from an important position would . . . be the cause of hundreds of shipwrecks in a single night." An earlier *Household Words* article, "The Preservation of Life from Shipwreck," (3 Aug. 1850) had explored a similar political shipwreck issue. This article calls for the planning and training for better procedures for rescue when shipwrecks occur and mirrors Dickens's consciousness of the shipwreck rescue situation that he had already so powerfully described in the deaths of Steerforth and Ham in *David Copperfield*.

Shipwrecks even have a way of sneaking into articles on completely different subjects. In "On Duty with Inspector Field" (14 June 1851), Dickens goes on a tour of the London underworld with Inspector Field of the Metropolitan Protectives and enters a house in which all of the rooms "were decorated with nautical subjects. Wrecks, engagements, ships on fire, ships passing lighthouses on iron-bound coasts, ships blowing up, ships going down, ships running ashore . . . sailors and ships in every variety of peril, constitute the illustrations of fact."

In two other feature articles, "Life and Luggage" (8 Nov. 1851) and "A Sea-Coroner" (13 Mar. 1852), Dickens's writers quote shipwreck statistics from Parliamentary bluebooks as arguments for legislation regarding better rescue procedures and more lighthouses as a means of reducing the shocking loss of life from shipwrecks around the English coast. In "Life and Luggage," referring to 1850, the writer notes that

> [L]ast year, six hundred and eighty-one English and Foreign vessels were wrecked on the coasts, and within the seas of the British Isles. Of these, two hundred and seventy-seven were total wrecks; eighty-four were sunk by leaks and collisions. . . . As nearly as can be ascertained, seven hundred and eighty lives were lost. . . . In the single month of March, 1850, not less than one hundred and thirty-four vessels were wrecked on our coasts, or the average for the month of more than four a day . . . no doubt, many [shipwrecks] occur which never appear in *Lloyd's Lists* or other public records. They are lost at sea with every soul on board.

In "The Sea-Coroner," shipwreck statistics again bolster the argument:

> In the Parliamentary Report on Shipwrecks for the year 1836, the loss of property in British shipping wrecked or foundered at sea, is estimated on an average of six years, at three million sterling per annum. . . . The annual loss of life by the wreck or foundering of British vessels at sea is estimated at one thousand persons each year.

All of these numbers were leveled at the terrible irony of the methods and motives of shipwreck salvage and rescue that Dickens set out to expose in *Household Words*. In "Life and Luggage," the title of which clearly defines that irony, the writer argues:

> While our system of lighthouses, lightboats, and beacons, and the matchless judgement, skill and daring of our boatmen, on many parts of the coast, are the admiration of all, whether natives or foreigners, who have any opportunities of experiencing or testing their merits, there has at the very same time existed the fact, that the preservation from shipwreck of a man's portmanteau receives, as a lawful demand, a proportionate reward—and the preservation of his human trunk, nothing whatever.

All during Dickens's career as a journalist he was involved with political causes that attempted to expose and change the savagery of everyday English life: public hangings, government bureaucracy, labor and educational inequities, and shipwreck salvage regulations. He used *Household Words* as a forum in his many attempts to transfigure the commonplace, to make fairer and civilize what he saw as the accepted barbarism and inhumanity of so many aspects of English life, including the astounding number of lives lost in shipwrecks.

By 1852, articles about shipwrecks and the use of shipwrecks as a source for descriptive analogy had become a recurring motif in *Household Words*. In an article titled "Margaret Fuller" (24 April 1852) the shipwreck that took the title subject's life and the lives of all her family is described. In "The Life of Poor Jack" (21 May 1853) the dangerous carelessness of shipboard life is indicated and the article's author ends by stating that the "consequences of all this carelessness is, as I find in my blue books, that of every seventeen sailors who die, twelve are drowned or lost by shipwreck."

By late 1853, *Household Words* had begun to publish shipwreck fiction. Two shipwreck stories (31 Dec. 1853 and Feb. 1854) were published within two months of each other. Late in 1854, a two-part anthology of true shipwreck narratives titled "The Lost Arctic Voyages" (2 Dec. and 9 Dec. 1854) proved extremely popular with *Household Words* readers. These articles simply describe a series of Arctic shipwrecks, but they are important because they serve as immediate sources and influences upon the imagery of two works with which Dickens was to involve himself, *The Frozen Deep* and *A Tale of Two Cities*.

Finally, in "When the Wind Blows" (*HW*, 24 March 1855) and "Wrecks at Sea" (11 Aug. 1855) the magazine returned to statistical polemic to expose the hazards of shipwreck on the English coast, a subject that by this time had become almost a preoccupation of the magazine. When *The Household Narrative of Current Events* was installed as a monthly supplement to *Household Words*, a whole section of this news tabloid was devoted to "Narratives of Accident and Disaster," which each month listed shipwrecks individually with whatever information was available.

Thus, at the time that Charles Dickens was creating stunning scenes of shipwreck and metaphorical constructs of shipwreck imagery in his novels *Dombey and Son*, *David Copperfield*, *Hard Times*, and *A Tale of Two Cities*, his obsession with shipwreck facts and shipwreck narratives was also very evident in his everyday journalistic work. He took all of the shipwreck information that he absorbed in his editing—first of the *Daily News*, and then of *Household Words* and *The Household Narrative of Current Events*—passed it through the magic of his alchemic imagination and thus transfigured it into the symbolic stuff of his fiction.

David Copperfield

In a sense, *David Copperfield* is Dickens's most historical novel. Its historical consciousness is two-pronged. In its exorcism of the blacking factory episode and in its representation of Victorian marriage, it dwells more closely than any other of his novels on its author's personal history. But in its characterization of Steerforth and in the elaborate motif of shipwreck imagery that emerges out of that characterization, *David Copperfield* creates an intense commentary on England's class exploitation. It offers a harsh warning about the direction that the social history of the Victorian age is taking. *David Copperfield* is one of Dickens's most heteroglossic novels. The voices of every class of Victorian society are represented, and those voices interact in terms of power relationships. The metaphor that Dickens chose to represent those power relationships is the metaphor of shipwreck.

In *Images of Crisis: Literary Iconology*, George P. Landow has written the seminal work on the descriptions and symbolic function of shipwrecks in the literature of the last 240 years. Landow presents both a theory defining the literary iconology of shipwrecks as well as a great deal of applied criticism analyzing the meaning of shipwreck scenes, images, and metaphors in major works. For some inexplicable reason, however, Landow does little with the novels of Charles Dickens. Landow even fails to remark upon the most famous and elaborate shipwreck in the Dickens canon, the shipwreck off Yarmouth in *David Copperfield*.[48]

Perhaps one reason why Landow does not spend much time with Dickens involves the difference between iconology (which combines metaphorical signification with religious signification) and imagery. While for Landow shipwrecks and shipwreck language consistently present an iconology of existential and spiritual crisis, for Dickens, shipwrecks form, in different novels, images of apocalypse and desolation (as in the famous shipwreck of *David Copperfield*), images of social and existential abandonment, alienation, and emptiness (as in *Hard Times*), images of utter social and political chaos leading to social apocalypse (as in *A Tale of Two Cities*), and, finally, images of retribution and rescue embodying the sort of religious iconic significance that Landow espouses (as in Dickens's last completed novel, *Our Mutual Friend*). When Dickens employs the imagery of shipwreck, especially in the fiction of the second half of his career, it almost always represents some aspect of Victorian social history. In fact, along with the imagery of the prison, it may be Dickens's most historically based metaphor.

The controlling shipwreck imagery of *David Copperfield* demonstrates Dickens's employment of this motif to signify, both metaphorically and objectively, the apocalyptic violation and desolation of nature (including human nature) due to one man's immoral tampering with the Victorian concepts of family and social class. In the prefigurative construction of their controlling metaphors culminating in their apocalyptic resolutions, Dickens's *David Copperfield* and George Eliot's *The Mill on the Floss* are nearly identical in both structure and theme. Four-fifths of the way through each of these novels, the controlling imagery—of shipwreck in *David Copperfield* and of flood in *The Mill on the Floss*—builds to a violent apocalyptic scene that sweeps away all pretense of human control, free will, aspiration, and redemption to leave its victims either physically or spiritually dead to the world around them, ostracized from society, rendered helpless by the surge of social history that has carried them away, and shipwrecked them on the desolate strand of Victorian life.

In both novels, when the apocalyptic event subsides, the victims who have been swept away in the grip of its terrible force wash up on the sort of desolate beach that Matthew Arnold repeatedly describes in his poems as representative of the Victorian world's moral desolation (compare "Dover Beach," and "To Marguerite"). For Steerforth, Ham, and David (who powerless looks on), the desolation of the apocalyptic shipwreck is complete; it offers only the waxen after-image of shipwrecked human beings, drowned and washed up on the beach like the broken spars and shattered hulls of fragile barks. Ham and Steerforth perish in the violent maelstrom of their emotional lives in an unemotional age. David is their witness, the failed salvager of the moral shipwreck of his age. He can only stand by and claim the corpses once the apocalypse has spun its victims through its vortex.

The flood in *The Mill on the Floss* and the shipwreck near the end of *David Copperfield* are the inevitable deconstructions of fragile, ill-designed, morally shaky worlds. In *The Mill on the Floss* Maggie Tulliver is a flirt, but her flirtations with the men in her life are nothing in comparison to her flirtation with the narrow catwalks of Victorian morality. When, through her sexual flirtations, she repeatedly walks too near the edge, she must inevitably slip and be swept away. When Steerforth plots a course that ignores not only the charted meridians of Victorian morality but also those of Victorian social class, inevitably he too will run aground.

Where Landow sees shipwrecks as images of crisis, Dickens's shipwrecks go beyond crisis to become metaphors for the apocalyptic destruction of the past, of a life, of a society, of a relationship, or of the status quo. Dickens methodically prepares the reader for each apocalyptic moment. He builds his historicist metaphors upon repetition. He constructs meticulously a pattern of shipwreck imagery, often, as in *David Copperfield*, beginning on the very first page of the text and continuing until the crucial moment when he either employs a full-blown shipwreck or laces a plot event so strongly with shipwreck imagery that the analogy is unmistakable. It is thus that he shows the total destruction of the world of the characters and the novel. George Eliot later would accomplish a similar imagistic development using the river in *The Mill on the Floss*. In *David Copperfield*, after this apocalyptic shipwreck, Dickens proceeds to attempt to salvage what he can from the apocalypse, but most often he fails, becoming a beach-bound observer forced to collect the flotsam and jetsam of the wrecked world when it washes up on the desolate beach. Thus, Dickens's imagery (and David's, the narrator /novelist inside the text) not only represents the events, emotions, and outcomes at work in the lives of his characters, it simultaneously represents the history of his age, the temper of his times, the "Condition of England." The image of the shipwrecked world in Dickens's "dark novels"[49] is a particularly modernist image that foreshadows the empty visions of later Victorian novels—such as *The Mill on the Floss* and Thomas Hardy's *Jude the Obscure*—as well as those of T. S. Eliot's twentieth-century wasteland world. It is in *David Copperfield* that Dickens most stolidly establishes himself at the fulcrum of that history of ideas that balances the eighteenth-century philosophy of benevolence with the visionary sense of modernist angst that makes his later fiction so historically engaging. In *David Copperfield*, Dickens gives the first strong evidence of his position as a novelist caught between two historical worlds, as a troubled mediator between the past and the future.

"I was born with a caul," David, the hero of his own life, announces on the first page of his autobiography. What is interesting, however, is that he goes on to tell how his caul, "was advertised for sale, in the newspapers, at the low price of fifteen guineas," because "among sea-going people" (*DC*, 1) birth cauls are a good-luck charm against drowning. Thus, from page one of *David Copperfield* the shipwreck imagery is in place.

The shipwreck imagery of *David Copperfield* takes a number of different forms to serve a number of different purposes, all of which ultimately converge to form the texture of tone and theme that culminates in the apocalyptic shipwreck off the beach at Yarmouth. For example, throwaway references to shipwrecks and shipwreck lore surface frequently in offhand conversations. At the very beginning of the famous "Brooks of Sheffield" conversation between Murdstone and his cronies, after Murdstone has introduced his soon-to-be stepson simply as Davy, one of the gentlemen asks, "Davy who? . . . Jones?" (2). Later, when David is being encouraged to study law at Doctor's Commons in London, Steerforth defines "ecclesiastical law" as "about people's wills and people's marriages, and disputes about ships and boats." David thinks that Steerforth's definition is preposterous: "Nonsense, Steerforth! . . . You don't mean to say that there is any affinity between nautical matters and ecclesiastical matters?" (23). This seemingly offhand comment becomes highly ironic in the light of the novel's later developments. David will, indeed, find himself right in the middle of a distressing situation involving marriages and boats.

Like many of his predecessors in the Dickens canon—such as young Martin Chuzzlewit and Tom Pinch in *Martin Chuzzlewit,* and Sol Gills and Walter Gay in *Dombey and Son,* David Copperfield is well versed in the literature of shipwreck at a very early age. To escape Murdstone's oppressive presence, young David retires to "that blessed little room" where, from his father's books "Roderick Random, Peregrine Pickle, Humphrey Clinker, Tom Jones, the Vicar of Wakefield, Don Quixote, Gil Blas, and Robinson Crusoe, came out, a glorious host, to keep me company." He goes on to describe how "I had a greedy relish for a few volumes of *Voyages and Travels* . . . the perfect realization of Captain Somebody, of the Royal British Navy, in danger of being beset by savages, and resolved to sell his life at a great price" (*DC,*4).

The imagery of shipwreck, however, serves a more serious purpose when it begins to function prefiguratively in reference to Steerforth's ultimate fate. As David and Steerforth approach the Peggotty houseboat for the first time, Steerforth remarks on the setting: "Dismal enough in the dark . . . and the sea roars as if it were hungry for us" (21). Later that same evening, "Steerforth told a story of a dismal shipwreck (which arose out of his talk with Mr. Peggotty) as if he saw it all before him—and little Em'ly's eyes were fastened on him all the time, as if she saw it too" (21). This passage carries the irony of prefiguration one step further than usual. Both Steerforth and Em'ly are actually seeing their own fates, the shipwrecks of their future lives. The irony of prefiguration is generally not understood by either character or reader until after the prefigured event has occurred, but in this case the tone is so ominous that the characters and the readers are apprised of the connection between shipwrecks and their futures. David, the narrator, warned his readers of the irony of prefiguration earlier when he cryptically intruded into his narrative with this ominous flash forward: "would it have been better for little Em'ly to have had the waters close above her head that morning in my sight . . ." (3).

These three different functions of shipwreck reference in *David Copperfield*—offhand conversational reference, familiarity with shipwreck literature, ironic prefiguration of shipwreck disaster—are, however, only secondary functions of the shipwreck imagery of the novel. The primary function of that shipwreck imagery prior to the ultimate apocalypse is as the controlling metaphor that defines the Yarmouth houseboat world of the Peggottys. The Peggotty houseboat sits on "the dull waste" (3) between the sea and the river at Yarmouth. As David is introduced to the various members of the household, Mr. Peggotty regales him with the past history of the place and its former inhabitants, a number of whom are "Drowndead" (3). Perhaps David should have kept his "caul" instead of selling it. Perhaps if he had, he might have been more successful in rescuing his loved ones from the fate of being "Drowndead."

What the Peggotty's have managed is the ramshackle construction of a positive alternative world in the midst of the wasteland world of Victorian life. They have moored a fragile bark in the destructive element. That positive world, however, is vulnerable from the moment David first comes on board: "I'm afraid of the sea," little Em'ly tells David, "I have seen it tear a boat as big as our house all to pieces" (3). In *David Copperfield*, Dickens employs different metaphors for the different worlds of the novel much as he did to underline the oppositions between Fagin's world and Brownlow's world in *Oliver Twist*. The Peggotty's Yarmouth world is a fragile one existing always under the threat of shipwreck, whereas the world of the city and David's illusory romantic life with Dora is one of fairy tale enchantment. As David lies in bed in the houseboat, "instead of thinking that the sea might rise in the night and float the boat away, I thought of the sea that had risen, since I last heard those sounds, and drowned my happy home" (*DC*, 10). When, after Em'ly has eloped with Steerforth, David asks "Will you desert the old boat, Mr. Peggotty?" that worthy answers in almost exactly the same shipwreck terms that David used earlier in reference to his first home. "My station, Mas'r Davy," he returned, "ain't there no longer; and if ever a boat foundered, since there was darkness on the face of the deep, that one's gone down. But no, sir, no; I doesn't mean as it should be deserted" (32).

All of these associative images of shipwreck define the fragility of the Peggotty's familial world in the exploitative sea of Victorian life that makes drifting castaways of every individual. All of the various shipwreck analogies converge in the final apocalyptic event that defines the novel's central theme: the individual's isolation and utter helplessness in the maelstrom of a destructive world gone mad. The storm, the shipwreck, the rescue attempts, the powerlessness of the onlookers not only comprise one of Dickens's most memorable tour-de-force action scenes, but also offer an elaborate metaphor for man's struggle to survive, to contribute morally, to affirm existence in the face of an unnatural, anti-existential world whose power dooms him ultimately to fail. It is a Sisyphean scene of struggle involving rebellion against a malevolent nature and ultimate, ever predictable, defeat. It is also one of the finest examples in the Dickens canon of the working of his alchemic imagination, the transfiguration of common knowledge into social historical myth. The shipwreck apocalypse begins:

> I now approach an event in my life, so indelible, so awful, so bound by an infinite variety of ties to all that has preceded it, in these pages, that, from the beginning of my narrative, I have seen it growing larger and larger as I advanced, like a great tower in the plain, and throwing its fore-cast shadow even on the incidents of my childish days.[50]

Thus David, the narrator, and Dickens, the metanarrator within David the narrator, begin the shipwreck apocalypse of *David Copperfield*. That opening passage is one of those instances sprinkled throughout Dickens's fiction in which he either loses control or intentionally intrudes to explain what he has been doing throughout the construction of his self-reflexive text. That passage is David (and Dickens) forcibly clasping the reader by the lapels and barking into his face, "Here it comes! Pay close attention!"

For David, the up-coming shipwreck is "an event in my life . . . so awful" that it throws a "shadow over my childish days." But for Dickens it is the culmination of the structuring of his text, "indelible . . . bound by an infinite variety of ties to all that has preceded it, in these pages . . . from the beginning of my narrative." For David it is a culminating event in a life, but for Dickens it is the climax of a text, a word construct, "these pages." As meta-fictionist, he defines the up-coming shipwreck as a rhetorical event, not a human event. It is a language apocalypse prepared for "from the beginning of my narrative" and "growing larger and larger as I advanced" and meticulously "fore-cast" throughout the writer's rhetorical construction of his text.

Thus Dickens's most memorable shipwreck narrative begins in a most uncharacteristic manner. The attention is deliberately diverted from the introduction of the shipwreck as event and directed toward Dickens's self-reflexive consciousness of the shipwreck as the culmination of the rhetorical structure of his text. In beginning this way, Dickens is making sure that his readers are aware of the text/subtext nature of David's narrative. *David Copperfield* is about navigating and surviving the shoals of Victorian life, but it is also about charting the voyage through a sea of words and the perils the writer must face before reaching the safe harbor of white at "The End" of his voyage. The very length and uncharacteristically parenthetical nature of David the narrator's introductory passage underlines the clear distinction Dickens is making between David's and his own interests in the upcoming scene. For David the text is an attempt to justify himself as "the hero of my own life," (1), but, as this cunningly chosen moment of self-reflexive intrusion shows, the subtext is Dickens's own attempt to justify the writer's art as equally heroic. For Dickens, the ability to create a compelling and meaningful text out of a sea of words is heroic, not in a Carlylean sense of the writer as hero, but in the Dickensian sense of imaginative alchemy as heroism.

To Dickens the metafictionist's credit, he, after this initial single paragraph of subtext intrusion, immediately relinquishes the stage to his primary text narrator; but the layered identity of this crucial scene has been established. After this intrusion, the scene moves back into David's voice. The reader, however, has been alerted to listen to what the waves are saying beneath the surface of that primary text voice. For example, the shipwreck is described by David as a lasting "association between it and a stormy wind, or the lightest mention of a sea-shore, as strong as any of which my mind is conscious. As plainly as I behold what happened, I will try to write it down." As the evidence of Dickens's canon demonstrates, the fact and the symbolic possibility of shipwreck is certainly an "association . . . as strong as any of which" Dickens's "mind is conscious." The strength of that association surfaces in all the outlets for his writing, from his journalism to his novels. But Dickens's interest is that of an alchemic writer, not merely the chronicler that David claims to be when he says "as plainly as I behold what happened, I will try to write it down." Dickens's shipwreck association becomes an elaborate trope throughout his whole canon, an ongoing representation of his vision of man's relationship to the turbulent and treacherous Victorian world. But that same shipwreck association also controls this most graphic of Dickens' shipwreck scenes.

Throughout this shipwreck scene, beginning with his intrusive opening, Dickens forms an elaborate imagery of apocalypse, of the storm at sea and the wrecking of the ship and of the sea's destruction of human life, as representative of the manner in which the Victorian social process has plunged human values into the depths of darkness, has ripped asunder Victorian moral life. While this apocalyptic shipwreck is occurring, the writer can only stand upon the beach and describe the destruction. This shipwreck scene in David Copperfield is, on the level of his metafictional subtext, a grudging admission of the writer's relative helplessness in the face of the terrible problems in his society, in the face of England's rapidly deteriorating condition. From this point on in his novels, Dickens will portray in increasingly desolate terms the manner in which the Victorian social process batters and drowns the better nature, the best intentions, the romantic dreams of the individual. In the shipwreck scene in David Copperfield,

Dickens presents his first and most violent (as well as most passionately constructed) of a series of apocalyptic nightmares revealing the fragility and moral desolation of Victorian society.

The oft repeated word in Dickens's violent description of the sea off Yarmouth is the adjective "great." In Dickens's intrusion in the scene's opening, the impending shipwreck is an event that the text is moving toward "like a great tower in a plain." When David actually confronts the storm, the wind is rising with "an extraordinary great sound" and "it blew great guns" tearing "great sheets of lead" off of the church tower and plucking "great trees . . . out of the earth." The storm is acknowledged by all to be "the greatest ever known to blow upon the coast" and brings upon the world "a great darkness." The storm batters the foundered ship with "great waves" and the misery and desolation of the people on shore forced to watch helplessly as this violent destruction takes place is expressed first by "a great cry" and then by "another great cry of pity from the beach." Finally, Ham and Steerforth are "beaten to death by the great wave" and Dickens's first major, exterior-world apocalypse is complete.

In this scene, Dickens's repeated magnification of a mad nature's power as well as his magnification of human misery and helplessness in the face of that power signals his heightened consciousness. This pivotal point in his writing career and in this most introspective and self-reflexive of all his books, illustrates the breaking up of his world, the shipwreck of the light, humorous, sentimental, and hopeful world of Pickwick, the Brownlows, Tom Pinch, and even Little Nell. In his earlier novels, apocalypse had taken the form of individual failures, individual deaths, individual betrayals and suicides and temptations; but in *David Copperfield* Dickens finds in the imagery of shipwreck a trope for superseding small personal desolations and representing the apocalyptic desolation of the whole Victorian world.

Aside from this repeated rhetoric of magnification, the shipwreck scene develops an elaborate language of apocalypse to describe the breaking up of both David and Dickens's worlds. This language develops throughout the shipwreck passage in terms of three imagistic motifs: first, the descent into the void of the underworld; second, nature going utterly mad and thus reshaping itself; and third, the abstract (as opposed to the quite realistic aspect of the first two motifs) image, inserted by David the writer standing helpless on the shore of the whole event, of a dark tower looming over his life.

When the storm first breaks on David as he's traveling in the coach to Yarmouth, the clouds have "depths below them to the bottom of the deepest hollows in the earth, through which the wild moon seemed to plunge headlong." The waves offshore rise "above the rolling abyss . . . as if the least would engulf the town." The biggest waves seem "to scoop out deep caves in the beach, as if its purpose were to undermine the earth." Some violent waves "dashed themselves to pieces before they reached the land, every fragment of the late whole seemed possessed . . . rushing to be gathered to the composition of another monster." The storm, the raging sea, the terrible dilemma of the sailors, the terrible frustration of those watching from the shore is represented as a descent into a hallucinatory, shape-shifting underworld, into a "black void."

The second motif, that of nature gone mad in the throes of apocalypse, represents the world as losing its coherent shape and reforming into monsters and grotesque shapes. The waves "plunge headlong, as if in a dread disturbance of the laws of nature" and "every shape tumultuously rolled on, as soon as made, to change its shape and place and beat another shape and place away . . . the clouds fell fast and thick; I seemed to see a rending and upheaving of all nature." This shape-shifting demolition of all of nature and its laws mirrors the confusion and turmoil in David's mind as he observes the shipwreck of his world. "I had lost the clear arrangement of time and distance," David admits. "Something within me, faintly answering to the storm without, tossed up the depths of my memory and made a tumult of them." The storm's rending and upheaval of the natural world is directly equated with the upheaval of David's unconscious mind. Figuratively and psychologically, David is caught in the undertow and dashed in the surf of the shipwreck of the Peggotty's world just as Ham and Steerforth are battered and killed by the storm's real waves.

The third motif that makes up the language of apocalypse in this passage belongs to the self-reflexive subtext that was introduced in the opening paragraph of the chapter. That motif, of looming dark towers, begins with the doubled narrator's (David the character/narrator, and David the novelist representing the intrusive Dickens) characterization of the real shipwreck and the writing of the shipwreck scene as "growing larger and larger as I advanced like a great tower in a plain." The same monstrous waves that created the "abyss," the "black void," and rended and reshaped the natural world in the first two apocalyptic motifs are, in this third abstract motif, "like glimpses of another shore with towers and buildings." As the sea pounds itself into grotesque shape after shape, this "ideal shore on the horizon, with its towers and buildings, rose and fell."

The "tower in the plain," the towers on that "ideal shore," are images intrusively inserted by Dickens. Sentimentally, from his position of frustrated helplessness as mere observer and recorder of the shipwreck of Victorian life, he stands on the shore watching the world pound itself apart and longs to pass through that metaphoric turmoil to a safer world on the other side where the tower seems to offer shelter. But the subtext narrator quickly realizes that his metaphoric ideal world is but a fluttering mirage compared to the reality of storm and shipwreck. He returns to the "dark gloom of my solitary chamber," moves inside to escape the buffeting of the real world and, entering the world of dreams, reaches his tower on the other side of the raging sea. But that tower offers no solace to the shipwrecked wordman. Idealized sentimentality in the context of the apocalyptic shipwreck of Victorian society is immediately rejected by the writer's unconscious. Fleeing from "the black void" of the storm, the wordman falls "off a tower and down a precipice—into the depths of sleep." The apocalyptic descent into the abyss of the real external world cannot be avoided by flight into any seemingly secure and safe inner world of the imagination. The same "depths" wait for the writer within himself. Though only an observer, he is still a participant in the inevitable shipwreck of his society.

This elaborate construction of a language of apocalypse in the shipwreck scene culminates in a return to a succession of sublime words of magnification and disbelief. Near the end of the passage, the storm becomes "infinitely more terrific," the waves beat each other to pieces "in interminable hosts," and the whole world is thrown into "unspeakable confusion" by "a violence quite inconceivable." It is a language of sublimity consciously employed in series to magnify the apocalyptic destructiveness of the storm. What is happening to the world in this shipwreck scene, to both David's Yarmouth world and Dickens's Victorian world, has overreached the normal articulative power of words. Thus, the subtext's observer/writer is frustrated in yet another way. The apocalyptic desolation of his world has gone so far with such violence that he can no longer even describe it, much less do anything about it; he simply hasn't powerful enough words at his disposal and he must resort to words of indeterminate magnification, meaningless words such as "infinitely," "unspeakable," and "inconceivable."

But the subtext's narrator is not alone in his utter helplessness. In the real shipwreck of the primary text, the waves rolling over the foundering ship "carried men, spars, casks, planks, bulwarks, heaps of such toys, into the boiling surge." Caught in the shipwreck of Victorian life, the writer, and all men, are but "toys" helpless in the grip of the dehumanized, materialistic surge.

The shipwreck scene from *David Copperfield* ends with the whole community standing on the shore watching the ship go down:

> I found bewailing women whose husbands were away in herring or
> oyster boats, which there was too much reason to think might have

foundered before they could run in anywhere for safety. Grizzled old sailors were among the people, shaking their heads, as they looked from water to sky, and muttering to one another; ship-owners, excited and uneasy; children, huddling together, and peering into older faces; even stout mariners, disturbed and anxious, leveling their glasses at the sea from behind places of shelter, as if they were surveying an enemy. (55)

The whole community, from the "bewailing women" to the "old sailors" to "ship-owners" to "children" to "stout mariners," is out to bear witness to this shipwreck, to join David the narrator and Dickens the meta-narrator as they stand helplessly on the shore observing the apocalypse. All segments of society, every gender and generation is represented. The shipwreck scene's tableau is perfect for articulating the point that Dickens, with his doubled narrator, is intent on making: The whole community, all of Yarmouth society, stands and watches as the world falls apart before its eyes: The whole community, especially the writer, stands helpless on the shore as its world deconstructs.

In *Bleak House* the same type of intrusive narration occurs when Poor Jo dies. In that novel, the metanarrator lets out an apocalyptic howl that can be heard to the top of the dome of St. Paul's:

Dead, Your Majesty. Dead, my lords and gentlemen. Dead, Right Reverends and Wrong Reverends of every order. Dead, men and women, born with heavenly compassion in your hearts. And dying thus around us every day. (47)

In both *David Copperfield* and *Bleak House*, when the moment arrives when the intrusive narrator, the author himself feeling the frustration of his own helplessness, must speak out in his own voice about the deconstruction of the world that he has been trying so hard to order, the whole community bears witness to both the apocalypse and the writer's frustrated helplessness (which the community must share) in the face of that apocalypse.

David's role in the shipwreck scene is that of the writer in relation to the events of history, of a bystander on the shore forced to watch as the sea of life pounds all around, of trying to order the chaos of nature and salvage some hope from that chaos. In *David Copperfield*, there is little hope to be salvaged. At the end of that shipwreck scene, the Peggotty family's boathouse (like the House of Dombey and the two houses of *Bleak House*) is directly compared to the shipwreck that has occurred offshore:

But, he led me to the shore. And on that part of it where she and I had looked for shells, two children—on the part of it where some lighter fragments of the old boat, blown down last night, had been scattered by the wind—among the ruins of the home he had wronged—I saw him lying with his head upon his arm, as I had often seen him lie at school! (*DC*, 55)

David's past, David's home, David's friend, all have been wrecked and cast back up on the shore in fragments that cannot be reordered, given new life. For both David the narrator and Dickens the metanarrator, all that remains is post-apocalyptic desolation.

"I went away from England," David writes of his life after the shipwreck, "not knowing, even then, how great the shock was that I had to bear. . . . As a man upon a field of battle will receive a mortal hurt, and scarcely know that he is struck, so I, when I was left alone with my undisciplined heart, had no conception of the wound with which it had to strive" (*DC*, 58). David wanders Europe in a state of shock like Byron's Childe Harold, but gradually the "desolate feeling with which I went abroad, deepened and widened hourly." This feeling of post-apocalyptic desolation begins as "a heavy share of loss and sorrow" but by "imperceptible degrees, it became a hopeless consciousness of all that I had lost—love, friendship, interest; of all that had been shattered—my first truth, my first affection, the whole airy castle of my life; of all that remained—a ruined blank and waste, lying wide around me, unbroken, to the dark horizon" (58). After the shipwreck of his world, David is marooned in a hopeless, dark wasteland where, if he wanders around a while, he will probably meet characters out of the poetry of Matthew Arnold and T. S. Eliot.

The Shipwreck of Revolution: *Hard Times* and *A Tale of Two Cities*

Every Dickens novel that follows this apocalyptic shipwreck in *David Copperfield* builds toward a similar apocalyptic event. In *Bleak House*, Lady Dedlock will be cast adrift, with Inspector Bucket and Esther Summerson trying to save her. In *Hard Times*, the imagery of shipwreck takes a different, more abstract, apocalyptic turn. W. W. Watt describes the style of *Hard Times* as Dickens's employment of a "symbolic shorthand."[51]

The major symbolic shorthand of *Hard Times* is a hard, metallic imagery of machines and the novel's dehumanization into machines of so many of its characters. However, working parallel to this mid-nineteenth-century Victorian imagery of the Industrial Revolution is an eighteenth-century imagery of shipwreck. The same imagistic parallelism occurs in *Dombey and Son* where the controlling imagery of shipwreck is paralleled by the imagery of the acquisitive and destructive, ultimately apocalyptic, railway that gobbles up land and buildings and, finally, men. Perhaps the most graphic Victorian representation of this imagistic parallelism can be seen in J. M. W. Turner's famous painting, "The 'Fighting Temeraire' Tugged To Her Last Berth To Be Broken Up, 1838." In that painting, the ghostly eighteenth-century galleon is being towed by a black, squat, smoke-belching steamboat of the nineteenth century. The wreck of the 'Fighting Temeraire' due to the progress of the Industrial Revolution somehow seems more tragic than if she had wrecked in a storm at sea. For Dickens, the modern analog to his favorite shipwreck imagery is the imagery of the dehumanizing shipwreck of English life caused by the Industrial Revolution. That shipwreck is best represented by machines, the most prominent of which and the most available to Dickens's imagination was the railway train.

But the shipwreck imagery is perhaps a clearer example of Dickens's quicker-hitting, instantly expressive shorthand style of *Hard Times*. Images of shipwreck are employed in a much less elaborate and calculated fashion than they are, for example, in *Dombey and Son* and *David Copperfield*. They function as an isolated simile or metaphor and yet also serve a dualistic symbolic purpose. On one level, shipwreck similes describe the psychic dislocation and loss occasioned by the loveless marriage of Louisa Gradgrind and Bounderby coupled with Louisa's adulterous attraction to James Harthouse. On another level, however, that same shipwreck simile represents the apocalyptic desolation of Thomas Gradgrind Senior's philosophic vision of the Victorian world.

Thus, in *Hard Times*, the shipwreck imagery is not a controlling motif, prepared for from the very beginning, as it is in *David Copperfield*. Instead, it functions as a crucial metaphor at a climactic moment. Louisa Gradgrind, like little Em'ly, has been seduced by a slick urban drifter. Harthouse has the same type of two syllable symbolic name as Steerforth and is also a yachtsman. Almost by reflex, Dickens represents the breakup of Louisa's world by turning to the shipwreck metaphor that appeared in so many of his earlier novels.

While these isolated shipwreck similes function on dual levels, the level of moral plot and the level of philosophic theme, they also consistently fulfill three ascending subfunctions. First, characters such as James Harthouse, in both their physical and moral existences, are defined through the use of shipwreck images. Second, shipwreck similes define the relationship of one character to another; for example, that of Harthouse to Louisa

Gradgrind. Third, shipwreck similes and metaphors expand and define the world of the novel in which these characters live and act.[52]

Shipwreck images serve as a commentary on the relationship between James Harthouse and Louisa Gradgrind. They generally appear at the end of a passage that describes the physical and/or moral makeup of one of these two characters, or they appear as a kind of marginal iteration, taking the form of an appropriately placed running headline.

After Harthouse has insinuated himself into the Bounderby household and "established a confidence" with Louisa, the narrator pauses briefly to describe him:

> . . . he had not, even now, any earnest wickedness of purpose in him. Publicly and privately, it were much better for the age in which he lived, that he and the legion of whom he was one were designedly bad, than indifferent and purposeless. It is the drifting icebergs setting with any current anywhere, that wreck the ships. (HT, II, 8)

The description's culminating metaphor sets Harthouse's character. He is an aimless, "drifting" man who reads a few blue books in order to gain the patronage of the "hard facts" men of the Gradgrind school. He is a man who projects a smooth and placid surface personality, but who is, beneath the surface, a completely impersonal opportunist. The image, however, also foreshadows the serious danger of his relationship with Louisa. Finally, this image shows Harthouse as an emblem of the moral shipwreck of the age; an age in which men indifferently follow their own inclinations no matter what harm their actions might cause to the lives of other people.

The proof of Dickens's conscious use of the imagery of shipwreck as an indicator of the result of the extramarital love relationship between Harthouse and Louisa can be found in the running headlines Dickens appended to chapter 12, Book Two of Hard Times. On the night of her meeting with Harthouse during her husband's absence, a meeting witnessed by Mrs. Sparsit, Louisa flees through a driving storm to her father. As she sinks in his arms, she begs him to save her, and the scene ends with Thomas Gradgrind looking at "the pride of his heart and the triumph of his system, lying, an insensible heap, at his feet" (II, 7). The running headline that Dickens appended to this page of Hard Times, "Shipwrecked," refers to the condition of both father and daughter. Louisa, because of her love for Harthouse, a love that can bring her nothing but ruin, has been cast adrift in the world. She can't return to a husband she despises nor can she accept an immoral relationship with the man she loves. "She has suffered the wreck of her whole life upon a rock"(III, 1).

For Thomas Gradgrind, the broken and insensible heap that lies before him symbolizes the shipwreck of his whole philosophy of life. In this pivotal scene, the shipwreck metaphor that represents Louisa's personal dislocation and desolation also represents the apocalyptic desolation of her father's intellectually constructed and rationally navigable Utilitarian world. The other running headline that appears in this chapter, the "Great Failure of the House of Gradgrind," is reminiscent of the failure of another great house, the house of Dombey, which also failed because of a shipwreck caused by the obstinacy and insensitivity of its proprietor, its Captain. That running headline is also prefigurative of the apocalyptic fall of the House of Clennam in Little Dorrit. In all three cases, the houses that fall, the worlds that are shipwrecked, are steered on to the rocks because their Captains are navigating by maps drawn from social illusions and dehumanizing philosophies that lack the lighthouses of compassion, imagination, and love.

Ironically, the shipwrecks that occur in Dombey and Son, Hard Times, and Little Dorrit, the apocalyptic breaking up of their flawed worlds, prove to be the ultimate salvation for both captain and crew (excepting, of course, the fanatic Mrs. Clennam, who goes down with her ship like Captain Ahab in Moby Dick). Only after the great houses of Dombey and Gradgrind have fallen can these two men realize the error of their similarly fanatic philosophies of life; and through that realization, in both cases accomplished by a loving but rejected daughter, open themselves for the first time to love. Dickens shows Louisa at the moment of personal shipwreck and her father at the moment of the shipwreck of his philosophic world, but those moments of shipwreck also prove to be the first step in the process of their salvation.

The concentrated metaphorical explosion of shipwreck imagery at this crucial moment in Hard Times is much in keeping with the extremely different conception and style of Hard Times from that of the three longer novels—Dombey and Son, David Copperfield, and Bleak House—that immediately precede it in the Dickens canon. Shipwreck imagery as isolated metaphor representing the apocalyptic desolation of the lives and worlds of Harthouse, Louisa, and Thomas Gradgrind Senior is not, however, introduced completely unannounced at this crucial scene. Early in the novel Louisa and Sissy Jupe talk about their problems with "statistics" that form the basic subject matter of McChoakumchild's curriculum and are the cornerstone of Thomas Gradgrind's blue-book philosophy of life and society.

"Statistics," said Louisa.

"Yes, Miss Louisa—they always remind me of stutterings, and that's another of my mistakes—of accidents upon the sea. And I find (Mr. McChoakumchild said) that in a given time a hundred thousand persons went to sea on long voyages, and only five hundred of them were drowned or burnt to death. What is the percentage? And I said, Miss," here Sissy fairly sobbed as confessing with extreme contrition to her greatest error; "I said it was nothing."

"Nothing, Sissy?"

"Nothing, Miss—to the relations and friends of people who were killed." (HT, III, 9)

In light of the sudden accretion of shipwreck images around the later moment of the "Great Failure of the House of Gradgrind," the early association of statistics to shipwrecks becomes highly ironic. The reef upon which Gradgrind's philosophy of life runs aground is the jagged pile of cold numbers, blue books, and statistical abstractions toward which he constantly steers. In Sissy's mind, statistics and shipwrecks go together but mean nothing, because statistics cannot take into account the human suffering caused by a shipwreck. That is why the house of Gradgrind—like the house of Atreus of Greek myth, the houses of Montague and Capulet of Shakespeare's *Romeo and Juliet*, the house of Dombey, and the house of Sutpen of Faulkner's *Absalom, Absalom!*—is doomed to wreck, because it fails to navigate by the heart as well as the head.

At the beginning of another earlier scene, a similar confrontation in which Louisa announces to her father her decision to marry Bounderby, the imagery of shipwreck metaphorically sets the situation. Louisa, facing her father, "sat looking at him fixedly" and "was impelled to throw herself upon his breast, and give him the pent-up confidences of her heart." But Thomas Gradgrind is utterly oblivious to the emotional uncertainty and terror that his daughter feels at the prospect of this marriage. Gradgrind sees nothing because

> to see it he must have overleaped at a bound the artificial barriers he had for many years been erecting, between himself and all those subtle essences of humanity which will elude the utmost cunning of algebra until the last trumpet ever to be sounded shall blow even algebra to wreck. (I, 25)

In this zany mixed metaphor, the "last trumpet" becomes a wind that blows that sturdy ship "algebra to wreck." This metaphor, however, rather

clearly prefigures the crucial confrontation scene at the end of the novel
when the shipwreck imagery bursts out. It predicts that Gradgrind will never
be capable of understanding or establishing any relationship with his daughter until his whole algebraic vision of the world has been wrecked.

This early confrontation ends with Louisa's realizing that her father is
not capable of seeing into the turmoil of her heart; "and the moment shot
away into the plumbless depths of the past to mingle with all the lost
opportunities that are drowned there" (I, 15). Louisa's hope that her father
might understand and tell her not to marry Bounderby is drowned in
Gradgrind's indifference, and the course is set for the rocks on which both
daughter's and father's lives will be wrecked.

The third participant in the shipwreck of the "Great House of
Gradgrind," James Harthouse (though he was previously described as the
iceberg upon which the family wrecks) is also a hopeless victim of the
metaphorical shipwreck just as Steerforth was the victim of the real
shipwreck off Yarmouth in *David Copperfield*. When Louisa flees to her father
and collapses, "Shipwrecked," as the running headline characterizes the
scene, she is not only rejecting her husband, Bounderby, but also her
would-be adulterous lover, Harthouse. When Harthouse receives the news
of this rejection, he reacts with a description of the state of his own
metaphorical shipwreck. "The drowning man catches at the straw," Harthouse pleads, "I cling to the belief that there is yet hope that I am not
condemned to perpetual exile from that lady's presence" (*HT*, III, 2).
Harthouse, like Steerforth, is not the malevolent moustachioed villain of
Victorian melodrama, but merely aimless and careless in his morality (like
the "drifting icebergs . . . that wreck the ships.") When Louisa rejects him
as well as Bounderby, he becomes a "drowning man" clinging to a spar
adrift in the vast emptiness of the Victorian social world.

In *Hard Times* the shipwreck imagery is used in a different manner for
different purposes. No longer is it a controlling symbolic pattern in both the
language and the plot action of the novel as it was in both *Dombey and Son*
and *David Copperfield*. In *Hard Times* this imagery is employed in two ways, as
isolated simile/metaphor and as marginal running headline, for two similar
purposes: first, to figuratively emphasize moments of apocalyptic desolation
for both the characters and the world of the novel and, second, to give visual
emphasis in the margins of those pages on which these scenes of personal
and philosophic apocalypse appear. On the stage of *Hard Times* the imagery
of shipwreck plays a supporting role, only coming on at crucial moments in
the play to deliver its isolated apocalyptic lines, which give metaphoric
emphasis to the event.

In *A Tale of Two Cities,* however, Dickens's imagery of shipwreck moves back to center stage mainly because *A Tale of Two Cities* is set in an eighteenth-century past where the imagery of ships is much more appropriate than amidst the mechanistic imagery of the Industrial Revolution. In *Images of Crisis,* George P. Landow asserts: "With the French Revolution, perhaps the central event of modern history, the imagination of Europe, now politicized in an entirely new way, had changed forever."[53] In noting the use of images of storm and shipwreck to analogize revolution in novels such as George Eliot's *Felix Holt,* Elizabeth Gaskill's *North and South* and, of course, Dickens's *A Tale of Two Cities,* Landow scolds that "participants in the French Revolution, and not nineteenth-century authors, invented this representation of the masses as a raging ocean that sweeps all before it."[54]

Landow's disinterest in the metaphorical applications of images of shipwreck in these novels is understandable, because he is not interested in shipwreck as metaphor but is interested in shipwreck as myth. For Landow, when "certain basic structures function as cultural codes that communicate culturally relevant information, one can begin to construct an archaeology of imagination."[55] Landow is interested in unearthing the origins of ship-wreck imagery with a focus on Christian mythology whereas the Dickens critic avoids archaeology for the study of the alchemy of imagination. However, nowhere in Dickens's canon is the metaphor of shipwreck more powerfully at work than in *A Tale of Two Cities.*

In keeping with the gravity of its subject matter, the French Revolu-tion, *A Tale of Two Cities* moves the shipwreck metaphor back to center stage from its supporting role, in *Hard Times,* as an off-stage voice functioning as part of the "symbolic shorthand." In *A Tale of Two Cities* the shipwreck imagery never takes objective form as it does in the very real shipwrecks of *Dombey and Son* and *David Copperfield,* nor does it burst out at crucial times with off-stage crescendoes of analogic metaphor, as in *Hard Times.* Rather, the ship-wreck imagery in *A Tale of Two Cities* functions as pure metaphor, an image pattern shaping itself in the mind of an omniscient narrator intent on describing the apocalypse of revolution. As the omniscient narrator's prin-cipal analogic tool, the shipwreck metaphor functions in the same two ways that it functioned in *David Copperfield:* first, as a metaphoric pattern of ominous prefiguration of storm and impending shipwreck as the central characters are magnetically "Drawn to the Loadstone Rock" as the title of Book II, Chapter 24 of *A Tale of Two Cities* augurs; and second, as pure metaphor of the apocalypse of revolution.

In other words, the French Revolution becomes the event over which the apocalyptic metaphor of shipwreck is laid, as it was laid over the objective shipwreck scene in *David Copperfield* and over the simultaneous emotional shipwrecks of daughter and father in *Hard Times*. In *A Tale of Two Cities*, the metaphor has moved out of the microcosmic existential realm into a macrocosmic political realm. The shipwreck metaphor embodies the actual destruction of a world, not a personal family world, but a whole nation, a whole society, a way of life.

In *A Tale of Two Cities*, the imagery of shipwreck as apocalypse gathers force in Book II, Chapter 21 as the French Revolution begins with the storming of the Bastille. The chapter opens with echoes "afar off and scarcely audible" to the Manette household in their quiet house in London. But they are "advancing echoes" occasioning frightening thoughts in the minds of Lucie Manette that "swelled her eyes, and broke like waves."[56] The echoes in the chapter opening are the messages of Lucie's husband's past history that form the reefs upon which her family life will run aground while attempting to navigate the storm of the French Revolution. But, in facing the threat of shipwreck, Lucie is not alone. Sydney Carton is "like a boat towed astern" in the great steamship Stryver's wake and because "the boat so favored is usually in a rough plight, and mostly under water, so, Sydney had a swamped life of it." Thus, as the Revolution hovers over their lives, both Lucie Manette and Sydney Carton are already beleaguered and taking on water. Already vulnerable, when the storm of Revolution hits, they will be among the first engulfed.

As the Revolution begins, it is described "as of a great storm in France with a dreadful sea rising." When the bloodthirsty residents of the St. Antoine district mount their attack, they are "a whirlpool of boiling waters" that like "the living sea rose, wave on wave, depth on depth, and overflowed the city . . . the sea raging and thundering on its new beach." At the drawbridge to the Bastille, "the raging storm" and "the raging sea," the sea of people caught in the storm of Revolution, takes possession of a single man: "suddenly the sea rose immeasurably wider and higher, and swept DeFarge of the wineshop over the lowered drawbridge. . . . So resistless was the force of the ocean bearing him on," that he was like a shipwrecked mariner "struggling in the surf at the South Sea."

The metaphor is multileveled, holographic. It begins as a storm representing the abstract political concept "Revolution" that blows like a high wind over France, stirring up the waters and giving them force. That abstract metaphorical storm then becomes an objective physical sea of people aroused by that concept into a raging maelstrom. Thus, the metaphor of apocalypse begins with an idea, gives that idea objective physical form, then proceeds to show how that idea brings about the shipwreck of society, the apocalypse out of which a new world must be salvaged. As this chapter proceeds, the idea of Revolution, the storm, is forgotten and only "the living ocean," "the raging flood . . . surging and tossing" remains. The abstract political idea only serves to stir up the angry waves of violence that, once aroused, become a "sea of black and threatening waters and of destructive upheaving of wave against wave, whose depths were yet unfathomed," a "remorseless sea," an "ocean of forces" so violent that "never did sea roll which bore more memorable wrecks with it." Thus, the apocalyptic event of the novel, the objective scene of violent Revolution, like the apocalyptic shipwreck of *David Copperfield,* takes the form of a wind, a storm arousing the sea, which then destroys the previously secure world.

As was the case with Dickens's "symbolic shorthand" and running headlines in *Hard Times,* at this crucial juncture in the middle of *A Tale of Two Cities,* Dickens makes offstage statements by means of his chapter and book titles. With Book II, Chapters 22 and 24, and with the title of Book III, Dickens's chapter titling manifests a different strategy. All of the chapter titles of Book I are nouns preceded by the article "the" denoting the central object of the chapter. All of the chapter titles in Book II preceding Chapter 21 (wherein the Revolution begins) are words or phrases objectively descriptive of either the time ("Five Years Later," "Nine Days"), the person ("Monseigneur in Town," "The Honest Tradesman"), or the action ("Congratulatory," "Knitting") of that particular chapter. However, suddenly, with Chapter 22, the titling becomes metaphorical and the metaphor that Dickens chooses is that of an angry sea and an impending shipwreck. Chapter 22 is titled, "The Sea Still Rises," which is appropriate because it continues the violent, revolutionary action of Chapter 21 in which the raging sea metaphor for the Revolution was introduced. Chapter 24 is also titled metaphorically, but the metaphor has changed as has the time and the omniscient narrator's focus.

Chapter 24 is titled "Drawn to the Loadstone Rock" and begins:

> In such risings of fires and risings of sea, the firm earth shaken by the rushes of an angry ocean which had now no ebb, but was always on the flow, higher and higher, to the terror and wonder of the beholders on the shore—three years of tempest were consumed. (*TTC,* II, 24)

Revolution has been underway for three years, but, for the first time since the apocalyptic metaphor of revolution was introduced three chapters earlier, the omniscient narrator shifts focus from the violent events taking

place on that raging sea to the "beholders on the shore," to those who, like
David Copperfield helplessly watching the shipwreck off Yarmouth, will be
greatly affected by this shipwreck of revolution, even though they are not
on board when it occurs.

The mythic, magnetic title of this chapter, "Drawn to the Loadstone
Rock," clearly defines the shipwreck situation of those characters in the
novel who may think themselves safe from the storm and the rising sea of
the Revolution, but who nevertheless will be drawn magnetically into its
destructive power. Charles Darnay, safe in England, observing the storm of
the Revolution from a far shore, is one of those who, like Ham observing
the plight of the shipwrecked mariners in *David Copperfield*, cannot simply
look on helplessly from the shore as David did:

> Yes. Like the mariner in the old story, the winds and streams had driven
> him within the influence of the Loadstone Rock, and it was drawing
> him to itself, and he must go. Everything that arose before his mind
> drifted him on, faster and faster, more and more steadily, to the terrible
> attraction. . . .
>   Yes. The Loadstone Rock was drawing him, and he must sail on,
> until he struck. He knew of no rock; he saw hardly any danger. (*TTC*,
> II, 24)

Whereas the shipwreck metaphor first embodied the growth of a
political idea and the death by drowning of that idea in chaotic, apocalyptic
action, here, in this last chapter of Book II, the narrator abandons the
macrocosmic overview for the microcosmic focus on the individual characters whose fragile bark is forced to put off from the safety of the distant shore
due to the intervention of a mythic fate. In other words, the shipwreck
metaphor no longer represents either a political idea or a violent action, but
rather it represents some of those "cultural codes" or myths that Landow
finds the most comforting way of handling shipwreck imagery. Charles
Darnay and Lucie Manette, Dr. Manette (Lucy's father), Jerry Cruncher,
Miss Pross and, of course, Sydney Carton are drawn into the shipwreck of
the Revolution as ancient mariners were drawn magnetically, inevitably, to
the Loadstone Rock. Whereas, in *David Copperfield*, Dickens gave Ham a
choice as to whether or not he should attempt to rescue Steerforth, Dickens
gives Darnay little choice, representing his action (as George Eliot represents Maggie Tulliver's action in *The Mill on the Floss*) as fated. The whole
microcosmic action of *A Tale of Two Cities* is represented as a mythic shipwreck
just waiting to happen.

Thus, the macrocosmic world of the French Revolution, a world of political idea and mob action, is represented as a storm and a raging sea that shipwrecks an entire society, and the microcosmic world of the novel is represented as a doomed ship caught in the mythic, magnetic pull of that Revolution. The title of Book III then, "The Track of the Storm," ends this complex storm/sea/Loadstone Rock/shipwreck metaphor and turns the novel's focus back on the political idea of Revolution, which earlier had been drowned when the human sea rose out of control. In the crucial center of his novel, Dickens employs the imagery of storm and shipwreck to differentiate between his macrocosmic and microcosmic themes. However, unlike in *Hard Times*, this shipwreck imagery is by no means an intrusion or dramatic assertion for effect. The importance of the imagery of shipwreck has been prefigured from the very beginning of the novel.

As in both *David Copperfield* and *The Mill on the Floss*, the controlling imagery of *A Tale of Two Cities* is present from the very beginning of the novel. As the Dover Mail struggles up Shooter's Hill, the mist "made its slow way through the air in ripples that visibly followed and overspread one another, as the waves of an unwholesome sea might do" (*TTC*, I, 2). Jarvis Lorry and Jerry Cruncher survive the "eddying mist" (I, 2) on the Dover road but, when they reach the beach at the end of their journey, it is "a desert of heaps of sea and stones tumbling wildly about, and the sea did what it liked, and what it liked was destruction" (I, 4). Thus, the threat of shipwreck is prefigured in the early objective landscape of the novel, but it is also prefigured in the abstract metaphoric language of the omniscient narrator. For example, Doctor Manette, sleeping, is described as yielding "to the calm that must follow all storms—emblem to humanity, of the rest and silence into which the storm called Life must hush at last" (I, 6). Here, the imagery of storm and shipwreck is aligned with mythic metaphor for the first time and hints at the manner in which the macrocosmic significance of the storm and shipwreck metaphor will later develop. Like the macrocosmic significance of the storm and shipwreck metaphor, its microcosmic significance is also prefigured. The Manette household in London is described as "a very harbour from the raging streets . . . a tranquil bark in such an anchorage" (I, 6). But soon this safe harbor will no longer provide shelter from the raging streets of Paris and their "tranquil bark" will be inexorably drawn to the Loadstone Rock and wrecked on the shoals of the Revolution.

After the storming of the Bastille, the Manette household—Dr. Manette, Lucie, Charles, Miss Pross, Jerry Cruncher—become shipwrecked mariners adrift in the Revolution's terror and desolation. Caught in the vortex of the Revolution, Dr. Manette and Mr. Lorry view the giant grindstone from the window of their lodging, and what they see is "the vision of a drowning man, or of any human creature at any very great pass" (III, 2). Finally, the novel moves into the interior space of the prison and Sydney Carton's submission to the flood of history that has pulled him into the center of its vortex. At the moment of Carton's death, Dickens chooses a shipwreck image to represent this final, small, microcosmic apocalypse:

> The murmuring of many voices, the upturning of many faces, the pressing on of many footsteps in the outskirts of the crowd, so that it swells forward in a mass, like one great heave of water, all flashes away. Twenty three. (*TTC*, III, 15)

Carton is the only member of the shipwrecked crew of the microcosmic world to perish in the storm of Revolution. All the other members of the Manette household survive the shipwreck, make it back to the safe "harbour" from whence they originally sailed their "tranquil bark." But they are changed, marked, as Miss Pross's loss of hearing best illustrates. They have survived the Loadstone Rock by luck and a benevolent faith, not by any power or strength of their own. Like David Copperfield's helplessly watching from the beach, they have survived the apocalyptic shipwreck of their world, but they have also realized how ineffectual they truly are in a world gone mad and breaking apart.

If the second half of Dickens's career was marked by "dark novels," by a turning to a more cynical, despairing philosophical vision of man's relation to the realities of the postindustrial Revolution society, then these stranded observers of the shipwrecked world, which is similar to the situation of Matthew Arnold's speaker in the poem "Dover Beach," embody Dickens's frustration (and the Victorian social novelist's frustration) with his own helplessness. Nonetheless, in every novel, Dickens presents an antidote to that helplessness, and in every case it is a return to the eighteenth-century paradigm of selfless benevolence. Sydney Carton is willing to give up his life in resistance to his stranded situation, and that same positive conversion to hope and benevolence triumphs in *Our Mutual Friend.*

Shipwrecks, Lighthouses, Rescues: *Our Mutual Friend*

Dickens's last completed novel, *Our Mutual Friend*, begins in a boat and proceeds immediately to the telling of the story of a man overboard, presumed drowned. Can shipwreck be far behind? Like the shipwreck scene in *David Copperfield*, like the symbolic shipwreck of the Gradgrind philosophy in *Hard Times*, like the violent metaphorical shipwreck of the French Revolution in *A Tale of Two Cities*, *Our Mutual Friend* also builds to an apocalyptic resolution of the personal dilemma of at least two of its central characters, Lizzie Hexam and Eugene Wrayburn. In fact, it begins where *David Copperfield* ends—with the drowned man washing up on the beach—but, to steal a thematic phrase from *A Tale of Two Cities*, it is really about that man and a number of others being "Recalled to life" (the title of Book I). Whereas, in *David Copperfield*, Steerforth could not be saved, and David could only stand helplessly on the beach accepting his friend's death, in *A Tale of Two Cities*, partially, and *Our Mutual Friend*, wholly yet with qualification, resurrection is once again possible. Thus, *Our Mutual Friend* begins with a man overboard and ends on the water with a shipwrecked mariner who, like Steerforth, has harbored ungentlemanly designs on a working-class girl. This shipwrecked mariner ends up floating helplessly on the current and being rescued by an intrepid boatman who resuscitates him. The outcome is very different from that of the apocalyptic shipwreck of *David Copperfield.*

Near the end of *Our Mutual Friend*, while walking near the river at night in the contemplation of his potentially exploitative relationship with Lizzie Hexam, Eugene Wrayburn is suddenly attacked, beaten insensible and knocked into the river to drown. It is an apocalyptic breaking open of the world, the sky, both in the unexpected suddenness of the attack and in the language used to describe it. The attack occurs "in one instance, with a dreadful crash" and "the reflected night turned crooked, flames shot jaggedly across the air, and the moon and stars came bursting from the sky" (*OMF*, IV, 6). In this final Dickensian apocalypse, all creation is torn asunder in an explosion of flame and light. Luckily, however, Lizzie is nearby and, commandeering a handy boat, rescues Eugene, who is floating helplessly in the river.

Once again, as Eugene fights for his life after the attack and rescue, Dickens chooses to express this apocalyptic resolution in the language of shipwreck. As Eugene lies in bed fighting for his life, his struggle is the "frequent rising of a drowning man from the deep, to sink again," who, even in the course of "rising from the deep would disappear the sooner for fighting with the water, so he in his desperate struggle went down again" (IV, 10). As Stein, in Joseph Conrad's *Lord Jim*, will later advise, "in the destructive element immerse,"[57] so does Eugene face this sink or swim situation in *Our Mutual Friend*. As Eugene starts to slip away, he seems to be "quietly yielding to the attraction of the loadstone rock of Eternity" (*OMF*, IV, 11), an echo of a similar shipwreck situation in *A Tale of Two Cities*. Finally, the culminating image of this whole scene of apocalypse, rescue, and salvage is quite typically and predictably Dickensian. When Eugene finally awakens, the "utter help-lessness of the wreck of him that lay cast ashore here now alarmed her, but he himself appeared a little more hopeful" (*OMF*, IV, 11). In the end, Dickens always seems to return to his imagery of shipwreck as analogy for worlds apocalyptically broken up.

However, the major shipwreck imagery in *Our Mutual Friend* is not this familiar "dark" imagery of apocalypse, but rather the more optimistic imag-ery of that which can save the ships from running aground and breaking up on the rocks, the protective imagery of lighthouses. In setting the editorial policy and in the actual editing and writing of essays in *Household Words, The Household Narrative of Current Events,* and *All the Year Round,* Dickens had, during the seventeen years prior to the composition of *Our Mutual Friend,* become an active and outspoken polemicist for the building of additional lighthouses on the treacherous English coastline. The lighthouse as base metal for the imaginative alchemy of his novelistic pen would be readily available to a writer whose journalistic pen had spent so much time on it.

Early in *Our Mutual Friend,* the two young lawyers, Mortimer Light-wood and Eugene Wrayburn, sup alone in the middle of a London winter and discuss the boredom of their lives:

> "The wind sounds up here," quoth Eugene, stirring the fire, "as if we were keeping a lighthouse. I wish we were."
>
> "Don't you think it would bore us?" Lightwood asked.
>
> "Not more than any other place. And there would be no Circuit to go. . . . If we were on an isolated rock in a stormy sea," said Eugene. "Lady Tippins couldn't put off to visit us, or, better still, might put off and get swamped. People couldn't ask one to wedding breakfasts. There would be no precedents to hammer at, except the plain-sailing Prece-dent of keeping the light up. It would be exciting to look out for wrecks." (I, 12)

Eugene, in his fanciful lighthouse wish, which immediately metamor-phoses into a social metaphor, expresses four separate dissatisfactions with Victorian society from which he desires to be protected as a lighthouse protects ships from danger. First, he longs for isolation from the hypocritical buffeting of the London social "Circuit" as represented by Lady Tippins. Second, he longs for the "plain-sailing" and simplicity of the lighthouse-keeper's life, a life uncomplicated by the irresponsible and hypocritical role-playing of London social life. Third, he longs to take responsibility for something, make some sort of meaningful contribution to society. Finally, he feels it "would be exciting to look out for wrecks."

Eugene is one of the most ennui-afflicted characters in all of British literature, and his mere anticipation of excitement is almost a major character upheaval. Interestingly enough, his idea of the excitement of "looking out for wrecks" is what places him in a partially protective, though admittedly ambiguous, relationship to Lizzie Hexam after her father drowns and her brother jumps ship leaving her cast adrift and being drawn to the "Headstone" rock. For Lizzie, Eugene becomes the lighthouse keeper who, despite the great sexual power he as a gentleman holds over her, keeps the light up and steers her away from the shoals of exploitation both by Headstone and by himself. In other words, he lives up to his "plain-sailing" responsibility as lighthouse-keeper and rescues her from the metaphoric sexual shipwreck that, too often, drowns young working-class women in the "stormy sea" of London life. Ironically, in time, Lizzie will rescue Eugene from the physical shipwreck of Headstone's apocalyptic assault at the end of the novel.

What Mortimer Lightwood cannot understand is how Eugene, who constantly complains about the boredom of English life, could long for such an alternative:

> "Why, it was but now that you were dwelling on the advantages of a monotony of two."
>
> "In a lighthouse. Do me the justice to remember the condition. In a lighthouse." (I, 12)

For Eugene, the lighthouse offers a different, more meaningful monotony, a chosen monotony, that involves a clear-cut responsibility to society as opposed to the ambiguity, irresponsibility, and unchosen reality of his nonexistent law career. Later in *Our Mutual Friend*, the tension between Eugene's protective responsibility toward the drifting Lizzie and his gentleman's sexual attraction toward the vulnerable Lizzie momentarily causes him to let the light burn low. In an expressive image, Old Riah describes this lapse in the lighthouse-keeper's attention to "plain sailing:"

> "Sir, it was only natural that she should incline towards him, for he had many and great advantages. But he was not of her station, and to marry her was not in his mind. Perils were closing round her, and the circle was fast darkening. (III, 1)

However, in *Our Mutual Friend*, the shipwreck and lighthouse imagery is not reserved only for the definition of the relationship of Eugene Wrayburn and Lizzie Hexam. In employing lighthouse imagery to comment on the plight of Betty Higden, Dickens raises this motif of shipwreck and rescue to the level of Christian religious iconography, which George Landow argues is its most typical function in English literature and art. For Betty Higden the lighthouse imagery serves as a beacon of Christian salvation. As she flees the shipwreck of the Poor House, "all the Light that shone on Betty Higden lay beyond Death" (III, 8). Suddenly, the "light" that has guided the other castaway souls has been elevated to the upper case "Light." Set adrift, Betty struggles past the "gentlefolks and their children inside those fine houses" and "the humbler houses in the little street, the inner firelight shining on the panes as the outer twilight darkened" (III, 8). Finally, on the verge of death with "a bright fire in her eyes," she sits by the river and sees the lighthouse-like path of "the lighted windows, both in their reality and their reflection in the water"; and that water-reflected beam of light "brought to her mind the foot of the Cross, and she committed herself to Him who died upon it" (III, 8). For Betty, the lighthouse transfigures into the Cross, and Christ becomes the lighthouse keeper who protects her from the shipwreck of the Poor Laws and guides her across the bar into the safe harbor on the other side of "Death." Here, near the end of his writing career, Dickens gives the lighthouse imagery two distinct metaphoric forms. In the case of its representation of Eugene and Lizzie's relationship, it carries an existential, moral signification, a secular signification of personal and social responsibility. In the case of Betty Higden, however, the lighthouse imagery carries a religious, mythic signification of a higher protection, a higher rescue from the Victorian dilemma of spiritual shipwreck.

However, one other interpretation of Dickens's turning to the imagery of lighthouses and lighthouse-keepers in his last completed novel is worth exploring. In *David Copperfield*, he had presented a quite negative and frustrated image of the writer's role in Victorian society as that of a helpless observer on the shore. In *Our Mutual Friend* the image of the writer as lighthouse keeper is certainly qualified, yet it is also more positive than that of the powerless watcher on the shore in *David Copperfield*. The writer as lighthouse keeper is still alone, isolated from the "stormy sea" of Victorian life, but he is no longer powerless. His light can illuminate—and warn off from the dangers of Victorian life—the ships (the readers) that must navigate those treacherous seas. Near the end of his career, Dickens sees the writer as necessary and, to steal a term from Sartre and Camus, *engagé*—responsible for keeping up the light so that others can see.

If Dickens's later novels are so irredeemably "dark," then how does one explain his choice of strikingly "light" imagery in his final finished work. This imagery of lighthouses and rescue in *Our Mutual Friend* announces that Dickens, at the very end of his novelistic career, has no desire to stagnate in the self-pitying pessimism of *David Copperfield*, wherein the novelist is stranded on the beach. He has no desire to embrace the despair of Matthew Arnold's sad lover in "Dover Beach." Rather, Dickens sees himself as a novelistic beacon for a humanistic (and positive) postindustrial vision of existential perfectibility in the best Godwinian/Camusian sense.

Other characters in *Our Mutual Friend* also experience the dilemma of either spiritual or physical shipwreck. The Lammles, like two false Sirens, lure each other onto the rocks of a moneyless marriage. In an ironic echo of both Steerforth's final rest in *David Copperfield* and the lover's situation in Matthew Arnold's poem "Dover Beach," the Lammles find themselves washed up and marooned on a desolate beach: "The tide is low, and seems to have thrown them together high on the bare shore. A gull comes sweeping by their heads and flouts them. . . . A taunting roar comes from the sea and the far-out rollers mount upon one another, to look at the entrapped imposters, and to join in impish and exultant gambols" (*OMF*, I, 10).

While the Lammles's shipwreck is merely metaphorical, Rogue Riderhood is physically run over by a huge steamer driving downstream in the fog toward the sea. It is a much more ethereal, impersonal shipwreck than those that occurred in *David Copperfield* and *Great Expectations*. The scene takes place in a ghostly fog, and the steamer is characterized as a mechanical monster more akin to the railway train that runs down Carker in *Dombey and Son* than to the sailing ship on which Steerforth perishes. This shipwreck is described in much different, more violent, certainly less romantic terms than Dickens's earlier apocalyptic shipwrecks. The passage is somewhat similar to the shipwreck litany that Walter Gay and old Sol Gills recite in *Dombey and Son*, but the tone of the recitation by this waterside community is totally different. To these people, the shipwreck is not romantic or unusual, it is destructive, intentional, impersonal, and demonic. The outraged voices of the community members penetrate the scene as they go about the act of rescue:

> A cry for the lifebuoy passed from mouth to mouth. It was impossible to make out what was going on upon the river, for every boat had put off, sculled into the fog and was lost to view at a boat's length. Nothing was clear but that the unpopular steamer was assailed with reproaches on all sides. She was the *Murderer*, bound for Gallows Bay; she was the

Manslaughterer bound for Penal Settlement; her captain ought to be tried for his life; her crew ran down men in rowboats with a relish; she mashed up Thames lightermen with her paddles; she always was, and she always would be, wreaking destruction upon somebody or something, after the manner of her kind. The whole bulk of the fog teemed with such taunts, uttered in tones of universal hoarseness. All the while the steamer's lights moved spectrally a very little, as she lay-to, waiting the upshot of whatever accident had happened. (*OMF,* III, 2)

This uncharacteristic Dickens shipwreck is not an act of God or an unfortunate collision of circumstance with the aroused elements of air, water, and submerged stone. Rather, this shipwreck is described as a premeditated crime, a postindustrial Revolution act of mechanical aggression, an intentionally malicious wreaking of destruction. The world has changed and so has Dickens's perception of the nature of shipwreck, the nature of society, and the possibilities for protection and rescue from the "stormy sea" of Victorian life.

Despite Dickens's atypical use of the metaphor of shipwreck in *Our Mutual Friend,* it is somehow appropriate that, in one of the final shipwreck allusions of his career, Dickens returns to his favorite shipwreck narrative, *Robinson Crusoe. Our Mutual Friend* begins with a dinner at the Veneerings, and Dickens returns to their "bran' new" board for another dinner party at the end. When Mortimer Lightwood sits down at the Veneering dining table, he no longer can avoid that rapacious gossip, Lady Tippins:

> "Long banished Robinson Crusoe," says the charmer, exchanging salutations, "how did you leave the Island?"
> "Thank you," says Lightwood. "It made no complaint of being in pain anywhere."
> "Say, how did you leave the savages," asks Lady Tippins.
> "They were becoming civilized when I left Juan Fernandez," says Lightwood. "At least they were eating one another, which looked like it."
> "Tormentor. . . . You know what I mean, and you trifle with my impatience. Tell me something, immediately, about the married pair. You were at the wedding. . . . How was the bride dressed? In rowing costume?"
> Mortimer looks gloomy and declines to answer. "I hope she steered herself, skiffed herself, paddled herself, larboarded and starboarded herself, or whatever the technical term may be, to the ceremony?"
> "However she got to it, she graced it," says Mortimer.

Lady Tippins with a skittish little scream, attracts the general attention. "Graced it! Take care of me if I faint, Veneering. He means to tell us that a horrid female waterman is graceful!" "Pardon me, I mean to tell you nothing, Lady Tippins," replies Lightwood. (*OMF*, IV, "Chapter the Last")

Throughout this whole exchange, like Robinson Crusoe the shipwrecked mariner who returned from his desert island to supposed civilization, Mortimer is realizing that the true savagery, the true cannibalism, lies in the gossip of supposedly civilized "Society." Disdaining "Society," affirming the better post-shipwreck life that Eugene and Lizzie have built for themselves on their desert island of love, Mortimer refuses to participate in the savagery of Lady Tippins's "gossip-mongering." Refusing to converse with the "Voice of Society," as Lady Tippins christens this gathering of gossips, is a moral decision on Mortimer's part, and he finds an unexpected ally in the innocuous Twemlow. Thus, the final word in *Our Mutual Friend* is the rejection of supposedly civilized "Society" by this intrepid Robinson Crusoe and his man Friday (Twemlow) and a return to Eugene and Lizzie's post-shipwreck world of rebirth.

Social Shipwreck

Throughout his canon, Dickens uses the reality and the metaphorical possibility of shipwreck in myriad ways. In *Barnaby Rudge* and *A Tale of Two Cities*, he uses shipwreck metaphor as a symbol of both violent social upheaval and the vortical entrapment of the individual in that upheaval. In *Hard Times* the imagery of shipwreck serves as a commentary on the psychic dislocation and foundering of the central characters. In the Lammles's case in *Our Mutual Friend*, the shipwreck imagery becomes a comic expression of their fatal navigational error in marrying.

But, most importantly, from *Dombey and Son* on, the shipwreck imagery serves as the major symbolic component of each Dickens novel's building to an apocalyptic resolution. In *Dombey and Son*, all of the litany-like recitation of eighteenth-century shipwreck lore and the metaphoric representation of the sinking of the great merchant House of Dombey prefigures the postindustrial Revolution version of the shipwreck apocalypse, namely the pulverizing of Carker by the railroad train. In *David Copperfield*, a real, fully described shipwreck is the apocalyptic event on which all of the novel's action and relationships turn. *Bleak House* is the narrative of a series of failed salvage operations. All of the characters are ships lost in the fog, trying to avoid running aground and perishing. Only a few of those castaway mariners survive. *Hard Times* builds to the bilevel moral shipwreck of Louisa Gradgrind and her father's philosophy, which he had launched with high hopes but which runs aground on the shoals of the Industrial Revolution's dehumanization. Physical violence characterizes the shipwreck apocalypses of *A Tale of Two Cities* and *Our Mutual Friend.* In the maelstrom of the French Revolution and in Bradley Headstone's personal attack on Eugene Wrayburn, Dickens represents the social class struggle of Victorian life as an apocalyptic shipwreck that must be survived if any change into a more enlightened society is to occur.

At the most crucial moments in Dickens's novels, when moral action, human relationships, or social decisions need to be resolved, the danger and potential negative consequences of those actions, relationships, or decisions are most often couched either in real scenes of shipwreck or in a metaphoric language of shipwreck.[58] As each novel moves toward its apocalyptic resolution, Dickens's imagination is repeatedly fueled by the imagery of shipwreck. That imagery is perhaps the most appropriate representation of the cautionary nature of Dickens's vision of Victorian society. A tentative duality exists in Dickens's use of shipwreck as a way of representing the world. In a way, as Lionel Stevenson characterizes Dickens in the "dark novels" of the latter half of his canon, Dickens is a doomsayer, a frustrated chronicler of a society on the rocks, a sinking society struggling to stay afloat in the violent vortex of apocalypse. Yet, in his constant reshaping of this shipwreck imagery of apocalypse in the successive later works of his canon, Dickens comes to emphasize the marvelous powers and instincts for survival and rescue from the turbulent sea of Victorian life; and the result is a regenerative, positive vision for Victorian society. In the final analysis, Dickens found a metaphor for his age—that of a generation of shipwrecked mariners—quite similar to Albert Camus's eloquent metaphor for the struggle of mid-twentieth-century man—the myth of Sisyphus.

FOUR

Dickens and George Barnwell

While all of Dickens's novels are historical novels, his approach to the writing of historical fiction alternated throughout his career. Sometimes, as in *Barnaby Rudge* and *A Tale of Two Cities*, he is a traditional historical novelist setting his personal histories in the shadows of great events. Sometimes, especially in his panoramic social epics such as *Bleak House* and *Our Mutual Friend*, he is a writer of complex, heteroglossic social histories in which many voices on many levels of society are given the opportunity to express themselves. Thus, a New Historicist approach to Dickens's fiction that consistently asks the questions "how does Dickens employ history in his novels" and "how does Dickens define a philosophy of history in his novels" results in a portrait of an artist acutely conscious of his position at the fulcrum of history. A New Historicist reading of Dickens's fiction reveals his consistent positioning of his art within a dialogic sense of historical flux and historical continuity. Dickens's sense of history is that of a flowing current that brings together past, present and future; that historicizes time.

While New Historicism's approach to literary interpretation customarily examines the ideological or philosophical agendas of works of fiction to trace the emplotted language structures (such as the shipwreck metaphor) that define its dialogical tensions, this approach less often deals with the concept of historicist characterization. Yet, it seems only natural that New Historicist themes and metaphors ought to be embodied in New Historicist characters. In Dickens's fiction, they are. His characterizations emanate from past models that take on heteroglossic present voices that construct philosophies of history for England's future. Once again, time comes together in Dickens's characterizations. His characters emerge from the eighteenth-century prototypes to prefigure the twentieth-century motives and contingency of the New Historicist project.

Dickens employs a strong sense of eighteenth-century literary history as the source for many of his Victorian social characterizations. While the bulk of that eighteenth-century literary influence comes from the novels of Defoe, Fielding, Goldsmith, and Godwin, Dickens was also strongly influenced by the drama of that and earlier periods.

Dickens's interest in the theatre is legendary. He was a great lover of Shakespeare and Ben Jonson, but most often his novelistic characterizations turn to the stock characters and theatrical social voices that he knew best, those of eighteenth-century melodrama. He saw eighteenth-century melodrama's stock characters as ready voices for those socially marginalized by the mid-nineteenth-century rise of a Victorian middle class in England. One eighteenth-century play in particular presented Dickens with a group of allegorical characters who embodied the historical situation of Victorian England, and that play's historicist warning against amoral materialism consistently echoes throughout Dickens's fiction.

> Be warned, ye youths, who see my sad despair, Avoid lewd women, false as they are fair,
>> By reason guided, honest joys pursue. . . . By my example learn to shun my fate,
>> (How wretched is the man who's wise too late!) Ere innocence, and fame, and life be lost, Here purchase wisdom cheaply at my cost.[1]

George Barnwell, the patsy in George Lillo's eighteenth-century domestic tragedy *The London Merchant, or, The History of George Barnwell* delivers this cautionary speech as he is being carted off to prison. Again, on the eve of his death on the gallows, Barnwell delivers a dire warning to his fellow apprentices:

> If any youth, like you, in future times, Shall mourn my fate, though he abhor my crimes, Or tender maid, like you, my tale shall hear, And to my sorrows give a pitying tear:
>> To each such melting eye, and throbbing heart, Would gracious heaven this benefit impart, Never to know my guilt, nor feel my pain;
>> Then must you own, you ought not to complain; Since you nor weep, nor shall I die, in vain. (V, ii)

Despite George Barnwell's allowing himself to be seduced and manipulated into embezzlement by the town's lewd woman, Sarah Millwood, despite his murder of his kind rich uncle, some critics feel that George Barnwell should have been executed simply for the crime of delivering these ponderous warning speeches.

Nonetheless, the moral exemplum, cautionary didactic quality of *The London Merchant* did indeed give this simplistic domestic and commercial melodrama an extraordinary staying power on the London stage. Its century and a half longevity as a regular London and provincial theater production turned the name "George Barnwell" into a household and counting house word as well as generating a wide range of literary influence.

One hundred and five years after Lillo's play was first offered on the stage of the Drury Lane Theatre, Charles Dickens, a promising young journalist and writer of imaginative sketches of English life, partook of that theatrical influence at the most crucial moment of his literary career. The first three serial numbers of the young Dickens's *The Pickwick Papers* had enjoyed, at best, average sales. In the fourth number, however, Dickens introduced a sparkling new comic character, one Mr. Samuel Weller, a bootcleaning philosopher, and the sales of *The Pickwick Papers* and their author's career hit the highroad at the breakneck speed of one of DeQuincey's mail coaches.

As a lower class prodigy with a flair for language, Sam Weller was a lyrical, clearsighted "Everyman" in a world of quixotic dreamers. He provided Pickwick with everything from clean boots to perceptive snatches of literary criticism. In his very first appearance in the carriage yard of The White Hart Inn, Sam throws off this trenchant bit of drama critique as an eavesdropper on Pickwick's legal conversation:

> "Never mind George Barnwell," interrupted Sam, who had remained a wondering listener during this short colloquy; "everybody knows vhat sort of a case his was, tho it's always been my opinion, mind you, that the young 'ooman deserved scragging a precious sight more than he did." (*PP*, 10)

The fact of the matter is that by the time of Sam Weller's pronouncement in 1836, everybody—especially Dickens—indeed knew what sort of a case George Barnwell's was and what sort of a woman his seducer, Sarah Millwood, was as well.

Over the course of his long and prolific career, those two characters would haunt almost every succeeding Dickens novel. In some novels, allusions to these characters would merely serve as metaphoric references for moral statements and situations. In other novels they would serve as models for characters. But in some novels, the influence of these two Lillo characters and their actions would become a major impetus for the plot, structure, and language motifs of the entire work.

The London Merchant's Staying Power

The *London Merchant,* a "sentimental domestic tragedy" written by George Lillo, a real London merchant and dissenting jeweler who knew well his rising middle class audience, was first staged at Drury Lane on June 22, 1731. Based on *The Ballad of George Barnwell,* the play moved its audience to tears at "the distresses of young Barnwell" and edified them with "his exemplary end."[2] By 1733, only two years later, the anonymous author of *The Apprentice's Vade Mecum* was already recommending that the apprentices of London be edified each year by a revival of this play.[3] By the mid-eighteenth century, *The London Merchant* had become the traditional offering for the Christmas and Easter holidays in both London and the provincial theaters as well as for Lord Mayor's Day in November in London because it was "judged a proper entertainment for the apprentices as being a more instructive, moral, and cautionary drama than many pieces that had usually been exhibited on those days with little but farce and ribaldry to recommend them."[4] One critic speculates that "the frequent performance of *George Barnwell* was encouraged by influential citizens, not because they themselves enjoyed it, but because they thought young people should."[5] Sir A.W. Ward affirms these motives in stating that *George Barnwell* "came to be frequently acted in the Christmas and Easter holidays, being esteemed a better entertainment for the city prentices than the coarse shows with which they were at such seasons habitually regaled on the stage."[6] The most acidic critical reaction to the play came from Charles Lamb in the early nineteenth century. In his essay "On the Tragedies of Shakespeare," he referred to it as "the nauseating sermon of *George Barnwell.*"[7] By 1748-1749 *The London Merchant* had become such a standard offering in a theatre's repertory that in any given season it might be played only once to audiences specially summoned for its performance.[8]

After 1740, however, "the novel gradually became the chief literary form of the age, though novelists often drew upon the theatre for characters, situations and themes. . . . Among the advantages of the rising novel were leisurely development of plot, the possibility of detailed psychological analysis, and an increasingly flexible prose. The novel could and did more successfully continue Lillo's search for a hero."[9] For example, in Fielding's *Tom Jones,* in both name and action, Squire Allworthy is an obvious direct descendent of Lillo's Thorowgood. The story of George Barnwell, Millwood, Thorowgood and Trueman formed "the theme of a novel in three volumes which was published in 1796 and dedicated by the author, Thomas Skinner Surr, to Mrs. Siddons, who had recently appeared as Millwood. This was followed by *The Memoirs of George Barnwell, the Unhappy Subject of Lillo's celebrated Tragedy, derived from the most*

Authentic Sources, and intended for the Perusal and Instruction of the Rising Generations, by a Descendant of the Barnwell Family (1810). Ten years afterward, this prolix chronicle was abridged and appeared as *The Life and History of George Barnwell.*[10] By the 1840s, William Makepeace Thackeray "used the name George de Barnwell, though nothing but the name, in his *Novels by Eminent Hands*, for his travesty of the melodramatic criminal romances of Bulwar Lytton."[11] But the novel genre was not the only art form to imitate the domestic tragedy of Lillo's vision in *The London Merchant*. Hogarth's drawings of good and bad apprentices also mimicked the situations and themes of Lillo's play.

Despite these novel piracies and cannibalizations on into the nineteenth century, Lillo's original play continued to be performed on the London stage on special occasions and even more frequently in provincial theatres. The theatrical periodicals of the nineteenth century, such as *The Dramatic Magazine* (1829-31), *The Dramatic Gazette* (1830-31), *The Theatrical Inquisitor* (1812-21), *The Theatrical Observer* (1821-76) and *The Theatrical Journal* (1839-73), all chronicle the frequent productions of *The London Merchant*.[12] One magazine, *The Drama*, also known as *The Theatrical Pocket Magazine*, appeared from 1821 to 1825 and chronicles, in detail, the consistent revival of Lillo's play on London stages.

In August of 1821, *The Drama* published an essay on Lillo's *Fatal Curiosity*.[13] One month later, under the heading "UTILITY OF THE DRAMA," an anonymous essayist wrote:

> It is desirable that the exhibition of dramatic performances should be as frequent as possible in all large and populous places. The common business of life too intensely pursued, makes man unmindful of precepts and maxims of virtue, which they are more apt to forget in the eager pursuit of their avocations, than to abandon through want of principle. The DRAMA awakens them to virtue; exercises all the kinder emotions; and by its kinder influence over the mind and feelings, prevents the moral stagnation, which so much tends to degrade and brutify.[14]

If this writer wasn't referring to the moral exemplum theater of George Lillo directly, he was at least very aware of the Utilitarian motive that kept *The London Merchant* such a popular revival choice more than a century after its first appearance. Yet, in the October issue, "a biography of Charles Kemble" appeared in which the writer gushed, "to dwell upon the points of his performance of George Barnwell would be merely to repeat a thrice-told tale; we may observe, however, that it is personated with every effective feature of an ingenious mind, imperatively hurried onwards to error, and yet virtuous in repentance; the whole progress of his seduction is marked by an exquisite variety of feeling and pathos, that wholly subdue the audience."[15]

The next year, 1822, *George Barnwell*, as the play had come increasingly to be called, was given a single performance at Drury Lane on April 8[16] and another at the New Drury Lane Theatre on December 26.[17] In the January 1823 issue of *The Drama*, the following summary of the offerings at the Cobourg Theater for recent weeks appears:

> We fear we can do no more at present than give a list of the pieces which have appeared at this house, since our last notice, and it will be perceived their titles are full of that "empty wordiness," for excelling in which the authors, adaptors, and managers of this theatre are so celebrated. The first was a melo-drama, founded on and called *George Barnwell, The London Apprentice* in which the whole of the characters were dressed in the habits of the times, and the scenery, consisting of ancient views in London, rendered it very interesting. Huntley as Barnwell, and Mrs. Stanley as Millwood, were never seen to more advantage. Their respective performances were indeed as high a treat as we ever witnessed at a minor theatre.[18]

In the February 1823 issue, *The Drama* reprinted a poem first published in *The Monthly Mirror* magazine in 1807 and titled "An Elegy, written in Drury Lane Theatre," that contained the following lines: "Ambition on our mimic stage will rise;/ Trueman survives when Barnwell yields his breath."[19] At the beginning of the March 1823 issue of *The Drama*, a one-paragraph mini-essay on "George Barnwell" appeared, and, at the end of the issue, under the heading "TOWN TALK," which signaled the magazine's gossip column, the following appeared:

> Cooke declared, that the greatest compliment he ever received from an audience was that of being hissed for his consummate villainy in the character of Iago. Lately, at the Bath Theatre, Mrs. Bunn was similarly rewarded for her powerful but just representation of the abandoned Millwood in the tragedy of George Barnwell.—The performers did right to interpret a somewhat equivocal expression into a compliment.[20]

In the December 1823 issue, under the heading "COUNTRY THE-ATRICALS," is a notice for the Redruth Theatre: "21st Nov. *George Barnwell* and *Tom and Jerry* (for the third time), Barnwell by Wilton, did him great credit; all the rest were below mediocrity."[21] In the January 1824 issue of this magazine, which listed performances of Nicholas Rowe's play *Jane Shore* at the Covent Garden Theatre and at Drury Lane on *George Barnwell's* usual

26th of December date, an essay on Rowe's melodrama appeared that bemoaned its substitution for Lillo's old warhorse:

> The theatre as at Drury Lane was crowded to excess. For what reason the trashy tragedy of Rowe's was selected at both houses we know not. A few years since it was the established rule to play '*George Barnwell*,' by way, we suppose, of a 'great moral lesson' to the apprentices of London. In this age of innovation this venerable custom has been broken down, but the principle seems not wholly to have been abandoned. '*Jane Shore*' has supplanted '*Barnwell*,' and the anxieties of the age are, it would appear, more directed toward the softer sex. [22]

In fact, this prediction proved not to be the case at all as the Covent Garden Theatre immediately reinstated *George Barnwell* for its December 26, 1824 performance, after its one-year experiment with *Jane Shore*.[23]

In *The Drama's* June 1824 issue, under the heading "COUNTRY THEATRICALS," this comic critique of *George Barnwell* done at the Great Malvern Theatre in April 1824 appeared:

> Some idea may be formed of the histrionic powers of the "company" from the following observation, made (by a friend of mine) in reply to a remark from a lady who had the evening before witnessed their representation of what the bills of the day "styled" the moral and instructive tragedy of "*George Barnwell*"—indeed Madam, for my own part, I think Barnwell was the most fortunate of the lot—he was only hung at the conclusion—whereas the rest of the characters were miserably mangled and executed throughout![24]

Despite these sorts of "histrionic" excesses of provincial theater groups, Lillo's play seems to have been every bit as popular in the country as it was on the London stage. Its popularity was probably due as much to its portrayal of the corruption and immorality of city life as to the efficacy of its moral exemplum message. As late as December 12, 1845, its title still bastardized, the play itself, foreshortened and newly subtitled *Barnwell, The London Apprentice; or, Fatal Love,* was still being offered at the Cobourg Theatre in London.[25]

Texts and Subtexts

Though Charles Lamb went to the trouble of contrasting *The London Merchant,* "the nauseating sermon of George Barnwell," to *Othello,* many (Dickens surely was one) in both the eighteenth and nineteenth centuries were much more sympathetic to the former play's themes, characters, and moral messages. Before *The London Merchant* even begins, in his dedication to Sir John Eyles, Lillo stresses that the major selling point of his play is its moral influence on all classes of society. He writes: "tragedy is so far from losing its dignity by being accommodated to the circumstances of the generality of mankind that it is more truly august in proportion to the extent of its influence." In that same dedication, Lillo quotes from Shakespeare's *Hamlet*

> I've heard that guilty creatures at a play,
> Have, by the very cunning of the scene,
> Been so struck to the soul that presently
> They have proclaimed their malefactions.

to illustrate the power of the theatre to deliver morally regenerative messages. It seems that, on into the mid-nineteenth century, Lillo and his audiences actually subscribed to the melancholy Dane's proposition that "The Play's the thing/Wherein I'll catch the conscience" of the whole society, from the lowest apprentices to the most powerful merchant "King."

The London Merchant is, first and foremost, a play about business. Its metaphor and mileu is the business world of England's rising middle class, and its primary text's moral message is unmistakably clear: Attend to thy business, young man, and you will attain success! Early in the play, Thorowgood admonishes Trueman "that if hereafter you should be tempted to any action that has the appearance of vice or meanness in it, upon reflecting upon the dignity of our profession, you may with honest scorn reject whatever is unworthy of it" (I, i).

Business is idealized throughout the play to the point where Barnwell's sins appear not to be against the morality of a Christian god but against the honor of business itself. In fact, young Barnwell's first perceived sin is, indeed, against business. Speaking to Sarah Millwood, he says: "I am sorry I must refuse the honor that you designed me, but my duty to my master calls me hence. I never yet neglected his service. He is so gentle and so good a master that should I wrong him, though he might forgive me, I never should forgive myself" (I, ii). Nonetheless, Barnwell accepts Millwood's invitation to neglect his master's business this night, and his fall from grace is accomplished.

As the evening proceeds in its seduction, Barnwell cannot retire to enjoy Millwood without tossing off one last commercial metaphor:

> I would not yet must on.—Reluctant thus, the merchant quits his ease

And trusts to rocks, and sands, and stormy seas; In hopes some
golden coast to find,
Commits himself, though doubtful, to the wind, Longs much for
joys to come, yet mourns those left behind. (I, ii)

At the end of Act I of *The London Merchant,* Lillo chooses this shipwreck
metaphor to drive home his point that a business man must not leave the charted
course to sail into unknown waters where he may find himself out of his depth.

"Business requires our attendance," Trueman pleads with Barnwell later
in the play; "business the youth's best preservative from ill, as idleness his worst
of snares" (II, i). Patterns of accounting imagery and long speeches extolling
the greatness of business are placed like stiles to be gotten over throughout
Lillo's play. His primary-text theme of attendance to business and the fall from
grace lies directly in the eighteenth-century's mainstream literature, as evidenced in Defoe's *Moll Flanders* and *Robinson Crusoe;* Fielding's Parson Square,
Partridge and, of course, the title character in *Tom Jones;* Goldsmith's *The Vicar
of Wakefield;* Godwin's *Caleb Williams,* and well into the nineteenth century, when
Dickens picked up the theme in *Oliver Twist, Nicholas Nickleby, Martin Chuzzlewit,
David Copperfield,* and, especially, *Dombey and Son* and *Great Expectations.*

A second primary-text theme of *The London Merchant* addresses betrayal
motivated by lust and greed. Drawn in lust to do Millwood's bidding, George
Barnwell betrays first his employer Thorowgood and then his family benefactor, his rich uncle. He steals from the former and causes the death of the
latter. Driven by greed, Millwood betrays Barnwell and her whole sex after
seducing him to her plan. Early in the play, Barnwell's loyal friend Trueman
exhorts him to resist the temptation, which "transports you from yourself"
(II, i). Thorowgood strikes the same chord as he warns Barnwell of the
dangers that ensue "when reason willingly becomes the slave of sense" and
when "vice becomes habitual, the very power of leaving it is lost" (II, i).
Barnwell's lust in the throes of Millwood's seduction ironically unmans him.
It takes away his selfhood, turns him into a slave, and nullifies any power to
resist her Svengali charms and commands. In fact, the characterization of
Millwood is a prototype for one of the most popular female type characters
of the twentieth century.

The London Merchant as Film Noir

The London Merchant is the eighteenth-century, dramatic version of twentieth-
century film noir. Like Billy Wilder's *Double Indemnity* (1944) and Lawrence

Kasden's *Body Heat* (1981), it is a conspiracy melodrama in which a femme fatale seduces a young man to commit her crime and take the fall. It follows closely the three-part film noir structure: the seduction into conspiracy; followed by the actual planning and committing of the crime; followed by the falling out of the lovers, the betrayal motivated by greed, and the revelation of the diabolical nature of the fatal woman. Lillo's play resonates with the classic film noir themes of betrayal motivated by lust and greed, woman's employing sex for the purposes of exploitation, the exploitation of the male victim's business involvement for the femme fatale's purposes, and the revelation of the dark side of the human condition. Lillo peoples his play with classic film noir characters. George Barnwell is no different from Billy Wilder and Raymond Chandler's insurance salesman Walter Neff in *Double Indemnity* or Lawrence Kasden's lawyer Ned Racine in *Body Heat*. The three respective female characters, Sarah Millwood, Phyllis Dietrickson, and Mattie Walker are all cast from the same die.

The aspect of *The London Merchant* that most closely parallels the film noir genre convention is the characterization of the femme fatale as both representative of and betrayer of her sex. In *Body Heat* this theme of the woman's betrayal of her whole gender is physically embodied in Mattie Walker's blowing up of her double and only friend, Maryann, in the boathouse as a means of covering her own escape. In *The London Merchant*, Lillo, in the speeches of almost every character, makes clear the noirish treachery of the female sex and places the blame on a longstanding history of male sexual exploitation. "It is a general maxim among the knowing part of mankind," Millwood declares, "that a woman without virtue, like a man without honor or honesty, is capable of any action" (I, ii). Later, Trueman more vehemently castigates Millwood for her Lady MacBeth-like betrayal of her sex. "To call thee woman were to wrong the sex, thou devil!" he screams.

Millwood, however, like a true film noir femme fatale has her own clear rationalizations for her hatred and exploitation of both sexes. Her "had I been a man" will be directly echoed by Gertrude Morel in D. H. Lawrence's *Sons and Lovers* almost two centuries later. "What I have lost by being formed a woman! I hate my sex, myself," Millwood rants. "Had I been a man, I might perhaps have been as happy in your friendship as he who now enjoys it" (I, ii). In this speech she rejects her whole sex on terms of its social impotence. Lucy, Millwood's character foil in *The London Merchant*, who chooses not to follow her mistress's evil path, at one point talks of the susceptibility of men to a woman like Millwood's exploitation: "Let me see the wisest of you all as much in love with me as Barnwell is with Millwood, and I'll engage to make as big a fool of him" (III, ii). Lillo represents three types of women in

The London Merchant: Millwood, the femme fatale; Maria, the innocent virgin; and Lucy, the woman on the verge who is attempting to discover the direction in which she wishes her life to go. They are the same female character types who are so often juxtaposed in the novels of Fielding, Scott, Thackeray, and Dickens.

For Millwood, however, not a shadow of a doubt clouds her conviction of why she and all of her sex are justified in turning their Medusa beauty to the purpose of exploiting men. "We are but slaves to men," Millwood spits. "Slaves have no property; no, not even in themselves" (I, ii). The fatal attraction of Millwood's Medusa beauty is captured in one long exchange in which Lucy quotes Barnwell who repeatedly acknowledges the conflicting emotions and enticements generated within him by Millwood. The speech begins "Thou cursed fair!" It proceeds to describe his and Millwood's "cursed love." Lucy evaluates her mistress's "cursed design" and Barnwell then enters to have the final say on "this cursed design" (III, iii), which he has set forth upon at Millwood's bidding. Millwood's Medusa curse has, indeed, turned Barnwell into "such a monster" (III, iii).

George Barnwell also fits the male film noir type. His decree "She's got firm possession of my heart, and governs there with such despotic sway!" proves that he is, at least, clearsighted as to the course of his downfall and his own acquiescence to Millwood's seduction. "Aye, there's the cause of all my sin and sorrow. 'Tis more than love; 'tis the fever of the soul and madness of desire" (III, iii). Like Walter Neff and Ned Racine, George Barnwell is the willing victim, the eager patsy. "I will myself prevent her ruin, through my own," Barnwell tells Lucy just before he commits his first crime for Millwood, the embezzling of a bag of money from his employer Thorowgood. "You are my fate, my heaven, or my hell"; with this declaration, he surrenders both the bag of money and his soul to Millwood. In this eighteenth-century film noir, Shakespeare's "star-crossed lovers" have become Lillo's crime-bound lovers.

But these two primary-text themes of *The London Merchant*, of attendance to business and of film noirish betrayal motivated by lust and greed, are not the play's only concerns. Subtextual themes explore the myth of Cain and discuss the situation of women in eighteenth-century society (employing the metaphors of "slavery" and "prostitution"). But perhaps the most interesting subtextual theme is a Shakespearean metatheme that supports the didactic purpose that Lillo stressed so aggressively in his doggeral prologue verse to the play: that of life as a theatre. Lillo's characters actually see themselves as playing roles in the conspiratorial play within the play. At one point, observing the shifting dynamic of Millwood's seduction of Barnwell, Lucy decides, "this is a turn so unexpected that I shall make nothing of my part; they must e'en play the scene betwixt themselves" (II, i). Near the end of the play, after Barnwell has been arraigned at the bar, confesses, and yet refuses to implicate in any way his seductress, Millwood is described as "the shameless author of his ruin" (V, i). Finally, Barnwell, on his way to the gallows, bemoans how "life like a tale that's told, is passed away" (appendix to V). In text and subtext, George Lillo's *The London Merchant* provides enough themes, characters, plot elements, and image patterns to influence the next two centuries of writers (and filmmakers) with regard to the exploitative possibilities of sexual relationships.

Dickens and Lillo

Was Lillo Dickens's favorite playwright? Absolutely not. Shakespeare, everyone's favorite playwright, was. Was *The London Merchant* Dickens's favorite play? Though it is mentioned quite often throughout his canon, probably not. There are a number of contenders for the title of Dickens's favorite play. Perhaps it was the one at which he met the young actress, Ellen Ternan, backstage. Or perhaps it was John Gay's *The Beggar's Opera*, which he mentions every bit as frequently as *The London Merchant*. Or perhaps it was *Macbeth, Othello,* or *Henry the Fourth, Part One*. In fact, allusions to Shakespeare's plays do outnumber all others. Gay's *The Beggar's Opera* was surely a crucial influence, especially on *Oliver Twist*, for its portrayal of the criminal classes and lower-class London life. The plays of Oliver Goldsmith were particular Dickens favorites.

Of course, throughout his life, Dickens never faltered in his obsessive love of theatre in all its variety. Though, in his biography of Dickens, Fred Kaplan never mentions *"George Barnwell,"* one of the first base metals he notes as coming under the transubstantiating power of Dickens's imagination is the world of plays:

> The theatre was his model. In a culture unable to transmit voice or image except through print or illustrations, the living stage flourished. In the city and in the country, from serious drama and opera to light comedy, spectacle and musical, in established theatres and in temporary outdoor sites frequented by traveling companies, the theatre was a magical presence, a precious alternate world. The excitement of the stage and of the histrionic, of an exaggerated bright spectacle that heightened life, caught his imagination from an early age.[26]

Kaplan clearly traces how Dickens's love for the magic of theatre grew throughout his life. Sometime in 1817, when he was five years old, young Charles Dickens was taken to the Theatre Royale in Rochester. It was on this stage that he first saw Shakespeare performed[27] and was treated to performances by the great tragedian Edmund Kean and the comedian Charles Mathews.[28] But the young Dickens wasn't content simply to attend the theatre. Very early, he began writing, producing, directing, and acting in his own plays and pantomimes in the family living room, creating and taking control of "the entire world of performance, the clever child glowing with the satisfaction of being center stage."[29] Kaplan also tells of the "toy theatre" made for young Charles by James Lamert, the older boy who Charles became friends with while Matthew Lamert, James's father, was courting Dickens's Aunt Fanny, and how that "toy theatre provided continuity with his childhood theatrical obsession."[30]

Later in his life, that childhood obsession would continue to surface among the fondest of Dickens's childhood memories. In an essay titled "A Christmas Tree" written for *Household Words* in 1850, Dickens wrote:

> And now, I see a wonderful row of little lights rise smoothly out of the ground, before a vast green curtain. . . . The Play begins! . . . now, I learn . . . how George Barnwell killed the worthiest uncle that ever man had, and was afterwards so sorry for it that he ought to have been let off.[31]

One year later, in a *Household Words* article titled "Getting Up A Pantomime," Dickens offered this description:

> Seven o'clock, and one last frantic push to get everything ready. . . . The footman and the housemaid are smiling in the pit; and Joe Barrikin is amazingly jolly and thirsty, with his "missus" in the gallery. Now then, "Music!" "Play up!" "Order, order!" and "Throw him over!" "*George Barnwell,*" or "*Jane Shore,*" inaudible of course. . . . Fun, frolic and gaiety . . . and I hope success and crowded houses till the middle of February.[32]

Thus, despite the great variety of Dickens's theatrical sophistication, knowledge, and preference, Lillo's *The London Merchant,* more fondly known as "*George Barnwell,*" continued to surface both in Dickens's memory and in his fiction.

In the novels, he consistently alludes to the play, but he also uses the play conceptually by basing characterizations, character relationships, plot structure and themes upon it. The primary reasons he is so strongly attracted to *George Barnwell* are probably moral. The play melodramatically couches a didactic moral message in a sensational context. That is exactly the tack that Dickens most often sails in his didactic novels as well. As a cultural document, a representation of social history, *The London Merchant* was kept alive by the morally didactic message it was able to continue to deliver to the societies of both the eighteenth and nineteenth centuries. The cautionary moralism of the play continued to be appropriate for the edification of young Victorians, as it had been a century earlier. Its moral-message style fit well with the didactic intention, especially of the early stages, of the Dickens canon.

But Dickens clearly was attracted to Lillo's play for other reasons as well. As a struggling apprentice in Warren's Blacking Factory in London, perhaps he saw himself in the play's business-bound hero. As a proper Victorian gentleman, perhaps he was fascinated by the corruption of the high-class prostitute, Millwood. Certainly, as a theatre aficionado, he was drawn to the torrid melodrama of Barnwell's story. Whatever the reason, the myth of George Barnwell appears often in the Dickens canon.

One critic, Mowbray Morris, writing in *The Fortnightly Review* only twelve years after Dickens' death, though he does not mention George Barnwell by name, defines Dickens's technique as dependent on inspiration from plays like *The London Merchant* and characters like George Barnwell. Morris argued that "our descendants will have, we may be very sure, too frequent and too real claims upon their compassion to let them spare many tears for those rather theatrical personages which Dickens too often employed to point his moral."[33] The earliest modern critic to notice Dickens's use of *The London Merchant* was William Henry Hudson in *A Quiet Corner In A Library* (1915). This essay, on Lillo not Dickens, does nothing more than note a few allusions in the Dickens canon to the play and makes no attempt to analyze the influence. "For some reason or other," Hudson writes, "the play seems to have clung to the memory of Dickens, who makes various references to it as a piece of literature well known to he and his readers" and that, as evidenced by the elaborate use of the play by Mr. Wopsle in *Great Expectations*, "at the very end of his life Dickens still remembered vividly every detail of the play."[34]

Luckily, later critics rarely settled for Hudson's cavalier "for some reason or other" nonexplanation of why Dickens was so drawn to *The London Merchant*. Though, in *The Dickens Theatre*, Robert Garis argued that "anyone who opens one of Dickens's novels, then, is prepared to enter a 'theatre' and to cooperate with the 'theatrical mode'"[35] and that "I want to avoid the implication that it is the bad, the melodramatic, the trashy Dickens who is a theatrical artist,"[36] he never mentioned Lillo's play nor the George Barnwell character mainly because his argument focused on Dickens's style rather than the sources of his themes and characters. Though Paul Schlicke's *Dickens and Popular Entertainment* (London: Allen and Unwin, 1985) is the most thorough recent study of Dickens's uses of plays and entertainments in his fiction, its focus is on circuses, fairs, sporting events and itinerant repertory theatre more than on the legitimate stage. He also makes no mention of George Barnwell.

A few critics, in passing, have mentioned the influence of Lillo's play and the Barnwell character on Dickens's fiction. Harry Stone included "*George Barnwell*" in his rounding up of the usual suspects from the "little attic" in which Dickens did his childhood reading as described in *David Copperfield*.[37] Stone's listing of *Barnwell* in a chapter titled "The Fairy Tale Heritage," and amongst other titles such as "Jack the Giant Killer," "Little Red Ridinghood," and "Sleeping Beauty," is an interesting (and rather accurate though idiosyncratic) reclassification of *The London Merchant's* mode. In the long view, Lillo's play really is little more than a melodramatic moral fairy tale with its events compressed with fabular economy, its characters allegorically designated as moral types, and its message clearly drawn. Earle Davis places a more conventional attribution of influence on Lillo's play:

> Dickens saw many tragedies and melodramas. . . . The list of plays he refers to in his writings and his letters comes to more than a hundred titles. Besides the traditional tragedies of the poetic or Shakespearean kind, he enjoyed domestic tragedy; Lillo's *George Barnwell* and Moore's *The Gamester* illustrate this kind of play.[38]

While Stone and Davis merely mention that Dickens knew about *The London Merchant* ("*George Barnwell*"), as he knew of many other plays, novels, poems, songs, fairy tales, ghost stories, and legends, Sylvere Monod goes much further in his recognition of the play's importance to the Dickens's canon. "Yet, once more, Dickens has one favourite play," Monod writes, "it is George Lillo's *The London Merchant, or the History of George Barnwell* (1731), which he must have seen as a child and from which he quotes many times, usually with ironical comments on the personality of the chief character."[39] Though this favoritism on Dickens's part is declared outright, Monod is not very convincing, because within a page he wavers when he says: "In any examination of Dickens' sources, Shakespeare has to be placed in a category by himself because of his particular importance, but he has to be placed fairly close to the popular theatre."[40] Monod's is a characteristic waffle, one shared by both Schlicke and Garis. Popular drama and entertainment could have been Dickens's greatest theatrical love, but Shakespeare is the playwright that Dickens quotes more often than any other playwright or entertainer.

Only one critic, William Axton, has fully recognized the significant influence of Lillo's *The London Merchant* on Dickens. In *Circle of Fire: Dickens' Vision and Style and the Popular Victorian Theatre*, Axton devotes one chapter to analyzing the influence of *The London Merchant* on Dickens's *Great Expectations*. His reading of Dickens's alchemic transmutation of the play into the novel and of Dickens's motives for focusing on this particular source is brilliant. Axton first notes how "Dickens' use of such folk materials taken from the theatre is . . . both subtle and pervasive."[41] He then follows this statement by identifying *The London Merchant* as the primary source of plot, character, and (less convincingly) theme in *Great Expectations*. His meticulous comparison of the plot, characters and, especially, character relationships of *Great Expectations* is a state of the art influence study only limited by the critical theory limitations of the time in which it was written, not by the perceptions or discursive acumen of the critic. Writing in the fashion of similar major Dickens books by J. Hillis Miller (1959) and Steven Marcus (1965),[42] Axton's book (1966) did what these other Dickens critics of that time were doing. Dealing with the novels in chronological order of publication, one to a chapter, these 1960s critics typically chose one primary influence on each Dickens novel and based their readings of each novel on that influence. The late 1980s and the 1990s in Dickens criticism, however, is an era of canon reading as opposed to single novel reading. Thus, the influence of Lillo's play, as first defined by William Axton, can now be seen to be much wider and even more pervasive than Axton's fine single novel reading ever intimated. Dickens used *The London Merchant* throughout his career as allusion source material, characterization source material, and, in a number of novels, not just *Great Expectations*, primary text source material.

The Pickwick Papers

When Sam Weller, in the course of his very first appearance in the Dickens world, alludes to George Barnwell, an announcement is being made, a signal given. In revealing his knowledge of and interest in Lillo's play, Dickens is presenting one of many contributing sources for the issues that consistently haunt his fiction. Dickens's vision of the world is drawn from many such sources: his biographical experiences (such as the blacking factory), his daily (and nightly) stalking of London's streets, his sensitive pulsetaking of the political and social issues of his time, and his voracious childhood reading and attendance to all manner of plays and popular entertainments. The landscapes of his fictions are also drawn from these multifarious sources. Thus, traces of the Lillo influence, as announced by Sam Weller in the courtyard of the White Hart Inn, are everywhere in *The Pickwick Papers*.

Most prominent of these allusions to the *George Barnwell* story is, to use William Axton's invaluable term, the "burlesque" of Mr. Pickwick's seduction by Mrs. Bardell and his subsequent incarceration in the Fleet prison. In both Lillo's play and throughout Dickens's work, the seduction of innocents into committing crimes and their subsequent imprisonment as a mythic descent into the underworld in search of self-knowledge is a central theme. In Dickens's first two novels, the plots—the first comic, the second tragic—turn on the concepts and images of the seduction of the innocent and the underworld of prisons.

Why is Dickens, here at the very outset of his writing career and throughout (especially later in *Little Dorrit, A Tale of Two Cities,* and *Great Expectations*), so obsessed with the image of innocence imprisoned, of the prison as the landscape of self-knowledge? Following Edmund Wilson's lead, most critics would attribute this obsession to the traumatic psychological imprint on the young, innocent Dickens of his father's imprisonment for debt and the blacking factory experience. Others might attribute it to Dickens's acute observation of the situation of children both on the streets of London and in the prisons of the nation's burgeoning factory economy. Others, still, might point to other prominent influences from Dickens's early reading: certainly *Don Quixote* tells of an innocent who ends up in prison as do *Moll Flanders, Tom Jones, The Vicar of Wakefield, Caleb Williams, The Heart of Midlothian,* and even the hero of one of Dickens's clear favorites, *Robinson Crusoe,* who ends up in a symbolic prison cut off from all but himself. All of these possible sources, as well as the influence of *The London Merchant,* exist as contributors to this prominent theme.

In terms of characterization, Pickwick and Sam are much more quixotic than Barnwellian, but Pickwick's fall, due to his own naïveté and the dark despair that afflicts him in the Fleet, from which he is rescued by the loyal attendance of his true man Sam, is an eighteenth-century scenario previously played out in both Lillo's *The London Merchant* and Goldsmith's *The Vicar of Wakefield.* Whereas the George Barnwell story is but a shadow on *The Pickwick Papers,* its role is much more prominent in Dickens's second novel, *Oliver Twist.* Whereas in *The Pickwick Papers,* the George Barnwell story is a prominent allusion among many against which the plot, characters, and theme can be judged, in *Oliver Twist*, for the first time, it exercises strong primary-text influence.

Oliver Twist

While the sources most often pointed to for *Oliver Twist*, by both Dickens's contemporaries (such as Thackeray) and by twentieth-century critics, are Fielding and Ainsworth's "Newgate novels"[43] Gay's *The Beggar's Opera*, and Bunyan's *Pilgrim's Progress*,[44] in terms of similarity of plot and character, *this work* (even more closely than *Great Expectations*) is the Dickens novel that most nearly approximates the characters and circumstances of Lillo's play. After the opening sections in the workhouse and at Sowerberry's funeral parlor, *Oliver Twist* settles into a plot course parallel to that of *The London Merchant*. In both the eighteenth-century play and the nineteenth-century novel, a young, naive boy is seduced by a jaded exploiter. When that naïf gains a position of responsibility in a rich family, he is immediately seduced back into a life of crime and then driven to even more serious crime. But in *Oliver Twist* the seducer goes too far, and both the naïf and the seducer end up in prison in the shadow of the gallows.

In Dickens's version of Lillo's play, Fagin plays Millwood to little Oliver's George Barnwell. When the Artful Dodger first brings Oliver to Fagin, that old gentleman, "making a low obeisance to Oliver, took him by the hand, and hoped he should have the honor of his intimate acquaintance" (*OT*, 8). Fagin takes Oliver into his establishment and schools the child in thievery as does Millwood who makes it clear that "a house of entertainment like mine is not kept without expense" (*TLM*, II, ii). Both Millwood and Fagin clearsightedly turn their victims into potential contributors to the maintenance of their criminal enterprises. Both seduce their victims into committing crimes for them. As soon as Millwood ascertains that Barnwell resides in a position of trust and responsibility in Thorowgood's business, she counsels him to "shake off all slavish obedience to your master, but you may serve him still," so that he will maintain the opportunity "of fingering his cash" (*TLM*, I, ii). As Barnwell steals a bag of money from Thorowgood to supposedly save Millwood from "ruin," Oliver is sent out with the Dodger and Master Bates to be initiated into the reality of thievery and observes the pocket-picking of an "old gentleman . . . a very respectable-looking personage" (*OT*,10). While Oliver is suspected of this initial handkerchief theft, immediately after he is cleared of the crime he is entrusted by his benefactor with books to return to a shop; when he disappears without returning them, seduced back into Fagin's clutches, that crime also falls on his head.

But, as in *The London Merchant*, that initial breach of trust is but a misdemeanor in comparison to the major crimes toward which both Barnwell and Oliver are driven by their seducers. Both are sent out to the country to commit more violent crimes. Barnwell accidentally kills his uncle in the midst of a robbery, and Oliver gets himself shot while participating in a housebreaking.

Needless to say, both Lillo's play and Dickens's novel ultimately arrive at a prison cell where the criminals, Millwood and Fagin, face their final punishment. "It is the custom on the stage," Dickens's narrative voice intrudes in *Oliver Twist*, "in all good murderous melodramas, to present the tragic and the comic scenes, in as regular alternation, as the layers of red and white in a side of streaky bacon" (17). Inappropriate bacon similes aside, the murderous stage melodrama on which Dickens is modeling *Oliver Twist* is recognizably *The London Merchant*. All of the plot developments and characters of the play are reprised in altered form in the novel.

While Oliver is much younger than Barnwell and his attraction to Fagin is familial as opposed to Barnwell's sexual attraction to Millwood, they are mirror images in their naivete and their involvement in the plot events that follow their seductions. While Fagin is of a different sex than Millwood and his seduction of his victim is of a different nature, the result is the same, the crimes and the villain's motives are strikingly similar.

All of the other characters from Lillo's play are present in Dickens's novel as well. Brownlow is of the same type as Lillo's Thorowgood and Fielding's Allworthy, except that Dickens has chosen to demur on the obviousness of allegorical naming. Sikes, Dickens's brutal housebreaker, connected to Fagin through Nancy, is a large-writ character expansion of Blunt in *The London Merchant*. The parallel characterizations of Lillo's Lucy and Dickens's Nancy are, however, virtually exact: Both Lucy and Nancy begin as corrupt co-conspirators of the wily seducers. Both participate in the plots that occasion the unsuspecting hero's downfall. Both finally repent and betray their evil partner in crime in hopes of finding some salvation. Also, the roles of faithful friends to the beleaguered hero that Trueman and Maria Thorowgood play in *The London Merchant* are reprised by Harry and Rose Maylie in *Oliver Twist*.

But plot and character similarities are but a Barnwellian glaze on the surface of Dickens's *Oliver Twist*. The Lillo influence penetrates deeper into the historicized thematic structures of Dickens's novel. Like *The London Merchant*, which presents a world cleaved into antipathetic duality (the middle-class, honest, hardworking, loyal, business world of Thorowgood, Barnwell, and Trueman opposed to the corrupt, sensual, exploitative underworld of Millwood, Lucy, and Blunt), *Oliver Twist* also is divided into two worlds. The world of the Brownlows, the Maylies, and Oliver's fallen mother is a pastoral, Christian, green, well-lighted place while the world of Fagin, Sikes, and Nancy is an urban, labyrinthine, dark, corrupt, and hellish underworld.

In his preface to *Oliver Twist*, Dickens signals his juxtaposition of these two worlds. "I saw no reason," he wrote, "why the very dregs of life . . . should not serve the purpose of a moral, at least as well as froth and cream. Nor did I doubt that there lay festering in St. Giles's as good materials toward the truth as any to be found in St. James's." Dickens's plan in *Oliver Twist* (like Lillo's in *The London Merchant*) is to show "how Virtue turns from dirty stockings; and how Vice, married to ribbons and little gay attire changes her name, as wedded ladies do, and becomes Romance" (*OT*, Preface).

In Lillo's play, Millwood's world is where Barnwell becomes "the slave of sense" (*TLM*, II, ii). He pleads to Millwood: "Will nothing but my utter ruin content you?" (II, ii). In despair, Barnwell finally consigns himself to her underworld: "You are my fate, my heaven or my hell" (II, ii) where he ultimately is "Lost indeed!" (III, i). In Dickens's novel, little Oliver walks— as if protected by an aura—between these two worlds. As he and the Artful Dodger enter St. Giles, Oliver is "just considering whether he hadn't better run away, when they reached the bottom of the hill." They have begun their descent, but they have not yet reached the inner circle of hell. They descend further into Fagin's cave, "the walls and ceiling of the room . . . perfectly black with age and dirt" where "standing over them, with a toasting-fork in his hand, was a very old shrivelled Jew" (8), the devil with his pitchfork commanding this dark urban inferno.[45]

This underworld of Fagin contrasts directly to the pastoral felicity of Brownlow's "neat house, in a quiet shady street near Pentonville" (*OT*, 12). The difference between the opposed worlds of Millwood/Thorowgood and Fagin/Brownlow is the late eighteenth-century Godwinian concept of perfectibility and natural benevolence. This optimistic philosophy of man was not available to Lillo in the 1730s as it was to Dickens in the 1830s. Thus, the two writers' heroes find themselves consigned to quite different fates when caught between two worlds. The eighteenth-century world of Lillo, Barnwell, and Millwood is one in which, as Millwood states, "men of all degrees and all professions" are "alike wicked to the utmost of their power" and the law is dealt out by "suburb magistrates, who live by ruined reputations, as the inhospitable natives of Cornwall do by shipwrecks" (*TLM*, IV, ii). Barnwell cannot escape the punishment for his sin, so he accepts that punishment in repentance. But Oliver, who has escaped the wrath of the magistrate three times previously in the novel, is saved by the Godwinian natural benevolence of Brownlow's belief in perfectibility. Where Barnwell must hang with his seducer, Oliver is given the opportunity to learn from his. The one character in *The London Merchant* who is saved from the wages of Millwood's sin is Millwood's henchwoman, Lucy. Of all the characters in *Oliver Twist* who are modeled upon Lillo's characters, Nancy bears closest resemblance to this original. In play and novel, these characters follow a similar path. Both develop from gay conspirator into frightened and guilty outcast caught between two worlds into repentant sinner driven to betray the author of her corruption in hopes of saving the poor innocent whose seduction she was originally a participant in. Both take this path of repentance under the naturally benevolent auspices of a sympathetic middle class gentleman. Lucy goes to Thorowgood, who gives her an avenue of escape from Millwood, and Nancy goes to Brownlow, who offers her the chance for salvation from Fagin's underworld. In this case, Lillo is kinder to his character than Dickens. Nancy is unable to break her bondage to Sikes just as Barnwell is unable to break from Millwood.

Whereas the Barnwell story is a melodramatic examination of how business principles must be balanced against sensual temptations, how business honesty must be placed above emotional attraction, *Oliver Twist* is directly the opposite. Under the influence of the late eighteenth-century concepts of perfectibility and natural benevolence as exemplified in the writing of Goldsmith, Lord Shaftesbury, and William Godwin, Dickens's Oliver is protected from the corruption that overcomes Barnwell's soul. Oliver walks through Barnwell's world and no temptation or corrupt influence can penetrate his natural goodness. Comparison of *The London Merchant* and *Oliver Twist* shows the romantic tendencies of the young Dickens. At this point, he still believes in the romantic concept of unqualified perfectibility and, thus, is compelled to alter the realistic Hobbesian view of man's potential for evil that is presented in the characterization and fate of Lillo's Barnwell.

Finally, however, of all the plot, character, and theme similarities of Lillo's play and Dickens's novel, the one scene that both share most closely is that of the respective villains' final moments in prison waiting for the death sentence to be executed. Albert Camus's novel *The Stranger* also ends in a prison cell where a condemned man awaits the gallows. At the final moment of his life, Camus's Meurseult, will confront, all alone, a hostile yet festive crowd calling for, celebrating, his imminent death. *Oliver Twist* is not the only

Dickens novel that ends with this scene and all its complex components—
the dark cell, the totally alone, condemned man, the howling crowd. *A Tale
of Two Cities* will later reprise it, though with a completely different, much
more positive, spiritual cast. But, if this scene is somewhat different for
Sydney Carton, Millwood, Fagin, and Meurseult, this setting of existential
isolation and despair are all too similar.

In *The London Merchant,* the repentant Lucy describes Millwood: "She
goes to death encompassed with horror, loathing life, and yet afraid to die;
no tongue can tell her anguish and despair" (V, ii). Fagin sits in the same
sorry state in *Oliver Twist:* on "the night of this last awful day . . . a withering
sense of his helpless, desperate state came upon his blighted soul. . . . Those
dreadful walls of Newgate . . . never held so dread a spectacle as that" (52).
In the final scene of *The London Merchant,* Barnwell and Millwood address each
other as they are brought to the gallows. In the final scene of *Oliver Twist,*
Brownlow brings Oliver to Fagin's cell on the day before that worthy is to
die. It is in the issues presented by these scenes that the similarity lies.

In both scenes the innocent victim pleads with the guilty villain to
repent, not to despair, to pray to God. In both cases, the condemned villain
refuses, expresses her or his lostness, aloneness, hopelessness. "Life, like a
tale that's told, is passed away," Barnwell expresses his resignation to his fate
to Millwood at the gallows, but Millwood chooses instead to rail at God:
"Heaven, thou hast done thy worst!" she screams. When Barnwell implores
her to "bend your stubborn knees and harder heart," in repentance, she spits
at him in despair: "Why name you mercy to a wretch like me? Mercy's
beyond my hope—almost beyond my wish. I can't repent nor ask to be
forgiven" (*TLM,* Appendix). Oliver also begs Fagin, "'Let me say a prayer.
Do! Let me say one prayer. Say only one, upon your knees, with me, and we
will talk till morning" (*OT,* 52).

But Fagin faces Oliver "with a countenance more like that of a snared
beast than the face of a man." His is "a face retaining no human expression
but rage and terror" (*OT,* 52). By the time that Oliver arrives in Fagin's cell,
that villain has gone mad and is hallucinating in guilt, fear and despair. At
the very end of *The London Merchant,* Millwood also exhibits these nightmarish
symptoms of madness: "Chains, darkness, wheels, racks, sharp, stinging
scorpions, molten lead, and seas of sulphur are light to what I feel." Like
Fagin in his last quaking moments before Oliver is taken out of the cell,
Millwood bewails her plight: "Encompassed with horror, whither must I go?
I would not live—nor die. That I could cease to be, or ne'er had been!"
(Appendix). In both Lillo's play and Dickens's novel, the unrepentant villain
plays the last dramatic scene. Millwood and Fagin both run the gamut of

emotions from fear of death to hatred of society to existential aloneness to moral despair to anger at God to hallucinatory madness to defiance of the crowds who slaver for their public execution. In the melodramatic final gallows scene of *The London Merchant*, Dickens found a vehicle almost as useful as that old dramatic workhorse, the deathbed scene, for the final exposition of all sorts of moral, social, existential, and psychological issues.

Perhaps what is most interesting in the comparison of these dénouement scenes is the gradual shift of thematic emphasis from the eighteenth to the nineteenth to the twentieth century. Whereas the emphasis of both Lillo and Dickens is on the moral lesson to be learned from the condemned villain's plight and psychological state, in Camus's twentieth-century version of this scene—at the end of *The Stranger*—the emphasis shifts from the condemned criminal's need for repentance to his relationship with the crowd that clamors for his death. In all three versions of this scene, the crowd screams for the death of the criminal, greets those about to die with "howls of execration." In Camus's novel, the criminal gains sustenance from the rabid hatred of the crowd. Their reaction validates his existence. In *Oliver Twist*, "a great multitude had already assembled" to greet Fagin at the gallows. Dickens writes of how "the crowd were pushing, quarrelling, joking" and how "everything told of life and animation, but one dark cluster of objects in the center of all—the black stage" (52). Dickens ends this dramatic scene with a theatre metaphor. Even though *Oliver Twist* is a novel, condemned to the flat, one-dimensional essence of a page, still its characters play out their dramatic scenes before a chorus of social representations as Millwood (and most other protagonists going back to the Greeks) did on a stage.

In *Oliver Twist*, the Millwood character, in the form of Fagin, dominates Dickens's imagination. Little Oliver is not realistic; he never approaches the human emotion and weakness of George Barnwell. But Millwood and Fagin are real, are not burdened by having to carry a romantic philosophy of perfectibility on their shoulders. The influence of *The London Merchant* on *Oliver Twist* is focused in Dickens's use of Millwood to form Fagin. Later in his career, burdened himself with a greater sense of realism and a darker sense of human nature, Dickens's emphasis will shift from Millwood to George Barnwell, who will finally be expressed most fully in the characterization of Pip in *Great Expectations.*

Oliver Twist is the first Dickens novel in which the Barnwell influence moves from allusion to allegory, from motif to metaphor. It is the first novel in the Dickens canon upon which Lillo's play exerts primary-text influence. *The London Merchant* not only supplies Dickens with the material for the creation of his plots and characters, but it helps him to define the tone and meaning of the philosophic vision that he seeks to convey through his texts. First, the middle class allegorical figure of George Barnwell provides a well known moralistic model for the characterization of his bildungsroman characters, those recurrent young men—Nicholas Nickleby, Martin Chuzzlewit, David Copperfield, Richard Carstone, Tom Gradgrind, Pip—forced to survive in a hostile world and tempted to do it outside of the moral parameters of romantic perfectibility and Shaftesburian natural benevolence. Second, Lillo's Millwood provides a sociopolitical motivation for Dickens's villains. Whether they be women, jews, twisted dwarfs, or whatever minority group Dickens chose to symbolically exploit, their sociopathy is fueled by the need for revenge for sociopolitical oppression. Finally, Dickens's use of *The London Merchant* provides his fiction a subtext entrée into the exploration of the relationship between the business world, in which ethics and survival are always at odds, and the world of art, where morality and popularity contend.

Oliver Twist is but the first novel upon which Lillo's *The London Merchant* exerts primary-text influence. Later in the Dickens canon, it is clearly evident especially in *Dombey and Son, Bleak House, Hard Times,* and, as William Axton has pointed out, *Great Expectations.* From the very beginning of his novel-writing career, the George Barnwell story is constantly in Dickens's mind and in the texts of his novels.

Nicholas Nickleby and *The Old Curiosity Shop*

In *Nicholas Nickleby,* the Dickens novel that moves in the world of the theatre more than any other, young Nicholas has the opportunity to discuss with an unnamed literary gentleman the nature and ubiquity of literary influence:

> "When I dramatize a book, sir," said the literary gentleman, "that's fame for its author. . . ."
>
> "Shakespeare dramatized stories which had previously appeared in print, it is true," observed Nicholas.
>
> "Meaning Bill, sir?" said the literary gentleman. "So he did. Bill was an adapter, certainly, so he was; and very well he adapted, too—considering. . . ."
>
> "For whereas he brought within the magic circle of his genius traditions peculiarly adopted for his purpose, and turned familiar things into constellations which should enlighten the world for ages, you drag

within the magic circle of your dullness subjects not at all adapted to the purposes of the stage, and debase as he exalted." (48)

In this comic exchange, in the face of this pretentious literary gentleman's condescension to Shakespeare and to all original writers, young Nicholas presents the argument that art does indeed follow an alchemic process in which true artists work within a "magic circle" of "genius" that transmutes "familiar things" into "constellations" that "enlighten the world for ages." This whole exchange is Dickens's way of acknowledging that, yes, writers like himself do indeed gain inspiration from, even sometimes consciously imitate, the work of earlier writers or the material of every day life, but they do it creatively and with purpose, not slavishly and without artistic motive. Lillo's *The London Merchant* is just such a "familiar thing" that often is drawn into the "magic circle" of Dickens's genius and transmuted according to his artistic purposes.

Early in *Nicholas Nickleby*, just such a transmutation takes place. In contrasting Kate Nickleby to her ruthless uncle Ralph, an allusive metaphor reminiscent of the final scene of Millwood at the gallows and Fagin in his cell arises:

the warm young heart palpitates with a thousand anxieties and apprehensions, while that of the old worldly man lay rusting in its cell, beating only as a piece of cunning mechanism, and yielding not one throb of hope or fear, of love, or care for any living thing. (10)

While *Nicholas Nickleby* makes but shadowy allusion to the tone and scene of Lillo's play, *The Old Curiosity Shop*, in its Kit Nubbles subplot, is a true fable for apprentices just as is the George Barnwell story. In this Barnwellian subplot, however, as was the case with Mr. Pickwick, the Barnwell figure, Kit Nubbles, is framed for a crime, taken to law (as Pickwick was by Mrs. Bardell) and convicted. Kit Nubbles's crime of theft from his merchant master, Samson Brass, is exactly the same crime that George Barnwell committed one hundred years earlier. But in both the cases of Pickwick and Kit Nubbles, Dickens has diverted the Barnwell story from its original purpose of displaying the remorse of an apprentice who has violated the code of business ethics of the middle class to a new view of the power over the apprentice's life held by the merchant/master class. The message that Kit Nubbles delivers immediately after his conviction is a very different message than the one that George Barnwell delivers in his

cell before he goes to the gallows. "My innocence will come out," Kit
Nubbles assures his family, "and I will be brought back again; I feel a
confidence in that. You must teach little Jacob and the baby how all this
was, for if they thought I had ever been dishonest, when they grow old
enough to understand, it would break my heart to know it, if I was
thousands of miles away" (OCS, 63).

All through the trial, the prosecutor attempts to portray Kit Nubbles
as a George Barnwell figure; and he succeeds. Only Dickens's readers
perceive the "burlesque," as William Axton would later call it with reference
to Great Expectations, that Dickens is perpetrating upon the Barnwell story.
Kit Nubbles is, in fact, a good apprentice, and, in Dickens's little parable, it
is the society that is shown to be deficient; in Lillo's parable it was the
individual, the apprentice, who violated the social contract. The Barnwell
subplot of The Old Curiosity Shop once again demonstrates Dickens's youthful
romantic confidence in middle-class morality and human perfectibility. That
subplot is an affirmation of a "good apprentice" figure, as opposed to the
eighteenth-century "bad apprentice" paradigm of George Barnwell.

The Bad Apprentice Returns: Barnaby Rudge

In his next novel, Barnaby Rudge, Dickens would, for the first time, depart from
that "good apprentice" paradigm and show again, in a Barnwellian subplot,
the machinations of a "bad apprentice." In his early novels, Dickens writes as
though he simply could not accept the reality that good people could indeed
be tempted out of their souls and away from everything they valued and held
dear. Characters like Oliver Twist and Kit Nubbles read as if they were
created "before the fall." In Barnaby Rudge, Dickens acknowledged that "fall,"
and, for the first time, his Barnwellian apprentice character is portrayed
realistically rather than romantically.

But that realism resulted in a new historicist, revisionist view of the
Barnwell myth of the "unfortunate fall" of a "good apprentice." From Sim
Tappertit's point of view in Barnaby Rudge, the Barnwell story is that of a
"fortunate fall," one that allows the oppressed and exploited apprentice to
break out of the shackles of his apprenticeship and assert his freedom and
identity in a much more exciting world than that of work, duty, and a sense
of family or home, which Lillo's eighteenth-century play affirms. In this case,
however, the wayward apprentice is seduced to take part in the historical
dynamics of his time not by a woman's sexual allure but by the temptation
to political power.

Dickens looks at the Barnwell myth from both sides in *Barnaby Rudge*. Sim Tappertit's ridiculous physical characterization and insufferable pretentiousness affirm the eighteenth-century social censure of any apprentice who departs from the "good apprentice" paradigm. But when Sim speaks of his own feelings of oppression and lack of identity, despite his pretentiousness, a strong sense of his marginalization emerges. Sim is a "New Historicist" voice. Dickens, in the mere act of presenting these feelings, is amplifying another previously unheard voice that challenges the master text of history.

Of all of Dickens's novels, *Barnaby Rudge* most thoroughly exploits the Barnwell influence. Dickens is quite scrupulous in identifying his source for the Sim Tappertit, fall of the "good apprentice," subplot. The very first direct literary allusion made in *Barnaby Rudge* is to Lillo's George Barnwell. Sim Tappertit, who is an apprentice to good Gabriel Varden, the locksmith, is "reported to have said that in former times a stigma had been cast upon the body [of apprentices] by the execution of George Barnwell, to which they should not have basely submitted, but should have demanded him of the legislature . . . to be dealt with as they in their wisdom might think fit" (4).

Sim's is an appeal to the closed-mindedness of the master text of history and a revisionist evaluation of the lesson to be learned from the famous Barnwell case. While all of Dickens's earlier parallels to the Barnwell story— in *The Pickwick Papers, Oliver Twist,* and *Nicholas Nickleby*—had been affirmations of the "good apprentice" moral message of Lillo's eighteenth-century play, in the outspoken Sim Tappertit characterization of *Barnaby Rudge*, Dickens does what Lillo's play and his own novels had not hitherto done: he gives Barnwell a voice in his own defense, allows the "bad apprentice" to speak out and present a rationalization for the crimes against his master (and, by implication, society) of which he is accused (and, in fact, guilty).

Dickens's characterization of Sim Tappertit combines the conservative history of George Barnwell with the radical history of the French Revolution (as represented in the novel by the Anti-Catholic Gordon Riots in London in 1780). Sim is a character at once disloyal, ungrateful, and utterly seduced—as was Barnwell—yet intent on arguing quite forcefully for the rightness of his rebellion against his subjugated position in society. Sim is a true dialogic character who is torn between an eighteenth-century selfishness and a nineteenth-century marginalized historical consciousness.

Sim actually sees himself (and Barnwell) as political heroes for rebelling against their masters. "I'm never coming back here anymore" Sim Tappertit taunts his master, Gabriel Varden, who wants to protect him from the Army that is on its way to quell the riot and arrest the rioters. "Provide yourself with a journeyman; I'm my country's journeyman, henceforward that's my line of business." When Gabriel Varden persists in trying to protect his politically inflamed apprentice, Sim replies, "I hear you, and defy you, Varden. . . . This night, sir, I have been in the country, planning an expedition which shall fill your bell-hanging soul with wonder and dismay. The plot demands my utmost energy. Let me pass!" When Sim does escape, Gabriel can only watch him run away and think (as Thorowgood must have thought of George Barnwell), "I have done my best for thee, poor lad, and would have saved thee, but the rope is round thy neck, I fear" (BR, 51).

Thus, Sim Tappertit is directly identified as a latter-day George Barnwell, but his crimes are a bit more complex than were Barnwell's thefts and bungling murder, and his seducer is an idea, a desire for power, rather than a woman. In *Barnaby Rudge*, the Barnwell story has been fully transubstantiated from motif to metaphor. What is most interesting about the incorporation into *Barnaby Rudge* of the Barnwell story as political metaphor is the comment it makes on violent revolution, and the way that it prefigures the politics of the French Revolution in Dickens's great historical novel *A Tale of Two Cities*.

In fact, Sim Tappertit is a pass-through character leading from George Barnwell's weakness and moral failure to the high moral murderousness of Madame Defarge. In "the devil's cellar," the Boot, the low-life tavern that is the center of "the secret society of the 'Prentice Knights'," the toast "Death to all masters, life to all 'prentices'," is raised, and Sim Tappertit holds Star Chamber court just exactly as Madame Defarge does later in *A Tale of Two Cities*:

> "Write Curzon down. Denounced," said the Captain. "Put a black cross against the name of Curzon."
>
> "So please you," said the novice, "that's not the worst—he calls his 'prentice idle dog, and stops his beer unless he works to his liking. He gives Dutch cheese, too, eating Cheshire, sir, himself; and Sundays out, are only once a month."
>
> "This," said Mr. Tappertit gravely, "is a flagrant case. Put two black crosses to the name of Curzon."
>
> "If the society," said the novice, who was an ill-looking, one-sided, shambling lad, with sunken eyes set close together in his head—"if the society would burn his house down—for he's not insured—or beat him as he comes home from his club at night, or help me to carry off his daughter, and marry her at the Fleet, whether she gave consent or no—"

     Mr. Tappertit waved his grizzly truncheon as an admonition to
him not to interrupt, and ordered three black crosses to the name of
Curzon.
     "Which means," he said in gracious explanation, "vengeance,
complete and terrible." (BR, 8)

Madame Defarge's knitting and Sim Tappertit's black crosses of vengeance
are one and the same.

     However, if Sim is a clear precursor of Madame Defarge, his fate as a
result of all his conspiracy toward class revolution is the same as George
Barnwell's, though described by Gabriel Varden in a French Revolution
image: "your Great Association would have been to him the cart that draws
men to the gallows and leaves them hanging in the air" (BR, 51).

     But Sim Tappertit's sins (as were George Barnwell's) are not only
political or power-driven (as Barnwell's were sexual), they are also sins of
betrayal of the basic Dickensian philosophy of personal benevolence. Dickens places the definition of one of *Barnaby Rudge's* central themes in the hands
of that novel's Shakespearean holy fool and title character: "'Oh mother,
mother, how mournful he will be when he scratches at the door, and finds
it always shut!'"(46). Barnaby is talking about a neighborhood dog, but
Dickens, in one of those frequent authorial intrusions into his fiction for the
purpose of overt philosophizing (which almost always give terminal punctuation at the end of chapters and serial numbers), comments: "There was
such a sense of home in the thought, that though her own eyes overflowed
she would not have obliterated the recollection of it, either from her own
mind or from his, for the wealth of the whole wide world" (46).

     So many characters in the Dickens world are homeless (as was George
Barnwell) that it is doubly tragic when a Dickens character, such as Sim
Tappertit, who has been offered this "sense of home," rejects that home and
betrays the personal benevolence of that home's owner for some worldly
temptation. In the Dickens world, this is the original sin that expels all of
Dickens's Barnwells (such as Pip in *Great Expectations*) from the garden. When
they betray their own homes, as Sim Tappertit does the Varden household and
Pip does Joe Gargery's forge, they violate what, for Dickens, is the most sacred
space. When Sim Tappertit drunkenly screams in good Gabriel Varden's face
"'This family may all be smothered, sir'" (BR, 51), he is pronouncing what may
be the ultimate blasphemy in the philosophic structure of Dickens's world.

     Sim's blasphemy has its counterpart in *Barnaby Rudge's* larger historical
world as well. Immediately following Lord George Gordon's first bigoted,

anti-Catholic speech of the novel, Mr. Haredale confronts that demogogue in no uncertain terms: "'I hope there is but one gentleman in England who, addressing an ignorant and excited throng, would speak of a large body of his subjects in such injurious language as I heard this moment. For shame, my lord, for shame! . . . We have much in common . . . and common charity, not to say common sense and common decency, should teach you to refrain from these proceedings" (43). Haredale's point is that just as Sim (and Barnwell before him) are violating this English "sense of home" on a domestic, microcosmic level, Lord Gordon, in his religious bigotry and as a representative of English government, is violating that "sense of home" and human justice on a historical, macrocosmic level.

Thus, in *Barnaby Rudge*, Dickens makes significant progress in the presentation of the Barnwell theme. Many of the literal components of the Barnwell motif—the seduced innocent, the betrayal of the kindly benefactor, the cornered criminal—are present, but in this novel Dickens deals with elements more complexly, incorporating them into a multi-leveled, binary, New Historicist discourse. For the first time, Dickens gives a voice to the intense feelings of marginalization of the apprentice class (for which, previously, George Barnwell had only been a negative symbol). Dickens certainly makes it clear that Sim Tappertit is a "legend in his own mind" and that Sim's perceptions of his oppression and exploitation by his kindly master, Gabriel Varden, are fantastically over-blown. However, Dickens's expanded awareness that there are, indeed, two sides to this Barnwellian "apprentice" issue, that such oppression and exploitation of apprentices by masters does certainly exist, is a true revisionist acknowledgement. A decade later In *Hard Times* Dickens would further explore the terrible sense of marginalization among the working classes that was due to both the philosophical and physical exploitations of Utilitarianism. But first, in *David Copperfield*, Dickens decided to explore his own personal sense of marginalization, his own personal sense of being shut outside of history.

George Barnwell in the Blacking Factory

My father had left a small collection of books in a little room up-stairs. . . . From that blessed little room, Roderick Random, Peregrine Pickle, Humphrey Clinker, Tom Jones, the Vicar of Wakefield, Don Quixote, Gil Blas, and Robinson Crusoe, came out, a glorious host to keep me company . . . and the *Arabian Nights* and the *Tales of the Genii*. . . . I have

been Tom Jones. . . . I have sustained my own idea of Roderick Random.
. . . I had a greedy relish for a few volumes of *Voyages and Travels*. (DC, 4)

In this famous "blessed little room" catalogue from *David Copperfield*,
Dickens lists a great many of the literary influences on his fiction. Perhaps
the most prominent omissions from this list are the plays of Shakespeare and
Lillo's *The London Merchant*, the story of George Barnwell.

There is a quite obvious reason why these works would not appear on
the shelves of that "blessed little room." They are plays, not novels, and
would have been seen in the theatres of Dickens's youth rather than read in
the lonely isolation of his childhood during and after his Warren's Blacking
Factory experience. Yet, uncharacteristically, *David Copperfield* is the only
Dickens novel to that point in his career in which the story of George
Barnwell is not directly mentioned. That play and its characters do, however,
in a much more sinister and subtle psychological way drive both the novel's
characters and theme.

Why, after all the prominent overt attention Dickens had given in
earlier novels to the Barnwell influence did he choose to not mention this
text in his most overtly autobiographical novel? Precisely because it was
autobiographical! Dickens, who in each of his earlier novels had clearly
directed his readers to make comparisons with the notorious Barnwell
character and story, here, out of guilt and personal insecurity, chose to avoid
reference to the Barnwell parallel because it was too close to his own
experience in the Blacking Factory (and David's at Murdstone and Grinby's)
and too close to his personal sense of himself as a Barnwellian figure—an
apprentice who has risen against his master, an ungrateful son who has
betrayed the family trust.

Dickens's neglect to make a direct allusion to or comparison of David
Copperfield (his own autobiographical surrogate) to George Barnwell, as he
did for many of his protagonists and supporting characters in the novels
previous to *David Copperfield*, is a cover-up, an attempt to suppress the evidence
of his own psychological guilt and class insecurity at being a former apprentice
who has risen above his station in Victorian society. In short, Dickens
exhibited a primitive form of survivor guilt syndrome. Dickens's David has
actually committed the Barnwellian original sin of biting his master, Mr.
Murdstone, and, as a result, being expelled from the fallen Eden of Victorian
family life. Dickens, however, steadfastly refused to acknowledge David as a
Barnwellian miscreant. This refusal was an attempt to deny his own responsibility for his self-exile from family life in the years after his father's debtors'
prison experience and his own imprisonment in the Blacking Factory.

Even David, in one of his many intrusions as metanarrator (the voice of the novelist inside his novel) expresses this Barnwellian guilt at not being completely honest and forthcoming in his own portrayal. "Heaven knows I write this, in no spirit of self-laudation," David protests:

> The man who reviews his own life, as I do mine, in going on here, from page to page, had need to have been a good man indeed, if he would be spared the sharp consciousness of many talents neglected, many opportunities wasted, many erratic and perverted feelings constantly at war within his breast, and defeating him. I do not hold one natural gift, I dare say, that I have not abused. (42)

This passage is a repentant confession very much in the "George Barnwell at the gallows" manner. It ends with the following strong affirmation of Lillo's eighteenth-century values, which the Victorian age is striving so mightily to maintain: "there is no substitute for thoroughgoing, ardent and sincere earnestness" (42).

Dickens may be trying to cover up his and David's kinship to that traitor to the family and the work ethic, George Barnwell, but that cover-up is merely a means of avoiding his own guilt in his resentment over the Blacking Factory ordeal. Dickens feels this guilt because his own personal and literary identification with the Barnwell story, in all of its seductive motivation, criminal betrayal, and debilitating guilt, is so deeply engrained. The reason that Dickens so obsessively returns to the Barnwell character and plot all across the body of his work, in novel after novel, article after article, is because he too has lived the Barnwell story of the betrayal of middle-class Victorian values, he too has felt the Barnwell guilt of betrayal of the family, he too has been seduced by the irresistible passion for power and wealth and fame. Dickens so frequently alludes to the Barnwell story because that story parallels his own apprenticeship, calls up his own impatience at his fallen position in society, resentment toward his family for placing him in that position, and guilt for his rejection of his family over that forced humiliation. Dickens does not directly allude to the Barnwell story in *David Copperfield* because that novel is too close to his own story, and he chooses not to incriminate himself despite all the telling evidence that the text inevitably makes available. If Dickens is David, then both are Barnwell, except that the names are suppressed to protect the guilty.

When Dickens is pasting labels on bottles in the window of Warren's Blacking Factory and David is slaving away in Murdstone and Grinby's counting house, both are feeling all of the apprentice's oppression and resentment that George Barnwell, Kit Nubbles, and Sim Tappertit felt and expressed. David broods over "my ever being anything else than the common drudge into which I was fast settling down" and decides that "the life was unendurable." As a result David holds "no intention of passing many more weary days there. No. I had resolved to run away" (DC, 12). This terrible sense of powerlessness, of loss of the possibilities for an acclaimed life, of oppression, kindles the resentment that causes a George Barnwell, a Kit Nubbles, a Sim Tappertit, or a David Copperfield to run away from the drudgery and perceived humiliation of their apprenticeships. Because they feel they have been declassed, they strike out at the class that they perceive to be their oppressor. For the purposes of their own interiorized guilt, however, it is irrelevant whether that oppression is real (Sampson Brass), merely perceived (Gabriel Varden), or merely fostered by neglect and disinterest (Murdstone); it still occasions the Barnwellian need for rationalization, confession, and expiation.

"I now approach a period in my life, which I can never lose the remembrance of . . . and the recollection of which has often, without my invocation, come before me like a ghost" (10), David the novelist writes in dread. "Where my thoughts go back now, to that slow agony of my youth, I wonder how much of the histories I invented for such people hangs like a mist of fancy over well-remembered facts! When I tread the old ground, I do not wonder that I seem to see and pity, going on before me, an innocent romantic boy, making his imaginative world out of such strange experiences and sordid things" (11). Nothing is more "sordid" than the Barnwell story, and it is no wonder that the grown novelist (whether David or Dickens) wishes to exorcise that old "ghost" who haunts his every novel.

However, on a more literal level, there are, in fact, two Barnwells, two "bad apprentice" characters in David Copperfield: David/Dickens, attempting to flee from the Barnwell stigma and, of course, Uriah Heep, literally living out the Barnwell plot. Like Barnwell, Uriah Heep is the serpent in the garden of the Wickfield family. Like Barnwell, Heep manipulates and defrauds his friends and benefactors. Like Barnwell, Heep is described as "the most consummate villain that has ever existed" (52). And like Barnwell's, Heep's last scene is set in a prison. But he is a very different sort of cornered felon than were Barnwell, Millwood, Fagin, or Kit Nubbles. Uriah Heep, in the unctuous hypocrisy of his "turned-to-God" act in Creakle's jail, is George Barnwell as white-collar criminal, George Barnwell no longer as the red-blooded, lust-driven devil of the bawdy eighteenth century, but a bloodless, sycophantic George Barnwell of the Utilitarian Victorian age. David Copperfield's two Barnwells are quite different: One, David, is alive with his guilt;

the other, Uriah Heep, is dead in his utter surrender to the depravity of self-dramatization.

The Two Millwoods

After *David Copperfield* an interesting turnabout occurs in the Dickens canon. Commonly, *David Copperfield* is viewed as that turning point in Dickens's art where, after exorcising the personal demons of his past, he was able to redirect his energies toward the social abuses of his age. After *David Copperfield*, Dickens focused on the "Condition of England" question that his contemporary Carlyle had raised. In doing so, Dickens also turned toward more universal themes such as Justice and Identity in *Bleak House*, Utilitarianism in *Hard Times*, and Family and Government Bureaucracy in *Little Dorrit*. But both of these turns—to a higher social seriousness and focus and to a maturity of thematic vision—had previously been announced in *Dombey and Son*, the novel that immediately preceded *David Copperfield*. In fact, in many ways, *David Copperfield* can be seen as a regression for Dickens.

Immediately prior to *David Copperfield*, *Dombey and Son* had offered a panoramic critique of the ruthless business world of Victorian England (just as *A Christmas Carol* had offered a much more limited characterization of a Victorian businessman). *Dombey and Son* was also a novel based on the overarching theme of Pride. In the limitation of its first person narrative and its rather conventional bildungsroman plot, *David Copperfield* had failed to deliver on either of *Dombey and Son's* social or thematic promises. A much more interesting turnabout for the Dickensian imagination, which *Dombey and Son* also announced and *David Copperfield* also failed to fulfill was the much more analytic and intense characterization of a diverse group of women characters. In *Dombey and Son*, for the first time in any detail, Dickens confronted the gender issue of the condition of women in Victorian society.

For Dickens, then, *David Copperfield* was a pause from the advances in theme and especially female characterization made in *Dombey and Son*. *David Copperfield* was Dickens's farewell to the past, to Pickwick's generally carefree world, to Oliver's innocence, to the eighteenth-century need for the order of *Martin Chuzzlewit* and *Barnaby Rudge*. *David Copperfield* was meant to be that watershed point for Dickens's career where he finally exorcised his personal demons in order to move on, to "go about his society's business" to paraphrase the biblical parallel. But two years earlier in *Dombey and Son*, Dickens had already realized this necessity of putting his house in order and moving on in pursuit of bigger thematic game. He had already tested the water and launched his new contemporary social style.

Dickens's heightened interest in his female characters in *Dombey and Son* actually prefigures the change that the exorcism of *David Copperfield* will occasion. After the only male heir to the Dombey empire is killed off at the very beginning of the novel (as Dickens would proceed to kill off his own troubled childhood in *David Copperfield*), what is left are the women.

In fact, after little Paul Dombey dies so early in the novel—whose title ironically bears his name—it is clear that the Dickensian vision is going to have to undergo some revision if this novel is to be meaningfully completed. Out of the necessity created by his own irrepressible irony, Dickens was forced to turn to the women characters who had only populated the sentimental background of his earlier novels. Thus, he redirected all of the focus of *Dombey and Son* toward the relationship of Dombey to his daughter (and to his second wife).

This was a significant departure for Dickens (and one with which he was not altogether comfortable if the regression to uninspired female characterizations in *David Copperfield* is any indication). In order to accomplish this significant departure, he turned to an old familiar template, a text that many times before had proven valuable in helping him to articulate his vision of the world. That text, of course, is Lillo's *The London Merchant*, the story not only of George Barnwell, but also of one of the most striking and fully dramatized female villains in all of literature, Millwood.

> There was a criminal called Alice Marwood—a girl still, but deserted
> and an outcast. And she was tried, and she was sentenced. And lord,
> how the gentlemen in the court talked about it! And how grave the
> judge was on her duty and on her having perverted the gifts of nature.
> (*D&S*, 34)

Whereas both *Oliver Twist* and *David Copperfield* take for their inspiration the downfall of young George Barnwell, *Dombey and Son* is the first Dickens novel to be imbalanced in favor of playing out the lives of its female characters. *Dombey and Son's* central economic theme—that all of Victorian life and business are based on and driven by a paradigm of prostitution—and his complex triple-foil characterizations of young Alice Marwood to Edith Dombey to young Florence Dombey, are both governed by his alchemic transubstantiation of Millwood's eighteenth-century story into Victorian terms.

Alice Marwood, *Dombey and Son*'s forlorn prostitute, shares more with Lillo's Millwood than just the verbal echo of her name and the despair and cynicism attendant to her livelihood. She has traveled the archetypal road of the fallen woman in the footsteps of Defoe's Moll, Hogarth's Harlot, Lillo's Millwood, Cleland's Fanny, and Dickens's own Nancy. "When I was young and pretty," Alice Marwood tells how she was taken up by a gentleman who "thought to make a sort of property of me." But that gentleman did not fancy her for long: "Wretchedness and ruin came on me, I say. I was made a short-lived toy." But Alice Marwood, as was Millwood's case, goes on to tell how her initial sexual "ruin" led to other crimes. "His usage made a Devil of me," Alice continues her confession. "I sank in wretchedness and ruin, lower and lower yet. I was concerned in a robbery—in every part of it but the gains—and was found out, and sent to be tried, without a friend, without a penny" (53). The language of Alice Marwood's confession is that of the business world and that world's attendant obsession with objectification. She is made a piece of "property," a "short-lived toy," and after the robbery she, unfortunately, fails to share in the "gains."

It is this obsession with business, with all of life being dedicated to "gains," that so vexes Dickens in *Dombey and Son*. "'In short, we are so d____d business-like,'" says the mysterious gentleman who visits Harriet and John Carker's humble abode "in a state of extreme dissatisfaction and vexation" (33). *Dombey and Son* is a cautionary bourgeois tract in the best tradition of Defoe's eighteenth-century novels and Lillo and Gay's eighteenth-century plays. Like *Moll Flanders* and *The London Merchant* and *The Beggars Opera*, *Dombey and Son* is fueled by the false premise that business loss constitutes middle-class tragedy; whereas the real tragedy in all of these bourgeois texts is the manner in which human relationships have all become "so d____d business-like." In *Dombey and Son*, the central metaphor for the relationships between men and women, husbands and wives, parents and children, is that of prostitution, the theme that is embodied in and defined by poor Alice Marwood.

But Alice Marwood only exists in *Dombey and Son* to serve as a foil to the other Millwood character in the novel, Dickens's grand whore, Edith Dombey. "'What is it that you have to sell?'" Edith asks young Alice the first time they meet. "'Only this,' returned the woman, holding out her wares, without looking at them, 'I sold myself, long ago'" (40). Alice Marwood wears her prostitution on her sleeve, but Edith Dombey also is uneasy in her perception of her own situation in Victorian society and in her own marriage.

Moved by Alice Marwood's words, Edith Dombey realizes that her marriage to the rich Mr. Dombey, which she meticulously orchestrated and her mother so diligently brokered, is, in fact, an act of prostitution on a grand scale; no less an act of prostitution than those more common ones orchestrated by Alice Marwood and her hag of a mother, Mrs. Brown. Edith Dombey confesses:

> knowing that my marriage would at least prevent their hawking me up and down; I suffered myself to be sold as infamously as any woman with a halter round her neck is sold in any market-place. . . .
>
> From my marriage day, I found myself exposed to such new shame—to such solicitation and pursuit (expressed as clearly as if it had been written in the coarsest words, and thrust into my head at every turn), from one mean villain, that I felt as if I had never known humiliation until that time. (D&S, 54)

The language of prostitution is unmistakable in this passage: Edith has allowed herself to be "sold . . . infamously," and exposed to "shame . . . solicitation and pursuit . . . humiliation," expressed in "the coarsest words."

Edith's realization that her marriage is an act of prostitution (and Dickens's own judgement on the nature of the Victorian marriage contract in general) is an appropriate thematic note. Throughout the novel Edith has looked on Alice Marwood with growing uneasiness because she sees in this young confessed street prostitute an image of herself as a sold commodity as both wife and adulterer. Dickens is always very astute in his choice of metaphors (as his use of shipwrecks aptly demonstrates). Writing a novel about the Victorian business world, it made abundant sense that Dickens chose the oldest continuous form of contractual business, prostitution, as one of his controlling metaphors.

Edith Dombey is what, in the late twentieth century, is commonly called a "trophy wife." "'You know he has bought me,'" Edith challenges her mother. "'He has considered of his bargain; he has shown it to his friend; he is even rather proud of it; he thinks that it will suit him, and may be had sufficiently cheap; and he will buy tomorrow. God, that I have lived for this, and that I feel it!'" (27). In fact, Edith's sense of her prostitution is so strong that it actually turns her to stone. When Dombey informs Mrs. Skewton and Edith that "'the deed of settlement, the professional gentleman informs me, is now ready,'" Edith "sat like a handsome statue; as cold, as silent, and as still" (30).

After her marriage to Dombey, Edith's sense of it as a state of prostitution hangs heavy upon her. "The most innocent allusion to the power of his riches degraded her anew, sunk her deeper in her own respect, and made the blight and waste within her more complete" (35). The words "degraded" and "blight" in this passage are telling. She sees herself as no better than a street whore afflicted with the disease of her profession. "'What are you?'" Edith's mother asks her. "'I have put the question to myself,' said Edith, ashy pale, and pointing to the window, 'more than once when I have been sitting there, and something in the faded likeness of my sex has wandered past outside'" (30). Edith's answer is: I am a whore like those women who walk the streets. Edith Dombey's tragedy is that she sees herself in Alice Marwood, but her triumph is that she also sees the possibilities for marital prostitution in Florence Dombey's future, and she tries to keep Florence off the streets, so to speak. Unfortunately, and ironically, Edith becomes the very occasion of Florence's being driven out into the streets.

When Mr. Dombey finds out that his second wife, Edith, has betrayed him and run off with James Carker, he takes his anger for that act out on his innocent daughter, Florence. Unwittingly, Florence runs to him "with her arms stretched out, and crying 'Oh dear, dear papa!' as if she would have clasped him around the neck." But as she runs to him in love, he raises his heavy hand and strikes her down in the anger aimed at his adulterous wife: "And as he dealt the blow, he told her what Edith was, and bade her follow her, since they had always been in league." Thus, Dombey calls Edith a whore and tells Florence to become a whore like her stepmother, "and Florence, with her head bent down to hide her agony of tears, was in the streets" (47). Her own father has called her a whore and sent her out into the streets. In all three cases of the participants in this triple-foil female characterization, the parents serve as the panders in their prostitution of the daughters. In all three cases, the daughters recognize the "d____d businesslike" parenting at work and rebel against it, reject the female archetype of the fallen woman, and define their own existential identities in a world incapable of envisioning women as anything other than property.

Dickens defines his age as a ruthless marketplace where women are just another commodity to be bought and sold, used for one's purposes or entertainment and then thrown away. But Dickens is, perhaps, most sensitive to and empathetic with the existential tragedy of the loss of self-respect, which this societal reality occasions in its victims, the wives. "'There is no slave in a market; there is no horse in a fair: so shown and offered and examined and paraded, mother, as I have been,'" Edith clearsightedly characterizes herself as chattel, as an animal, as an object for sale. "'He sees me at the auction, and thinks it well to buy me. Let him! Where he came to view me—perhaps to bid—he required to see the roll of my accomplishments. I gave it to him. When he would have me show one of them, to justify his purchase to his men, I require of him to say which he demands, and I exhibit it. I will do no more. He makes the purchase of his own will, and with his own sense of its worth, and the power of his money'" (27).

This passage, with its analogies to slave auctions and horse auctions, uncannily echoes Mary Wollstonecraft's late-eighteenth-century feminist argument in *A Vindication of the Rights of Women* (1792). Dickens's complex triple-foil characterization of the "condition of women" in the mid-nineteenth-century and his clear and present critique of Victorian marriage as a respectable bourgeois form of prostitution places his gender consciousness in distinguished company. The 1846-1847 characterization of the situation of women in *Dombey and Son* predicts the arguments of the most powerful polemic statements of the Victorian feminist movement, which were to follow soon after. Harriet Taylor's *The Enfranchisement of Women* was published without attribution in *The Westminster Review* in July 1851 and was later credited by her husband John Stuart Mill as the basis for his feminist work *The Subjection of Women* published in 1869. The gender consciousness of *Dombey and Son,* and that novel's strident theme of marriage as prostitution, is one instance where Dickens was not simply a publicist for existing abuses in Victorian society, but was actually well ahead of the times in anticipating and calling early attention to the existence of those abuses.

Utilitarianism Deconstructed

Though every other novel to this midpoint in Dickens's career either alludes directly to the George Barnwell story as an influence or draws heavily on that story for its plot, characters, and major thematic issues, *Bleak House* does not. No direct allusion to Lillo's play raises its head in the novel. No dominant theme in *Bleak House* parallels Lillo's concerns. While there are many possible character parallels to the George Barnwell story in *Bleak House,* none echo as tellingly as the Marwood/Millwood parallel in *Dombey and Son.* Nonetheless, *Bleak House* does not completely demur from the Lillo influence.

Richard Carstone could be viewed as an insubstantial shadow of George Barnwell. He does, indeed, allow himself to be seduced by a powerful outside force that tempts him to pursue easy money. He does, as a result, turn against his benefactor and betray his trusted position in the household. But in Richard Carstone's case the seducer is a lawsuit and his crime against his benefactor is simply resentment, not theft and murder. "Jarndyce and Jarndyce has warped him out of himself, and perverted me in his eyes," John Jarndyce clearly evaluates the change that has taken place in his ward due to the seduction of the Chancery case. "I would rather restore to poor Rick his proper nature than be endowed with all the money the dead suitors . . . have left unclaimed" (BH, 35). As in the case of George Barnwell, an apprentice has undergone a complete perversion of "his proper nature" in pursuit of unearned wealth, but it does not drive him to theft and murder, only listlessness and loss of direction.

Lillo's eighteenth-century values are present in the relationship between John Jarndyce, who is the Thorowgood or Squire Allworthy of *Bleak House*, and Richard Carstone. Early in the novel, Jarndyce advises Richard, who is considering entering the legal profession, that the "course of study and preparation requires to be diligently pursued" (13). Like young Barnwell, Richard vows to do his best, and then disappoints everyone involved by doing his worst. And yet, Richard Carstone is never George Barnwell. He never commits a crime against his guardian for which he could be led to the gallows.

The only character in *Bleak House* who does commit such a Barnwellian crime is a woman, Hortense, Lady Dedlock's French maid. Hortense could have been yet another fallen female Dickens character based on Lillo's Millwood if Dickens hadn't had a much closer model at hand, the murderess Maria Manning whose public hanging he had attended only a year earlier. Hortense, like Millwood, is an utterly amoral beast with whom one must take great care, "especially when she is in an ill-humour and near knives" (12). Like Millwood, Hortense is "'powerful high and passionate; and what with having notice to leave, and having others put above her, she don't take kindly to it'" (18). Like Millwood, in the words of Lawyer Tulkinghorn, Hortense is a "jade" and "a vixen" (42), and he threatens to have her locked up in prison. But if she seems to be like Lillo's Millwood, her French descent, her pidgin English, and her bestial murderousness and utter lack of repentance for her crime make her much more an image of Maria Manning, who Dickens had spent a long night studying, and whose public hanging he had tellingly described in an outraged letter to *The Times*.

Some superficial parallels to the Barnwell story and characters do appear, but that hitherto almost obsessive influence does not seem to be uppermost in Dickens's mind during the composition of *Bleak House*. That eighteenth-century bourgeois myth, however, does seem to strongly reassert itself in Dickens's next novel, *Hard Times*, just as it certainly will later in *Great Expectations*.

Because it is a novel about work, set amidst the enunciation of the new work ethic of the Industrial Revolution, *Hard Times* is a text much more closely adapted to the cultural influence of the Barnwellian social myth. *Hard Times* is Dickens's ultimate critique of the philosophy of the Industrial

Revolution, Utilitarianism. But in order to critique that philosophy Dickens must adjust his thinking on the values that the Barnwell story professes. *Hard Times* is not only a reassessment of hard facts Utilitarianism, it is also a reassessment of the definition of the working class's relationship to management that had been so clearly, and simplistically, represented in moral black and white in Lillo's *The London Merchant* and in Dickens's earlier novels. *Hard Times* expands the profile of the apprentice and examines with greater insight and complexity the relationship of the apprentice to the master.

Clearly, as Dickens is finishing *Bleak House*, he is already thinking of *Hard Times* and Coketown. His description of Trooper George's journey to "the iron country"

> As he comes into the iron country farther north, such fresh green woods as those of Chesney Wold are left behind; and coalpits and ashes, high chimneys and red bricks, blighted verdure, scorching fires, and a heavy, never lightening cloud of smoke, become the features of the scenery. . . . At last, on the black canal bridge of a busy town . . . the trooper . . . asks a workman does he know the name of Rouncewell thereabouts? (*BH*, 63)

is almost a direct echo of Dickens's soon to follow description of Coketown in *Hard Times*:

> It was a town of red brick, or of brick that would have been red if the smoke and ashes had allowed it; but as matters stood it was a town of unnatural red and black like the painted face of a savage. It was a town of machinery and tall chimneys. . . . It had a black canal in it, and a river that ran purple with ill-smelling dyes. (I, 5).

This is the landscape to which Dickens adapted the George Barnwell story. In *Hard Times*, the story of the failed apprenticeship of young Tom Gradgrind is Dickens's first postindustrial Revolution pass at the Barnwell myth.

The concept of apprenticeship and the Carlylean fulfillment of work (the novel is, in fact, dedicated to Carlyle) are two of the earliest valorized themes in *Hard Times*. When one of Sleary's circus performers declares proudly that "I was apprenticed when I was seven year old," Bounderby decries his pride in work by scoffing that the speaker was apprenticed to "Idleness" (I, 6). Soon after, Mr. Sleary's parting advice to Sissy Jupe is: "My latht wordth to you ith thith, Thtick to the termth of your engagement, be obedient to the Thquire" (I, 6). He exhorts her to fulfill her apprenticeship properly.

But by far the apprenticeship that comes in for the most intense scrutiny in *Hard Times* is that of young Tom Gradgrind to Bounderby's bank. Tom sees his apprenticeship to Bounderby as an escape from the "hard facts" education and the severe work ethic lifestyle of his father's rigid Utilitarian household. "However, when I go to live with old Bounderby, I'll have my revenge," Tom declares. When his sister inquires what he means, Tom answers, "I mean, I'll enjoy myself a little, and go about and see something, and hear something. I'll recompense myself for the way in which I have been brought up" (I, 8). Thus, Tom Gradgrind goes into his apprenticeship with a bad attitude and the Barnwellian result, therefore, is rather predictable. His father's strict Utilitarianism has engendered in Tom a resentment toward the Victorian ethics of work and duty, and driven him to their opposites, profligacy and betrayal. Bitzer, the other apprentice in Bounderby's employ, makes the initial evaluation of young Tom Gradgrind's apprenticeship:

> "An individual, ma'am . . . has never been what he ought to have been,
> since he first came into the place. He is a dissipated extravagant idler.
> He is not worth his salt, ma'am. He wouldn't get it either, if he hadn't
> a friend and relation at court, ma'am." (II, 1).

But whelpish young Tom is not the only apprentice in Bounderby's employ. Bitzer is the other, supposedly model apprentice. He is no Barnwell! He does not steal from or betray his master. He simply betrays everyone else: "He held the respectable office of general spy and informer in the establishment. . . . His mind was so exactly regulated, that he had no affections or passions. All his proceedings were the result of the nicest and coldest calculation." (II, 1).

The ironic binary contrast that Dickens sets up between the two apprentices, Tom and Bitzer, deconstructs the simplistic, black and white Barnwellian myth of the good and bad apprentice. Here, the bad apprentice is a profligate thief like Barnwell, but the good apprentice is a jackal, a "general spy and informer," a Utilitarian automaton with "no affections or passions," his whole life based on the "coldest calculation." Dickens's brutal characterization of Bitzer almost makes Tom, the old-fashioned, eighteenth-century version of the failed apprentice, seem attractive.

In the gray light of Utilitarianism, Dickens seems to be reevaluating his Barnwellian paradigm, grappling with the anti-existential demands of this new bourgeois religion that teaches that in order to be good one must give up all "fancy," "wonder," passion, identity, and humanness and become a good apprentice, as Bitzer has, to the machines that rule society. The Barnwellian betrayal in *Hard Times* is less a betrayal of one's family or benefactor than it is a betrayal of a philosophy, a way of ordering the world. What Tom Gradgrind betrays is his education, the hard-facts Utilitarianism that is supposed to be the cornerstone of his family and business life. What Bitzer exposes is the betrayal of humanism that that same Utilitarian philosophy espouses. Whereas Tom's bad apprenticeship results in a Barnwellian crime against his employer and society, that employer and that society are so amoral, rapacious, and corrupt themselves that Tom's crime is mitigated as George Barnwell's could never be. Dickens allows him to escape to the continent in hopes that he can salvage some humanity. Tom Gradgrind has been shipwrecked on the rocks of Utilitarian opportunism and dehumanization.

In other words, in *Hard Times*, the simplistic morality of the Barnwellian failed-apprentice myth is muddied. Though similar to George Barnwell in appetite (profligacy) and action (robbing one's employer), Tom Gradgrind's motives are much more sophisticated, intellectual. Whereas Barnwell was seduced into his crimes by desire for a woman, Tom Gradgrind commits his crime out of rebellion against a philosophy. And Bitzer deconstructs the good apprentice paradigm (which Trueman had represented in *The London Merchant*) by adhering to the letter of that flawed philosophy. What Dickens is arguing via this binary deconstruction is that in the postindustrial Victorian world the simplistic moralities of his favorite myth are no longer operable. They must be reevaluated against the equally evil, dehumanizing, amoral myths of the brave new Utilitarian world.

In fact, perhaps the best analogy to the dialogic New Historicist project of *Hard Times* might well be the bloodless Utopian communities of mid-twentieth-century literature. *Hard Times* compares well to the parables of failed apprenticeship as crime against the state represented in Huxley's *Brave New World*, Orwell's *1984*, Margaret Atwood's *The Handmaid's Tale*, and Terry Gilliam's film *Brazil*. As in these twentieth-century futurist fictions, a political economy and its social philosophy turns Dickens's Tom and Bitzer into competing monsters. Tom is a monster whose "imagination had been strangled in the cradle" yet who is "still inconvenienced by its ghost in the form of groveling sensualities; but such a monster beyond all doubt was Tom" (*HT*, II, 3). Bitzer is not bothered by any such troublesome ghosts. He is utterly bloodless, empty, one of Conrad's papier-mâché devils, one of Eliot's "hollow men." Tom panders his sister and robs his employer, but Bitzer spies on and betrays everyone in slavish worship of an employer who is himself a monster. In *Heart of Darkness*, Conrad poses the same dilemma: Is it worse to be a "lusty, red-eyed devil" than to be a "papier- mâché Mephistopheles" who when you stick your finger through its insubstantial outer skin you find nothing inside? In fact, *Hard Times* is Dickens's *Heart of Darkness*, a descent down a dark river into a disturbing underworld where man must encounter the horror of what western philosophy has made of him. Tom Gradgrind is a clear precursor of Conrad's Kurtz: the product of Victorian philosophy, he becomes one of its greatest nightmares, its horror.

In every reincarnation of the Barnwell story, that monstrous horror finds its terminal punctuation in the public humiliation of the criminal, whether it be Barnwell or Millwood, in a climactic scene. In the original, both Barnwell and Millwood must go to the gallows while Barnwell also gets his prison cell scene. Fagin displays his descent into madness in a similar condemned cell scene in *Oliver Twist*. David Copperfield is publicly humiliated in the window of Murdstone and Grinby's wine warehouse, and Uriah Heep adapts his peculiar form of civility to jail society. In *Hard Times*, Tom's public humiliation takes a strikingly symbolic form as he is forced to confess his sins in black minstrel makeup in the middle of the ring in Sleary's travelling circus.

"Your brother ith one o' them black thervanth," Mr. Sleary announces as he leads them to the fugitive. When Mr. Gradgrind sees his son "in black face" and "so grimly, detestably, ridiculously shameful," he cannot believe that "one of his model children had come to this" (*HT*, III, 7). But, if Tom's humiliation is that of a marginalized outcast from society, Mr. Gradgrind is immediately faced with a second and clearly more dangerous product of the Gradgrind philosophy. In a chapter that Dickens titled "Philosophical" (III, 8), Bitzer reappears, and Mr. Gradgrind's educational philosophy comes back to haunt him. While Mr. Gradgrind views his son Tom as the greatest failure of his whole Utilitarian education system, Bitzer is one of that system's great successes. In this counterpoint, Dickens is clearly posing the question "Which is the greater of these two possible evils?"

> "Bitzer . . . have you a heart?" Mr. Gradgrind pleads. "Is it accessible . . . to any compassionate influence?"
> "It is accessible to Reason, sir," returned the excellent young man.
> "And to nothing else." (III, 8)

In the sharp sarcasm of the narrator's "excellent young man," Dickens makes clear his revisionist view of the Barnwell myth. Bitzer is by far the greater of the possible evils and, because of his emptiness, is beyond redemption. What both Dickens and later Conrad recognize is that there are much greater horrors than the sensual weakness of George Barnwell, Tom Gradgrind, or Kurtz. There are the bloodless Bitzers of the new postindustrial empire, the heartless bureaucrats who make the whole operation run on time and produce a profit. Indeed, in *Hard Times* the George Barnwell myth has come a long way from the moral simplicities of eighteenth-century melodrama.

A Postmodernist Pip

This extended discourse on the "New Historicist" significance of Lillo's George Barnwell story over 150 years of social and literary history as well as across the Dickens canon has all been generated out of William Axton's initial discussion of the influence of the Barnwell myth on *Great Expectations*. In his 1966 work, *Circle of Fire: Dickens' Vision & Style & The Popular Victorian Theater*, Axton wrote:

> As in *Dombey and Son, Great Expectations* goes to the theater for a folk archetype of an apprentice and for a pattern of action and character relationships that involve his unwilling betrayal of his friends and benefactors. In this case, the central allusion is to George Lillo's immensely popular sentimental drama, *The London Merchant, or The History of George Barnwell* (1731), a play so often revived and so widely imitated in the century following its debut as to become by 1860 a basic item in the Victorian common reader's cultural inheritance.[46]

In his analysis of the influence of this "archetype" on *Great Expectations*, Axton makes the proper comparisons of Pip to Barnwell as betrayers of family and of Estella to Millwood as seducers. He also discusses Lillo's story as a "play within the novel" exercise in metatheatre comparable to Shakespeare's similar, self-reflexive "play within a play" ploy in *Hamlet*. These discussions lead Axton to a two-pronged evaluation of the impact of Lillo's play on Dickens's novel:

> *The London Merchant* offers a pattern to hold up for comparison with the apprentice boy's progress that is both a serious burlesque and a grotesquely relevant prototype and that invests the novel with that universality that accrues to folk myth. At the same time, the novel offers a far more profound investigation into the themes of obsession, guilt, and

disenchantment than Lillo's play; and in this way *Great Expectations* constitutes an indictment of the comfortable cultural attitudes of which the play is an epitome. In the most serious sense of the term, then, this novel is as profound a burlesque of *George Barnwell* as Wopsle's plot is a frivolous burlesque of Pip's career.[47]

For Axton, this "play within the novel" provides a comic counterpoint to the much more serious Barnwellian social issues that the career of Pip the wayward apprentice raises. Axton's points about the Barnwell story and its two-pronged influence on *Great Expectations* could not be clearer or truer. Dickens has taken a quite available myth and tailored it to a complex purpose. Though Axton did not have the terms yet available to him in 1966, his discussion is still a deconstructive one. He argues that in *Great Expectations* Dickens consciously sets out to dismantle the easy and sentimental moralities of the Barnwellian paradigm, and in burlesquing that paradigm and those sentimentalities he is simultaneously attacking the easy acceptance of his Victorian Age's sense that eighteenth-century, preindustrial Revolution morality and thinking can still function in a postindustrial age. It cannot. It can only serve as a signpost signaling how far civilization has come and the extreme level of cynicism that has evolved.

In the world of *Great Expectations*, a bad apprentice doesn't end up on the gallows as Barnwell did, but, rather, becomes a partner in a quite respectable trading firm in the East Indies; and an utterly heartless seducer of youth like Millwood ends up with the distinct possibility of becoming a respectable Victorian wife. Dickens is quite conscious of the fact that swift justice and harsh punishment for crime and immorality is no longer possible in the Victorian age as it was in Lillo's eighteenth-century world. The postindustrial nineteenth century is a world where the betrayal of a Pip and the ruthlessness of an Estella are simply winked at as necessities of doing business in a utterly commodified world. Pip and Estella end up assimilated into a society where their strong profit-and-loss instincts serve them well; whereas Barnwell and Millwood were vilified and punished severely by an eighteenth-century society where moral law was still ascendant over the law of supply and demand.

Even though when Axton wrote his Barnwellian interpretation of *Great Expectations* in 1966, postmodernist critical theory was just beginning to find articulation, his binary argument for that novel as simultaneously a Barnwellian parable and parody is intuitively postmodernist and still wears well in 1997. If there is one flaw in Axton's discussion, it is its single clear focus on *Great Expectations* to the exclusion of Dickens's other treatments of the

Barnwell story—beginning with *The Pickwick Papers,* regularly appearing throughout the Dickens canon, and leading up to its culmination as a paradigm for *Great Expectations.*

The evolution of Dickens's treatment of the Barnwell story from novel to novel across his canon shows that, as Dickens matured, he became much more aware of the passage of the eighteenth-century values on which he had originally built his vision of the world and his moralistic literary philosophy. As did Matthew Arnold's protagonist in "The Stanzas From the Grand Chartreuse," he found himself wandering "between two worlds/One dead, the other impossible to be born." In his later, postindustrial novels, particularly *Dombey and Son, Hard Times, Great Expectations,* and *Our Mutual Friend,* Dickens is constantly aware of the necessity to develop a new, more flexible philosophy, a philosophy more dependent on the laws of profit and loss, a new philosophy of history that looks consciously forward to the twentieth century rather than backward to the world of George Barnwell. This new philosophy of history had to overcome the "impossible to be born" condition of Arnold's poem "Dover Beach" where mankind is stranded on a "darkling plain." It had to be a positive philosophy, a bright rather than a "dark" philosophy, that could carry the Dickens world into the postindustrial world of the twentieth century. Dickens' last completed novel, *Our Mutual Friend,* became the vehicle for the articulation of that new philosophy of history.

FIVE

The Movement of History in Our Mutual Friend

History as a cyclical experience of life is a preoccupation of the characters in Dickens's *Our Mutual Friend*. In the novel's opening scene, Gaffer Hexam defines the interrelationship between time and history as he tells Rogue Riderhood, "We have worked together in time past, but we work together no more in time present nor yet future" (I, 1). In making this break with Riderhood, Gaffer has "taken an unassailable position" (I, 1), because all historical time has converged within his simple mind. For Gaffer, in this scene the meaning of the past and its impact on the future is clearly intelligible, but for others in the novel there is no such easy understanding of the cyclical experience of history.

Many characters in *Our Mutual Friend* delve into past history, but invariably they misinterpret its meaning. The people at the Veneering dinner party express a morbid enthusiasm for hearing Mortimer Lightwood's story of "The Man from Somewhere," but, even when the past events of that story suddenly intrude into the present situation of the dinner party, no one realizes what impact, if any, this fragment of past history will have on their own lives. In another sense, the people around the Veneering dinner table are themselves involved in either the obliteration or the falsification of the past as a means of creating deceptive identities in the present. Twemlow subsists on the fiction that he is a close relation of Lord Snigsworthy. The mature young lady and the mature young gentleman, later to be Mr. and Mrs. Lammle, create false pasts in the present interest of fortune-hunting. Worst of all are the Veneerings, who are completely devoid of both past and future. Because "the Veneering fiction" (I, 10) has no basis and no prospects, those who believe in it show their utter dislocation from the reality of time and personal history.

By far the most singular delvings into past history are those undertaken by Noddy Boffin, one of the few characters who has a concretely realized past.

The essential knowledge acquired in his past life as "foreman at the Bower" involves the value of looking beneath the surface of things, of delving and sifting through every available fragment of material, in order to salvage what is usable and to discard what is obsolete, tainted, or false. When his station in life changes and he is master instead of foreman, his articulated past experience serves to stimulate his interest in the accumulated historical material of the past.

When he becomes proprietor of the Harmon holdings, Boffin expresses his desire to delve into the past by hiring Silas Wegg to unearth the mysteries of the "Decline-and-Fall-Off-The-Rooshan-Empire." Boffin's erroneous conception of the content of Gibbon's history gives vitality to his interest in the past. He looks "with beaming eyes into the opening world" that Wegg is unveiling for him in order to "see a way to our bettering ourselves" (I, 5). Boffin sincerely hopes that his study of the past can give direction to his actions as a rich and influential man in present-day England. But, as J. Hillis Miller observed in writing about this novel:

> It is clear that, for Dickens, nineteenth-century England is repeating the fall of Rome. . . . Modern England, like ancient Rome, is being slowly destroyed because it cannot find strength to rid itself of the tangible, material presence of the dead forms of the past.[1]

As he listens to the atrocities that the Romans took pleasure in visiting on one another, Boffin realizes the inadequacy of past forms. Through "intuitive wisdom" the lessons of the past are applied to the present and new forms begin to emerge. Mrs. Boffin defines the situation: "We have come into a great fortune, and we must do what's right by our fortune; we must act up to it. . . . It's never been acted up to yet, and, consequently, no good has come of it." And Mr. Boffin makes the distinction between the dead forms of the past and those new forms that are needed: "True, to the present time. . . . I hope good may be coming of it in the future time" (I, 9). As Gaffer Hexam had done in the opening scene, Boffin makes a clean break with what he has observed as false and immoral in the past, and he resolves to change the course of history in the future.

As Boffin's eccentric education continues, he becomes more and more involved with the dilemma of the truth of history:

> The Roman Empire having worked out its destruction, Mr. Boffin next appeared in a cab with Rollin's *Ancient History*, which valuable work being found to possess lethargic properties, broke down at about the period when the whole of the army of Alexander the Macedon (at that time about forty thousand strong) burst into tears simultaneously on his being taken with a shivering fit after bathing. The Wars of the Jews likewise

languishing under Mr. Wegg's generalship, Mr. Boffin arrived in another cab with Plutarch: whose *Lives* he found in the sequel extremely entertaining, though he hoped Plutarch might not expect him to believe them all. What to believe, in the course of his reading, was Mr. Boffin's chief literary difficulty indeed; for some time he was divided in his mind between half, all, or none; at length, when he decided, as a moderate man, to compound with half, the question still remained, which half? And that stumbling block he never got over. (III, 6).

Boffin, in his awareness of the falsity of past history, finally concludes that all of these dead forms of the past break down like the army of Alexander.

When Boffin begins his final foray into the realms of past history, his pseudo-obsession with the histories of misers, he is fully aware of the inapplicability of past history to human experience in his modern day. Thus, fittingly, he employs the histories of misers as a ruse, a type of history that to a person of perception can only demonstrate the deadness of the past. Boffin realizes the need for new forms through his study of past history, and he in turn uses the most preposterous past history available as a demonstration to others of the necessity of rejecting the values and conventions of the past. His choice of the history of misers as the main tool in his demonstration is also fitting because the most powerful and falsest value the past has raised—and that Boffin realizes must be replaced—is the Victorian reverence for money. Nowhere does the glorification of money show itself to be more absurd than in the histories of misers that Boffin parades before his audience.

The analysis of past history in *Our Mutual Friend* stimulates characters to benefit from the mistakes of the past. At the beginning of the novel, many of the characters do indeed have a sense of the deadness of past forms, but initially they are unable to see any means of replacing the past with a suitable new form. The major psychological action of *Our Mutual Friend* involves the attempts by troubled characters to place, in the twentieth-century terms of Jean-Paul Sartre, their "existence" before their "essence." Like Sartre's famous paper knife,[2] many of the characters in *Our Mutual Friend* live initially only in terms of an "essence" that "Society" has imposed on them. However, because man, unlike the paper knife, possesses subjectivity, he need not remain merely an object of predetermined "essence." Thus, man can humanize himself first by becoming aware of the potentiality in his nature for choice, then by realizing (or choosing) his own humanity, and finally by asserting his humanity by means of action in the world.

Sartre's twentieth-century humanism defines the existential dilemma that each central character in *Our Mutual Friend* must face. The movement toward new historical forms to replace the dead history of the past is dependent on the assertion of personal existence as precedent over the essences that "Society," the established world of the novel, is constantly trying to impose on individuals. The old forms of the past are imposed essences that the characters must rebel against before they can even begin to influence the movement of future history.

In *Our Mutual Friend* the majority of characters are described as object-like beings who inhabit an essence-dominated world. Often they are identified as pieces of furniture or as inanimate objects. Twemlow is "an innocent piece of dinner-furniture that went upon easy castors," which "at many houses might be said to represent the dining-table in its normal state," and "Mr. and Mrs. Veneering, for example, arranging a dinner, habitually started with Twemlow, and then put leaves in him, or added guests to him" (I, 2). Young Blight is a "clerkly essence" who makes "a great show" of his office "system" (I, 8), which is itself only a false form of action. After one of Podsnap's dinner parties, "big, heavy vehicles, built on the model of the Podsnap plate, took away the heavy articles of guests weighing ever so much." For Mr. Podsnap,

> nothing would have astonished him more than an intimation that Miss Podsnap, or any other young person properly born and bred, could not be exactly put away like the plate, brought out like the plate, polished like the plate, counted, weighed, and valued like the plate. (I, 11).

Because concern for the nonexistential, material quality of their lives rests uneasily on the minds of specific characters in *Our Mutual Friend*, they often express an interest in the course of future history, especially their own. However, for these concerned individuals a better future cannot come until a moral, rather than a material, change of form can be accomplished. Thus, Bella Wilfer cannot attain happiness in the future until her conventional belief in the power of money can be replaced by her realization of her own capacities for love and trust.

One inadequate way in which characters in the novel, who are uneasy with the past and yet unable to see their way into the future, attempt to adjust to their situation is by assuming an attitude of cautionary doubleness. In *Great Expectations*, the novel that immediately preceded *Our Mutual Friend* in publication, Wemmick and Jaggers display their adeptness at existing in this type of compromise role. In the harsh business world, they constantly maintain an elaborate facade of impersonality and ruthlessness. Only at home, where no one can see or exploit them, do they allow their natural selves to surface in the expression of sympathy and love. In *Our Mutual Friend* many characters feel the necessity of cautionary doubleness. John Harmon must assume a new identity in order to elicit from the people with whom he is involved sincere reactions not tainted by selfish motives. The power of the past is always at work on him. Old Mr. Riah is forced by Fledgeby to play the part of the inflexible money-lender, a historical stereotype, a guise that Riah casts aside immediately upon reaching the privacy, fresh air, and freedom of his roof garden. Both Mr. Venus and Jenny Wren display personalities, one unnaturally morose, the other exceedingly sharp, divorced from their very real yet frustrated capacities for love. The nature of the world of *Our Mutual Friend* demands that people become cautionary doubles in order to survive. The creation of that cautionary doubleness most often takes the form of a dialogic tension between a past and a present existence.

But clearly this type of day-to-day existence is not any sort of answer at all. These characters all realize that their uneasy compromise sustains the dead forms of past history. Each of them longs for a new form, a change in the emphasis of personal history, that will allow them to throw off their cautionary double personalities and become whole once again. Obviously the new form lies not in the dead past nor in the object-dominated present, but in the promise of the future. Thus, the potential history of the future captures the interest of all of the troubled and questing characters in the novel.

Future history in *Our Mutual Friend* takes shape only through the imaginative powers of characters such as Lizzie Hexam and Jenny Wren. In her ability to create images in "the hollow down by the flare" (I, 3), Lizzie is the most adept at seeing into the future. In its physical existence the fire embodies the vital interconnection of past, present, and future. As Charley Hexam notes, "the hollow down by the flare" is created by gas slowly seeping through a fissure in the ground and "coming out of a bit of forest that's been under the mud that was under the water in the days of Noah's Ark" (I, 3). Lizzie's fire arises out of the elemental material of the history of the world. It embodies history from primordial times into the present and it provides the vehicle for the imaginative projection of future history.

The fire is also, then, both a symbol of and a catalyst for Lizzie's imagination. It reveals her as a "deep rich piece of colour, with the brown flush of her cheek and the shining lustre of her hair, though sad and solitary" (I, 13). Here, the fire, like the sunbeam that darted through the window of M'Choakumchild's schoolroom and irradiated Sissy Jupe in *Hard Times*, reveals all of the pent-up vitality of Lizzie Hexam's inner life. As a symbol of imagination the fire is for Lizzie "where first fancies had been nursed, and her first escape made from the grim life out of which she had plucked her brother" (*OMF*, III, 9). Through her ability to create an imaginative future in the fire she can escape all of the deadness and squalor of her present life.

Also, as was the case with Louisa Gradgrind, who would spend long hours gazing into the dying fire, Lizzie's "hollow down by the flare" provides her with a natural education of the heart that even her perverse brother Charley recognizes: "I used to call the fire at home her books, for she was always full of fancies—sometimes quite wise fancies, considering—when she sat looking at it" (*OMF*, II, 1). This symbol in *Our Mutual Friend*, like Louisa's symbolic fire in *Hard Times*, expresses that dichotomy between the power of the imaginative world of the fire, the realm of fancy and wonder, and the inflexible, dead world of social convention. Charley Hexam, because he belongs to that dead world, repudiates the vision in the fire: "It was all very well when we sat before the fire—when we looked into the hollow down by the flare—but we are looking into the real world now" (*OMF*, II, 1). But the world that Lizzie is able to create in the fire exists because of her human capacity for love and for hope in the future, and these emotions are very real.

However, the most important function in *Our Mutual Friend* of the fire as symbol is the revelation of the new forms of personal history that are needed to replace the old. At one time, as they sit looking into the "hollow down by the flare," Jenny Wren begs Lizzie to "find a lady there," the lady who captivated the heart of Eugene Wrayburn. Lapsing into her own world of dreams, Lizzie sees that lady and describes her to Jenny Wren:

> "She is very rich. Shall she be handsome?"
> "Even you can be that, Lizzie, so she ought to be."
>   "She is very handsome."
>   "What does she say about him?" . . .
>   "She is glad, glad to be rich, that he may have the money. She is glad, glad to be beautiful, that he may be proud of her. Her poor heart—"
>   "Eh? Her poor heart?" . . .
>   "Her heart—is given him, with all its love and truth. She would joyfully die with him, or better than that, die for him. She knows he has failings, but she thinks they have grown up through his being like one cast away, for the want of something to trust in, and care for, and think well of." (II, 11)

This is Lizzie's first verbalization of her love, which can redeem Eugene Wrayburn from the monotony and aimlessness of his life. Her riches are the riches of the heart, and his poverty is his inability to love and to cast off the "essence" that society has imposed on him.

Later in the novel, Lizzie and Bella Wilfer sit together in a "dusky room," which is "lighted by the fire," and "the grate might have been the old brazier, and the glow might have been the old hollow down by the flare" (III, 9). Once again the visions of the future appear:

> "Shall I tell you," asked Lizzie, "what I see down there?"
>
> "Limited little b?" suggested Bella, with her eyebrows raised.
>
> "A heart well worth winning, and well won. A heart that, once won, goes through fire and water for the winner, and never changes, and is never daunted."
>
> "Girl's heart?" asked Bella, with accompanying eyebrows.
>
> Lizzie nodded. "And the figure to which it belongs—"
>
> "Is yours," suggested Bella.
>
> "No. Most clearly and distinctly yours." (III, 9)

Thus, Lizzie also sees the visionary history of Bella's future life in which Bella will discard her materialistic "essence" and will realize the natural "existence" of fully devoted love that Lizzie sees as soon to be awakened in her by John Rokesmith. In these two cases, the visionary history in the fire articulates the new forms needed to replace the false history that the dead forms of the past have imposed on the lives of Lizzie Hexam, Eugene Wrayburn, Bella Wilfer, and John Rokesmith.

Another type of imaginative future history in *Our Mutual Friend* is envisioned by Jenny Wren. She, however, is possessed of two very different conceptions of her own future. Her most dominant obsession is with the man whom she is going to marry. She plans many "various trials and torments" for this imagined lover, but she doesn't know who he is or when he will come or how he will look: she only has an immature conception of what she will do to him. This vision is extremely vague and indistinct because Jenny Wren is but a child who is trying to fulfill an adult vision, the actuality of which is wholly dependant on her action in the future. In order for her vision of married life to gain any sort of reality, Jenny must show herself to be qualified to participate in that vision. When she becomes an adult, not merely in terms of age but in mind, then this vision of future history might possibly come true.

But Jenny Wren also frequently envisions another possibility for her future. Her second vision is always a dream of great numbers of children "in white dresses, and with something shining on the borders, and on their heads," who "come down in long bright slanting rows, and say all together, 'Who is this in pain? Who is this in pain?'" When Jenny answers them, they reply, "Come and play with us!" and she always cries, "I never play! I can't play!" and they sweep in around her and take her up and make her "light" (II, 2). This second vision of future history that haunts Jenny Wren is a Blakean vision of heavenly children like that seen by little Tom Dacre in "The Chimney Sweeper" in *The Songs of Innocence*.[3] Like little Tom's vision in Blake's poem, Jenny's is a forlorn child's vision of salvation as a release from pain.

However, this type of salvation doesn't necessarily have to occur in future time. In the Dickens world, two types of salvation are possible: free entrance into heaven for the dead child or earthly salvation for the child who grows to feel and think as an adult and who becomes fully human by making moral decisions and expressing his or her own reality in the adult world. Jenny Wren sees these two different visions of future history and must choose which type of salvation she wants.

At the end of the novel, in her relationship with Sloppy, Jenny leaves behind her false life of self-pity and enters into a natural existence of human understanding. Her Blakean vision is one of despair and escape, but Jenny can still choose to reject the hopeless resignation of Blake's chimney sweeps, Little Nell, Paul Dombey, and Poor Jo. She can choose to grow out of her childish innocence and make a life for herself in the world of experience. When Jenny meets Sloppy she drops her singsong jargon of self-pity—"my back's bad, and my legs are queer" (II, 1)—in order to express her reality and humanity simply and truthfully—"'It [her crutch] belongs to me,' returned the little creature, with a quick flush of her face and neck. 'I am lame'" (IV, 16). When her beauty is acknowledged by Sloppy, she sees the futility of her self-pity and can finally express herself as a whole human being rather than a forlorn child or a warped cripple. Jenny's adult vision of future history ceases to be vague and indefinable and replaces the unearthly, purposeless Blakean vision of heavenly salvation.

For the morally concerned and questing female characters in *Our Mutual Friend*—Lizzie Hexam, Bella Wilfer, Jenny Wren—essence precedes existence. Each of them wants to replace the rules and attitudes under which they have been forced to live and make a new set of rules based on a completely different set of values. The central problem for each of these women who desire change is one of technique. At the outset none of them is quite sure of what technique to use in the development of a new life-style. This indecision, the anguish of trying to recognize the true values and the true modes of action necessary for the establishment of a new and better life-style is not shared only by these female characters; it is especially present in the separate predicaments of the novel's two protagonists, John Harmon and Eugene Wrayburn.

Each of these young men, in a different way, is involved in trying to establish his own mode of existence. From the very beginning of his relationship with the Boffins, John Harmon proves himself different from every other character in the novel. Using the name Rokesmith, he applies to Mr. Boffin for a job and stipulates that one of the conditions of his employment must be postponing "to some indefinite period the consideration of salary" (*OMF*, I, 15). This is the first relationship in the novel that is established for other than monetary considerations and it is directly contrasted to the earlier relationship established between Wegg and Boffin. John Harmon's presence in the Boffin household places in a different perspective the materialism of some of the other household members. However, throughout the greater part of the novel, John Harmon is really no more than a shadow who, under the protection of an assumed name, discreetly stands in the background while the main action goes on around him. He only becomes a substantial character when he is faced with the decision of whether or not to accept the responsibility of the great wealth that his dead father has left to him as the rightful heir. The inheritance represents the impingement of the past on John Harmon's present quest for identity.

As Boffin's secretary, John Harmon sees all of the distasteful responsibilities that accompany great wealth. During his own dark night of the soul, on that dreary evening when he returns to the waterfront in the clothes of the man who had replaced him in death, John Harmon remembers how he had arrived back in England caged in the power of the past, "shrinking from my father's money . . . mistrustful that I was already growing avaricious . . . knowing of nothing but wretchedness that my father's wealth had ever brought about" (II, 13). As these heavy memories draw to an end, he decides that perhaps it is better that he remain dead, because as a dead man at least he can see the truth clearly. In this decision John Harmon steps outside of himself and chooses a type of life that denies his real identity. Harmon's decision is a symbolic kind of suicide, a rejection of the possibilities of selfhood. The strange juxtaposition of death as a more desirable state of existence (or nonexistence) than life is a parallel to the same juxtaposition as it is found in the little game that Lizzie, Jenny Wren, and Riah play in the roof garden above Pubsey and Co. "Come up and be dead," they repeatedly shout to one another.

John Harmon's decision to avoid his own inheritance because he mistrusts himself and those around him is really indecision, and, as he lives with it, it weighs on him as "a gathering and deepening anxiety" (IV, 12).

Finally, he is forced to confront his own destiny and accept his responsibilities. As Mrs. Boffin observes, "It looks as if the old man's spirit had found rest at last. . . . And as if his money had turned bright again, after a long, long rust in the dark, and was at last beginning to sparkle in the sunlight?" (IV, 13). By facing all the responsibilities of being himself, John Harmon defeats the corruptive power of money in this darkened and decayed world. Eugene Wrayburn's problem of selfhood is even more acute than that of John Harmon. Whereas Harmon understands too well the problem involved in being himself, Wrayburn does not understand himself at all and refuses to make any effort toward changing the situation. In a conversation with Mortimer about Lizzie, Eugene displays his utter inability to understand himself:

> "Eugene, do you design to capture and desert this girl?"
> "My dear fellow, no."
> "Do you design to marry her?"
> "My dear fellow, no."
> "Do you design to pursue her?"
> "My dear fellow, I don't design anything. I have no design whatever. I am incapable of designs. If I conceived a design, I should speedily abandon it, exhausted by the operation."(II, 6)

Because it pertains directly to Lizzie, this is the most important of a number of conversations between Mortimer and Eugene in which the latter consistently displays a total ignorance of, as well as a lack of, concern for himself, his actions, and his motives. Eugene has actually given up trying to figure himself out:

> You know that when I became enough of a man to find myself an embodied conundrum, I bored myself to the last degree trying to find out what I meant. . . . The old nursery form runs, "Riddle-me-riddle-me-ree, p'raps you can't tell me what this may be?" My reply runs, "No. Upon my life I can't." (II, 6)

Eugene's aimlessness and lack of identity negate any possibility of action on his part. He cannot make choices because he has no criteria on which to decide. He cannot initiate any sort of moral action because he does not yet know whether or not he values morality. In the early stages of the novel, Eugene's total lack of concern for self freezes him into a state of motionless boredom.

Bored as he may be, Eugene Wrayburn still finds himself in conscious but hesitant rebellion against the "essence" that his father has arbitrarily determined and imposed on him. As Eugene describes it,

> M.R.F. having always in the clearest manner provided (as he calls it) for his children by pre-arranging from the hour of birth of each, and sometimes from an earlier period, what the devoted little victim's calling and course in life should be, M.R.F. pre-arranged for myself that I was to be the barrister I am (with the slight addition of an enormous practice, which has not accrued), and also the married man I am not. (I, 12)

Eugene, in his awareness of the need to assert his own "existence," must define himself in relation to that specific past form, social convention, and caste that has governed his whole life.

Throughout *Our Mutual Friend*, Eugene, "embodied conundrum" though he may be to himself, repeatedly shows a sensitivity and moral consciousness that sets him apart from the other members of upper-class "Society." At the Veneering dinner table, as Mortimer Lightwood reaches that point in the story of "The Man from Somewhere" in which John Harmon's sister dies, only Mortimer and Eugene share a "kindred touch" (*OMF*, I, 2) of feeling for the reality of the story. Later in this same evening, when Charley Hexam lets drop a few "words slightingly of his sister," Eugene takes "him roughly enough by the chin" (I, 3) in a spontaneous reaction against the ingratitude the boy has displayed.

But more important than these slight manifestations of his moral consciousness is Eugene's immediate awareness, after having seen her only once, of his moral involvement with Lizzie Hexam. As he and Mortimer sit in the Six Jolly Fellowship Porters waiting to witness the "taking" of Gaffer Hexam, Eugene expresses his spontaneous feeling of involvement with Lizzie:

> It was little more than a glimpse we had of her that last time, and yet I almost see her waiting by the fire tonight. Do you feel like a dark combination of traitor and pickpocket when you think of that girl? (I, 13)

Eugene's sense of involvement indicates the awakening of his latent capacities for feeling and for moral responsibility. As his relationship with Lizzie grows, his sense of moral responsibility undergoes a severe test.

In his relationship with Lizzie Hexam there are two alternatives open to Eugene Wrayburn, which Mortimer can see clearly but which Eugene himself does not wish to acknowledge. Either he can marry her or he can

pursue her and make her his mistress. All of the people who observe the
growing relationship between Eugene and Lizzie—Mortimer, Mr. Riah,
Bradley Headstone, and, especially, her brother Charley—naturally con-
clude that Eugene plans to "ruin" Lizzie. As Steven Marcus has noted, sexual
morality in the Victorian age was really not that much different from that
of any other period of English history, especially in regard to sexual
relationships between upper-class "gentlemen" and lower-class or servant-
class girls. Historically, all of the women of the lower classes were "fair game"
for London's "gents."[4]

Eugene Wrayburn and Lizzie Hexam are moving toward involvement
in precisely this sort of relationship: it is a type of liaison commonplace in
their time but toward which Eugene reacts in a strikingly uncommon
manner. He consciously refuses to seduce her. His reaction to Lizzie Hexam
serves to illustrate Marcus's evaluation of "how immensely humane a project
the Victorian novel was, how it broadened out the circle of humanity, and
how it represented the effort of Victorian England at its best."[5] The Victorian
novel was a mirror of public opinion in its reactions away from the standard-
ized motives and events of pornography. Pornography surely brings "a blush
into the cheek of the young person" (OMF, I, 11), but it also consistently
presents a dehumanized world. Women are portrayed as mere objects,
machines built only for the purpose of sexual gratification, while men exist
as beings devoid of any type of consciousness except animal passion.
Pornography, more than any form of literature, exalts the precedence of
essence over existence.

The one redeeming quality of Eugene Wrayburn's aimless and indeci-
sive existence is his inability to deny Lizzie Hexam's right to be treated as a
human being. At times in the novel Eugene takes great pride in being "so
faithful to her, as it seemed, when her own stock was faithless," but, because
he does not understand his own motives, he fully believes that his faithfulness
must be qualified. He knows "what an immense advantage, what an overpow-
ering influence" (OMF, II, 15) he holds over Lizzie, but he cannot bring
himself to exploit his power. Eugene Wrayburn is, indeed, to paraphrase
Matthew Arnold, "wandering between two worlds" where the dead power of
the past is contending with the powerlessness of the present to give birth to
the future. Mortimer thinks he understands Eugene and says, "you know you
do not really care for her." But Eugene answers, "I don't know that. I must ask
you not to say that, as if we took it for granted" (III, 10). Eugene is slowly
moving toward the understanding of that "embodied conundrum" that is
himself and this understanding will bring him to the crisis of his life.

That crisis occurs when Eugene finds Lizzie at the paper mill in the country. The two of them walk by the river and Eugene tries to seduce her. Twice Lizzie feels his arm "stealing around her waist" and she employs all of the clichés of the sexual jargon of the Victorian novel to defend herself. She charges that Eugene has come only to put her "to shame!" She states that she is "quite cut off" from him "in honour." She implores him:

> Remember that I have no protector near me, unless I have one in your noble heart. Respect my good name. If you can feel towards me, in one particular, as you might if I was a lady, give me the full claims of a lady upon your generous behaviour. (IV, 6)

From all of her pleading Wrayburn learns two things. He sees that she, too, thinks she understands him and his motives, just as Mortimer, old Riah, Bradley Headstone, and Charley Hexam think they do. He also realizes that he has "gained a wonderful power over her" (IV, 6).

The whole seduction scene is modulated between the dialogic consciousness that exists in each of the participating characters. Lizzie is deeply in love with Eugene, and yet she feels that his true motives are only sexual. And Eugene is also divided in his reaction to Lizzie. When he sees her attitude toward him he feels, "wearily out of sorts with one Wrayburn who cuts a sorry figure" (IV, 6), but he also exults in the power he holds over her. Both characters exist, then, in a state of divided consciousness, but before this scene ends both of them must choose which impulse to follow. Lizzie makes the typical choice of resignation as she reveals her love and then begs her lover to leave her forever. Eugene, however, makes the atypical choice. He refuses to press his advantage and he watches her as she leaves, walking alone through the soft, pliant grass in the gathering darkness.

As the scene ends, Eugene, in a kind of Shakespearean soliloquy, expresses his dilemma: "Out of the question to marry her, . . . and out of the question to leave her. The crisis!"(IV, 6). But he is wrong. The crisis has already passed and he has already conquered his passion and affirmed his love for Lizzie. In refusing to seduce her, he has recognized her right to humanity and bridged the gap between the classes. Thus, Headstone's brutal attack, which occurs at this very moment, is a highly ironic event. At the very moment when Eugene establishes moral order within his own consciousness by affirming his own and Lizzie's humanity, he is almost beaten to death by Headstone, the representative of moral anarchy and heartlessness in the world of the novel.

Finally, the love Eugene and Lizzie can now openly express toward each other restores him to health and he is able to say "of the healthful music of my pulse what Hamlet said of his. My blood is up, but wholesomely up" (IV, 16). Eugene chooses to be. He no longer has any regard for what "Society" might think; his only concern is for the affirmation of the love that exists between himself and Lizzie. As he expresses these feelings, the "glow that shone upon him as he spoke the words so irradiated his features, that he looked, for the time, as though he had never been mutilated" (IV, 16).

Our Mutual Friend ends with as unlikely a "Voice of Society" as Twemlow. After all is done, the conversation at the Veneering dinner table, always an exercise in hindsight, focuses on Eugene and Lizzie's marriage:

> Twemlow has the air of being ill at ease, as he takes his hand from his forehead and replies, "I am disposed to think," says he, "that this is a question of the feelings of a gentleman."
>
> "A gentleman can have no feelings who contracts such a marriage," flushes Podsnap.
>
> "Pardon me, sir," says Twemlow, rather less mildly than usual, "I don't agree with you. If this gentleman's feelings of gratitude, of respect, of admiration, and affection, induced him (as I presume they did) to marry this lady—"This lady!" echoes Podsnap.
>
> "Sir," returns Twemlow, with his wristbands bristling a little, "you repeat the word; I repeat the word. This lady, what else would you call her, if the gentleman were present?" . . .
>
> "I say," resumes Twemlow, "if such feelings on the part of this gentleman induced this gentleman to marry this lady, I think he is the greater gentleman for the action, and makes her the greater lady." (IV, The Last)

Twemlow is an "end-symbol" or "coda" that, like the fallen sheepfold in Wordsworth's "Michael," the river Oxus in Matthew Arnold's *Sohrab and Rustum*, or the Tyrian trader in "The Scholar-Gipsy," lingers expressively after the action of the novel has ended and punctuates the meaning of that action. Throughout the novel, Twemlow is the most insignificant of all the different pieces of furniture in the Veneering dining room, and he has never changed; through the whole course of the action, he has continued to perform his object-like function in the strictly systematized world of "Society." At the very end, however, he does change. He arises, directly opposes the implacable Podsnap, and, almost easily, conquers him, merely by asserting the value of good and true emotions in the world. The terminal emphasis that Dickens gives to Twemlow in *Our Mutual Friend* is the strongest affirmation he can give to his theme of the value of personal salvation. If the very least, most insignificant member of the world can redeem himself and assert his own existence this forcibly, then the world is not "dark" at all, and all of mankind can look to the future "gaily" (IV, The Last).

SIX

Dickens's Philosophy of History

Major Swindon: "What will History say?"
Gen. Burgoyne: "History, sir, will tell lies as usual."
— George Bernard Shaw,
The Devil's Disciple, Act III

Never, never underestimate the power of corruption to rewrite history.
— Oliver Stone, Filmmaker

History is just a gigantic whitewash after all, and we shouldn't accept it.
— Mudrooroo, Australian Aboriginal Writer

While George Bernard Shaw's character, Gentlemanly Johnny Burgoyne in *The Devil's Disciple*, writes off history in the tone of his author's legendary devil-may-care cynicism, and Oliver Stone subverts history from the perspective of a true believer (and proliferator) of deeply entrenched conspiracy theories, and Mudrooroo speaks from the conviction of two hundred years of Imperialist-driven racial oppression, their statements all represent the essential suspicion of Traditional History that has fostered the New Historicist consciousness.

New Historicism is a dialogic correction of the course of the historical consciousness. It is not revisionist because it does not attempt to recast history from a single point of vantage, economic or otherwise. Rather, New Historicism is an approach to history that attempts to counteract the sorts of omissions and abuses and tunnel visions that Traditional History made. It is an attempt to "thicken"[1] the historical consciousness, to fill out the extant story of history with new, neglected, suppressed voices and to interpret history in terms of the dialogic relationship between these new texts and the extant historical texts.

One of the contributions that the novel genre has made over the short three hundred years of its history is to serve as exactly this sort of corrective to the power-centered texts of Traditional History. More often than not, literature, whether it takes the form of poetry, theatre, or prose fiction, is written from the margins; even if it is written from the inside of society or the inside of a power-centered institution—such as a social class (the aristocracy who funded Pope's patronage), a religion (such as Protestantism in Swift's case), or a profession (such as the law in Fielding's case)—it is suspicious, subversive, often satiric or intent on exposing, correcting, reforming. Thus, one great advantage that a novelist writing historically has is that art is not subject to the same power-centered biases, political agendas, and distortions that plague the composition of Traditional History.

Traditional History, more often than not, has functioned like Empire. Traditionally, those in power have dictated history's composition. Because those in power have always controlled the documents on which Traditional History has been traditionally based, the power center has been able to control what texts are read, what voices are heard by the historians. In the past, history, as controlled by those at the centers of power, has been able to suppress the voices of the marginalized in the same manner that Imperialism was able to rule over subject peoples and turn whole indigenous populations into slaves. Traditional History has composed a narrow narrative. The New Historicist strives to "thicken" that narrative, to find those voices that can show another side of the extant narratives that have been long accepted because they were the only ones available.

In *Bleak House*, Dickens seems acutely aware not only of the heteroglossic "thickening" goal of the New Historicist project, but also of the interpretive responsibility that the New Historicist brings to each text included in his or her history. "What connexion can there have been," Dickens writes, "between many people in the innumerable histories of this world, who, from the opposite sides of great gulfs, have, nevertheless, been very curiously brought together." In the nineteenth century, other nonprofessional, untraditional historians composed new, adversary readings of Traditional History. Wordsworth and Carlyle both articulated new voices and presented new readings of the French Revolution. Byron and Thackeray offered utterly dialogic views of the Battle of Waterloo as seen from the vantage of the noncombatants. But of all those who in the nineteenth century sought to "thicken" the narrative of history, Dickens, especially in the realm of social history, was the most attuned to the marginalized voices (in characters like

Poor Jo in *Bleak House* or Daniel Doyce in *Little Dorrit*), the suppressed documents (such as those buried in Krook's shop in *Bleak House* or in the Harmon Dust Heaps in *Our Mutual Friend*), and the tremendously complex networks of dialogic oppositions within the nuanced and intricately sub-classed Victorian society.

As a novelistic social historian, Dickens firmly grounds his vision in two of the major objectives of the New Historicist project. First, across his canon he is intent on revealing the social history of the Victorian Age by liberating all of the multivarious voices from all levels of society, from both the centers and the margins, who can describe that history. But second, he also, by means of historical patterns of metaphoric representation (such as the symbolic motif of shipwreck in all its evolving meanings) or historicist characterizations (such as the evolving use of the George Barnwell stereotype as a paradigm for the marginalized working class), develops a dialogic philosophy of history. That philosophy actively participates in the general spirit of reform with an eye to England's future that characterized the social, political, intellectual, and literary history of the Victorian Age.

In *The Order of Things*, Michel Foucault presents a brief history of history that culminates in the nineteenth century and explains why the New Historicist impulses toward the "thickening" of the historical narrative were germinating in that time. "Thus the old word 'history' changes its value," Foucault begins. He then proceeds to define those changes over time up to the Victorian Age:

> the historian, for the Greeks, was indeed the individual who sees and who recounts from the starting point of his sight, it has not always been so in our culture. Indeed, it was at a relatively late date, on the threshold of the Classical age, that he assumed—or resumed—this role. Until the mid-seventeenth century the historian's task was to establish the great compilation of documents and signs—of everything, throughout the world, that might form a mark, as it were. It was the historian's responsibility to restore to language all the words that had been buried. His existence was defined not so much by what he saw as by what he retold, by a secondary speech that pronounced afresh so many words that had been muffled.

In the sense of Foucault's first definition of a historian, then, Dickens, in his heteroglossic liberation of those who don't have a voice or whose words are muffled in Victorian society, is returning to the original historical project as defined by Foucault.

But Foucault proceeds with his history of history:

> The Classical age gives history a quite different meaning; that of
> undertaking a meticulous examination of things themselves for the first
> time, and then of transcribing what it has gathered in smooth, neutral-
> ized, and faithful words.

This second evolutionary step in the historical process signals the involvement of the historian in the act of interpretation, in finding meaning in the
things of the world and expressing that meaning in language. But then another
change occurred

> at the end of the eighteenth century in the classification of words,
> languages, roots, documents, records—in short, in the constitution of
> a whole environment of history in which the nineteenth century was
> to rediscover, after this pure tabulation of things, the renewed possibil-
> ity of talking about words.

The result of this three-step evolution from the Greek's collecting of
historical documents to the eighteenth century's ordering of historical
documents under the principles of words, language—"the establishment of
archives, the reorganization of libraries, the drawing up of catalogues,
indexes, and inventories"—to "the historians of the nineteenth century" who
"were to undertake the creation of a history that could at last be 'true'—in
other words, liberated from Classical rationality, from its ordering and
theodicy: [was] a history restored to the irruptive violence of time."[2]

This history of "irruptive violence" is exactly the sort of history that
Dickens undertakes to write in his fiction. From below, from outside, from
the margins, he is trying to "thicken" the historical narrative of his time by
making it truer, more inclusive. In doing so, he rather clearly defines himself
as a historian and his Victorian Age as located at a fulcrum point of the
historical consciousness. But not only are Dickens's novels historical, they
are also metahistorical.

Just as Foucault takes the opportunity to present a "history of history,"
Dickens's novels are about the nature of history itself. Not only do his novels
deal with historical events, personages, social settings, and issues, they also
analyze how history works, what history contributes to culture and society,
how history enlightens us about ourselves, and how history gives a culture,
a society, direction for the future. Within his historical fiction, Dickens is
also a historiographer, a metahistorian, who extrapolates the meanings of
history and articulates its philosophical ideas. Every Dickens novel contem-

plates the nature of the historical consciousness and attempts to formulate a self-reflexive philosophy of history.

"One of my principle aims," Hayden White wrote in his preface to *Metahistory*, "has been to establish the uniquely poetic elements in historiography and philosophy of history."[3] White's interest is epistemological. His focus is on "the possible ways of conceiving history."[4] Dickens's novels consistently demonstrate this same concern for the "poetic elements" of historical style and for the formulation of a clear philosophy of history. Just as White's *Metahistory* concerns itself with defining and analyzing the agendas emplotted within the style of the great nineteenth-century histories, Dickens's philosophy of history involves finding extended metaphors and characterizational paradigms to embody his vision of history as a current of ideas flowing steadily out of the past toward the future.

More acutely than any historian of his epoch, Dickens's philosophy of history is attuned to and formulated from the temper of his times, his familiarity with his readership, the voices of all the age groups, genders, levels, and classes of his society. As a historian, Dickens knows exactly what books his readers are reading, what plays they are attending, what news they are reading daily in the newspapers, what language they are using to express their joy, dissatisfaction, and curiosity, what strategies for social survival they are employing, what prejudices and charities they are supporting. Dickens did not just walk the streets of London at night for post-prandial exercise. He prowled those streets stalking the cultural information that would inform his social histories.

But Dickens never limited his historicist vision only to the action of presentist social reform. He was most definitely concerned with the social abuses of his age and intent on exposing and correcting them. However, he was simultaneously and consistently also intent on formulating a philosophy of history—a way of ordering experience and acting in social humanist terms that would guide the Victorians into the postindustrial age of the twentieth century.

In Dickens's philosophy of history, the realism of his representation of the social world is always dialogically complimented by his optimism, his "light" rather than "dark" vision. His novels express the firm belief that the world can be perfected, changed, can evolve into a brighter future. Much as Tennyson does in his prophetic poem "Locksley Hall," Dickens actually offers his readers a vision of that future near the end of his most historical novel, *A Tale of Two Cities:*

> I see a beautiful city and a brilliant people rising from this abyss, and,
> in their struggles to be truly free, in their triumphs and defeats, through
> long, long years to come, I see the evil of this time and of the previous
> time of which this is the natural birth, gradually making expiation for
> itself and wearing out. (III, 15)

A novel that began in a dialogic present—"It was the best of times, it was the worst of times"—ends in a bright vision of the future. Dickens has accomplished a full dialectical work of historical fiction.

Dickens's philosophy of history is, above all, positive, grounded in the positive concepts of perfectibility and benevolence as articulated in the eighteenth century by philosophers such as Lord Shaftesbury, Bishop Butler, and William Godwin (all of whom stood in opposition to Thomas Hobbes) and popularized by the eighteenth-century novelists Fielding, Goldsmith, Sterne, and, again, Godwin. But Dickens was not a Pollyanna optimist or Romantic transcendentalist (like Wordsworth or Shelley). He was a social realist who clearly saw the dangers that were the byproducts of the Industrial Revolution—dehumanization, rampant materialism, interior marginalization within the middle and working classes—and moved to protect his society against those dangers not only by exposing them, but also by offering a new agenda of personal humanism as an alternative to those dangerous ways of conceiving history. Dickens's philosophy of history saw the Victorian Age (including his own works of social realist history) as a fulcrum, a balance point between the past and the future.

If Dickens's philosophy of history, then, could be captured in a catchphrase, he might be characterized as a "realist evolutionary humanist," a social historian of the marginalized who is capable of existing in the current of constant flux and embracing progressive change while never losing sight of the importance of the individual's power for good. In this sense, his sense of history is much like his contemporary Charles Darwin's sense of human evolution. Thus, while Dickens was always quite aware of the power of the past, he was also acutely conscious of his existence as a historical novelist caught in the powerful pull of the future. In his novels, he consistently expressed his desire to participate in the forward movement of that powerful future force. In other words, he was powerfully drawn to the Loadstone Rock of history.

When Dominick LaCapra described philosopher/critic Mikhail Bakhtin's attitude toward history, he might have been describing Dickens's own philosophy of history. He wrote of Bakhtin's basic conviction . . . that the context of folk culture and festive popular celebration "reveal the deepest meaning of the historical process." The festive, carnivalesque attitude shapes time to its own image as a destructive, regenerative force that opens the dialectic at both ends and supplements it with the ambivalent power of laughter.[5]

Dickens's night walks served as his vehicle into the Victorian version of Bakhtin's carnival world.

Dickens's philosophy of history is always dialogic. For every shipwreck there is a rescue, for every treacherous Loadstone Rock there is a lighthouse, for every marginalized worker there is a member of the struggling middle class willing to listen to that worker's voice and act on that worker's ideas. Above all, Dickens's philosophy of history is always open to change, to evolution, to perfectibility. His Victorian Age is represented as a carnivalesque world in which the grand play of human interaction is always a progress toward a frightening yet invigorating future.

Out of the postindustrial Revolution squalor, exploitation, materialism, and class snobbery that Dickens portrayed as the diseases of his age arose a philosophy of history focused on the existential individual who is capable of curing all those diseases by means of his own movement out of darkness into enlightenment. For Dickens, history was a narrative of awakening. So many of his characters are like the troglodytes emerging from Plato's cave, seeing the clear light of reality for the first time, and embracing it in all its possibility.

Notes

CHAPTER ONE

1. William Wordsworth, "Preface" to *Lyrical Ballads*, 2nd. Ed. (1800).

2. Mikhail Bakhtin in *The Dialogic Imagination* (Austin, TX: University of Texas Press, 1981), 272, writes that "the authentic environment of an utterance . . . is dialogized heteroglossia, anonymous and social as language, but simultaneously concrete, filled with specific context and accented as an individual utterance." Dominick LaCapra in *Rethinking Intellectual History* (Ithaca, NY: Cornell University Press, 1983), 312, defines Bakhtin's concept of "heteroglossia" more clearly as "the objective condition of language marked by a plurality of perspectives and value-laden, ideological practices that are in challenging contact with one another."

3. Michel Foucault, *Discipline and Punish: The Birth of the Prison*, trans. Alan Sheridan (New York: Pantheon, 1978), 129.

4. Quoted in "Doctorow's City," *The New Yorker* (June 27/July 4, 1994): 41.

5. Joseph W. Childers, "History, Totality, Opposition: The New Historicism and *Little Dorrit*," *Dickens Quarterly* 6, no. 4 (December 1989), 150.

6. Dominick LaCapra, *History and Criticism* (Ithaca, NY: Cornell University Press, 1985), 18-19.

7. For an extended reading of *The Official Story* in these terms, see William J. Palmer, *The Films of the Eighties: A Social History* (Carbondale and Edwardsville, IL: Southern Illinois University Press, 1993), 147-49.

8. Susan R. Horton, "Swivellers and Snivellers: Competing Epistemologies in *The Old Curiosity Shop*," *Dickens Quarterly* 7, no. 1 (March 1990), 212.

9. John W. Kronik, "Editor's Column" to *PMLA* special issue "The Theory of Literary History," *PMLA: Publications of the Modern Language Association* 107, no. 1 (January 1992): 9.

10. Stephen Bann, "The Sense of the Past: Image, Text, and Object in the Formation of Historical Consciousness in Nineteenth-Century Britain," in *The New Historicism*, ed. H. Aram Visser (New York: Routledge, 1989), 102.

11. Quoted by Bann in *The New Historicism*, 103.

12. Ibid., 103.

13. LaCapra, *History and Criticism*, 113.

14. Robert Newson, *Dickens on the Romantic Side of Familiar Things: Bleak House and the Novel Tradition* (New York: Columbia University Press, 1977), 18.

15. Jonathan Arac, "The Struggle for the Cultural Heritage: Christina Stead Refunctions Charles Dickens and Mark Twain," in *The New Historicism*, 127.

16. Quoted by Arac in *The New Historicism*, 127.

17. Hayden White, *Tropics of Discourse: Essays in Cultural Criticism* (Baltimore: Johns Hopkins University Press, 1978), 1.

18. Marlon Ross, "Contingent Predilections: The Newest Historicisms and the Question of Method," *The Centennial Review* 34, no. 4 (fall 1990): 485.

19. Ross, "Contingent Predilections," 492.

20. Theodore B. Leinwand, "Negotiation and New Historicism," *PMLA: The Publications of the Modern Language Association* 105, no. 3 (May 1990): 477.

21. Robert Garis, *The Dickens Theatre: A Reassessment of the Novels* (London: Oxford University Press, 1965), 13.

22. Robert B. Partlow, Jr., ed., *Dickens the Craftsman: Strategies of Presentation* (Carbondale, IL: Southern Illinois University Press, 1970), xxi.

23. J. Hillis Miller, *Charles Dickens: The World of His Novels* (Bloomington, IN: Indiana University Press, 1969; reprint of 1958 Harvard University Press edition), 191.

24. Quoted by Barry Paris, "Maximum Expression," *American Film* (October 1989): 32.

25. H. M. Daleski, *Dickens and the Art of Analogy* (New York: Schocken Books, 1970), 32.

26. Mario Vargas Llosa, "Updating Karl Popper," *PMLA: The Publications of the Modern Language Association* 105, no. 5 (October 1990): 1022.

27. Joseph Conrad, the Stein section of *Lord Jim* (New York: Norton, 1968).

CHAPTER TWO

1.   Albert Camus, *Lyrical and Critical Essays*, ed. Phillip Thody, trans. Ellen Conroy Kennedy (New York: Alfred A. Knopf, 1968), 199.

2.   See T. A. Jackson, *Charles Dickens: The Progress of a Radical* (London: Lawrence and Wishart, 1937); Jack Lindsay, *Charles Dickens: A Biographical and Critical Study* (New York: Philosophical Library, 1950).

3.   Joseph Gold, *Charles Dickens: Radical Moralist* (Minneapolis: University of Minnesota Press, 1972).

4.   See J. Hillis Miller, *Charles Dickens: The World of His Novels* (Bloomington, IN: Indiana University Press, 1969; reprint of 1958 Harvard University Press edition).

5.   See Edmund Wilson, *The Wound and the Bow* (Cambridge, MA: Harvard University Press, 1941), 40; Lionel Stevenson, "Dickens's Dark Novels 1851-1857," *Sewanee Review*, 51 (summer 1943); 398.

6.   Edgar Johnson, *Charles Dickens: His Tragedy and Triumph* (Boston: Little, Brown and Co., 1951).

7. I have elsewhere discussed the positive images of light/imagination/love in "*Hard Times:* A Dickens Fable of Personal Salvation," *The Dalhousie Review*, 52 (spring 1972).

8. Taylor Stoehr, *The Dreamer's Stance* (Ithaca, NY: Cornell University Press, 1965), 98ff. Robert A. Donovan, one year later, makes an even stronger assertion of the rightness of the "dark" novel descriptor in *The Shaping Vision: Imagination in the English Novel from Defoe to Dickens* (Ithaca, NY: Cornell University Press, 1966), 208.

9. For a discussion of Jarndyce and Jarndyce as an image of the Dickens world in *Bleak House,* see Miller, *Charles Dickens: The World of His Novels*, 196; and for the cure of the absurdity of that world see ibid., 206 and 217.

10. Stevenson, "Dickens's Dark Novels 1851-1857," 398.

11. J. Hillis Miller, "The Geneva School," *The Virginia Quarterly Review*, 43 (summer 1967): 465.

12. Humphry House, *The Dickens World* (London: Oxford University Press, 1941), 40.

13. Louis Cazamian, *Le roman social en Angleterre* (Paris: H. Didier, 1934), I, 237.

14. Ibid., 240.

15. From Lord Shaftesbury's preface to his edition of Whichcote's *Select Sermons* (1698), as quoted in Basil Willey, *The Eighteenth-Century Background*, (London: Chatto and Windus, 1946), 59.

16. Anthony Ashley Cooper, Third Earl of Shaftesbury, *Characteristics of Men, Manners, Opinions, Times* (London, 1711), I, 115-16.

17. William Godwin, *Enquiry Concerning Political Justice*, ed. F. E. L. Priestley (Toronto: University of Toronto Press, 1946), 436. Hereinafter, all quotations to this particular text will be noted by page number in parentheses within the text.

18. See Philip Collins, "Dickens's Reading," *The Dickensian*, 60 (autumn 1964): 143; and Edgar Johnson, *Charles Dickens: His Tragedy and Triumph*, II, 1130.

19. Quoted by George H. Ford in *Dickens and His Readers* (Princeton, NJ: Princeton University Press, 1955), 151.

20. The most famous statement of Dickens's acquaintance with eighteenth-century literature is the oft quoted passage in Chapter IV of *David Copperfield*. Reiterations of and additions to this list can be found in Philip Collins, "Dickens's Reading," 138, and in Edgar Johnson, *Charles Dickens: His Tragedy and Triumph*, I, 270 and II, 1131. Earle Davis, *The Flint and the Flame* (Columbia, MO: University of Missouri Press, 1963), 12, also adds a name that is important for this study, William Godwin.

21. Laurence Sterne, "Philanthropy Recommended," in *Sterne*, ed. Douglas Grant (London: Rupert Hart-Davis, 1950), 653.
22. Henry Fielding, *Joseph Andrews*, Ch. 1. Hereinafter, all quotations will be noted by abbreviated title and chapter number within the text.
23. Laurence Sterne, *Tristram Shandy*, Ch. XXXIV. Hereinafter, all quotations will be noted by abbreviated title, book number, and chapter number within the text.
24. Steven Marcus, *Dickens: From Pickwick to Dombey* (New York: Basic Books, 1965), 29-30.
25. Joyce Cary, *The Horse's Mouth* (New York: Harper and Row, 1958), 4.
26. Tobias Smollett, *Roderick Random*, Ch. XV. Hereinafter, all quotations will be noted by abbreviated title and chapter number within the text.
27. William Godwin, *Caleb Williams*, Postscript. Hereinafter, all quotations will be noted by abbreviated title and chapter number within the text.

CHAPTER THREE

1. Keith Huntress, ed., *Narratives of Shipwrecks and Disasters, 1586-1860* (Ames, IO: Iowa State University Press, 1974), x.
2. Ibid., xviii.
3. Ibid., xx.
4. John Fowles, *Shipwrecks* (Boston: Little, Brown and Co., 1975), 8.
5. Ibid., 7.
6. Huntress, *Narratives of Shipwrecks*, xix.
7. R. H. Thornton, *British Shipping* (Cambridge, UK: Cambridge University Press, 1959), 49.
8. Fowles, *Shipwrecks*, 9.
9. Thornton, *British Shipping*, 37-39.
10. Ibid., 215.
11. Fowles, *Shipwrecks*, 7.
12. Thornton, *British Shipping*, 7.
13. Ibid., 29.
14. Francis E. Hyde, *Liverpool and the Mersey: The Growth of a Port, 1700-1970* (Newton Abbot, UK: David & Charles, 1971), 40-41.
15. Erich W. Zimmerman, *Ocean Shipping* (New York: Prentice-Hall, 1923), 223-24.
16. Ibid., 230.
17. Ibid., 226

18. Quoted in Ibid., 223.
19. M. M. Beeman, *Lloyd's of London: An Outline* (Kingswood, UK: Windmill Press, 1937), 14-15.
20. Zimmerman, *Ocean Shipping*, 378.
21. Ibid., 363.
22. Ibid., 355.
23. Quoted in Beeman, *Lloyd's of London*, 6.
24. Sir Joseph Broodbank, *History of the Port of London*, 2 vols. (London: Daniel O'Connor, 1921), 100.
25. Hyde, *Liverpool and the Mersey*, 8.
26. Broodbank, *History of the Port of London*, 100.
27. Thornton, *British Shipping*, 144.
28. Beeman, *History of the Port of London*, 15.
29. Richard Altick, *The English Common Reader* (Chicago: University of Chicago Press, 1957), 344.
30. Huntress, *Narratives of Shipwrecks*, xii.
31. Altick, *The English Common Reader*, 21.
32. Huntress, *Narratives of Shipwrecks*, x.
33. Altick, *The English Common Reader*, 119, 218.
34. Ibid., 269.
35. Ibid., 268-69.
36. Ibid., 220.
37. Ibid., 217.
38. Ibid., 160.
39. Ibid., 63.
40. Ibid., 95.
41. Ibid., 159.
42. Ibid., 169.
43. Fowles, *Shipwrecks*, 9-10.
44. Huntress, *Narratives of Shipwrecks*, xiii-xiv.
45. Muriel Spark, *The Prime of Miss Jean Brodie* (New York: Dell, 1961), Ch. VI.
46. Other critics have circled and briefly touched on the subjects and issues concerning both Victorian culture and the novels of Charles Dickens that are raised in this essay. Garrett Stewart, in "The Secret Life of Death in Dickens," *Dickens Studies Annual* 11 (1983): 177-207, discusses the motif of drowning in *The Old Curiosity Shop, Dombey and Son*, and *A Tale of Two Cities*. Martin Postle, in "Dickens and The Fighting Temeraire," *Dickensian* 81 (summer 1985): 95-102, talks of the eighteenth-century affinities for ships of both Dickens and J.M.W.

Turner. E. Pearlman, in "David Copperfield Dreams of Drowning, in *American Imago* 28 (winter 1971): 391-403, and reprinted in *The Practice of Psychoanalytic Criticism*, edited by Leonard Tennenbaum (Detroit, MI: Wayne State University Press, 1976), takes a Freudian pass at the novel that I approach from the viewpoint of metafictional self-reflexivity and social consciousness. G.W. Kennedy, in "The Uses of Solitude: Dickens and *Robinson Crusoe*," *Victorian Newsletter* 52 (fall 1977): 25-30, also deals, in a more limited context, with Dickens's use of his favorite shipwreck narrative. Peter I. DeRose, in "The Symbolic Sea of *David Copperfield*," *Proceedings of Conferences of College Teachers of English of Texas* 41 (1976): 44-47, also discusses the sea imagery in *David Copperfield*. Janet Larson, in "Apocalyptic Style in *Little Dorrit*," *Dickens Quarterly* 1, no. 2 (1984): 41-49, analyzes the Dickensian style in much more depth than is attempted in this essay with the emphasis on its use of metaphoric language in *Little Dorrit*. Her essay looks at the structural movement of Dickens's plots, characters, and imagery toward consistent apocalyptic resolutions. All of these sources have noted similar Dickensian preoccupations with the sea, shipwrecks, and apocalyptic resolutions.

47. *Household Words: A Weekly Journal. 1850-1859, Conducted by Charles Dickens* (London: Bradley and Evans). All references to this will hereinafter be noted as "*HW*" in parentheses within the text. This reference is to (*HW*, 7 December 1850).

48. George P. Landow, *Images of Crisis: Literary Iconography* (London: Routledge and Kegan Paul, 1982).

49. Lionel Stevenson, "Dickens's Dark Novels," *Sewanee Review* 51 (summer 1943), 398-409.

50. All of the following references to the shipwreck scene in *David Copperfield* are, unless otherwise noted, from Chapter LV.

51. W.W. Watt, ed. "Introduction" to *Hard Times* (New York: Holt, 1958), xxxii.

52. Recast, the argument of the following three and one-half paragraphs originally appeared in my essay, "*Hard Times*: A Dickens Fable of Personal Salvation," *Dalhousie Review* 52, no. 1 (1972): 67-77.

53. Landow, *Images of Crisis*, 23.

54. Ibid., 114.

55. Ibid., 15.

56. All quotes in this paragraph and the two paragraphs that follow are taken from (*TTC*, II, 21).

57. Joseph Conrad, *Lord Jim* (New York: Norton, 1968), Chapter 20.

58. If the traumatic event of the Staplehurst train wreck hadn't occurred so late in his life (1865), perhaps train wrecks or lethal train accidents like that in *Dombey and Son* might have been a more prominent metaphorical choice. Dickens, however, by more than just the evidence of this essay, was much more comfortable with late eighteenth- and early nineteenth-century images than with postindustrial Revolution images such as the railway in *Dombey and Son* and the machines in *Hard Times.*

CHAPTER FOUR

1. All quotations from *The London Merchant* or *The History of George Barnwell* by George Lillo are from *Six Eighteenth-Century Plays*, ed. John Harold Wilson (Boston: Houghton, Mifflin Co, 1963) and will hereafter be noted by "*TLM*" and the corresponding Act and Scene in parentheses within the text. This speech is from IV, ii.

2. John Harold Wilson, "Introduction" to *The London Merchant* in *Six Eighteenth-Century Plays*, 181.

3. Claude M. Newlin, "The Theatre and the Apprentices," *Modern Language Notes* 45 (spring 1930): 453.

4. William H. McBurney, "Introduction" to *The London Merchant* in the *Regents Restoration Drama Series* (London: E. Arnold Ltd., 1965), xii-xiii.

5. Ernest Bernbaum, quoted in McBurney, *Regents Restoration Drama Series*, xiii.

6. Sir A.W. Ward, "Introduction" to *The London Merchant* and *Fatal Curiosity* in the *Belles Lettres Series*, (London: E. Arnold Ltd., 1967), xiii; also quoted by Newlin, "The Theatre and the Apprentices," 451.

7. Quoted in William Henry Hudson, *A Quiet Corner in a Library* (Chicago: Rand, McNally and Co., 1915), 121.

8. Allardyce Nicoll, *A History of English Drama, 1660-1900* (Cambridge, UK: Cambridge University Press, 1952, 3rd edition), II.

9. McBurney, "Introduction," xxv.

10. Hudson, *A Quiet Corner in a Library*, 122.

11. Ibid., 123.

12. Nicoll, *A History of English Drama* IV, 7.

13. *The Drama, or, The Theatrical Pocket Magazine*, published in London from 1821-1825 in 7 volumes. This reference is to the first issue (August 1821); 174-77.

14. *The Drama*, 1 (September 1821): 243.

15. Ibid., 1 (October 1821): 326.

16. Ibid., 2 (April 1822): 298.

17. Ibid., 3 (December 1822): 395.
18. Ibid., 4 (January 1823): 42.
19. Ibid., 4 (February 1823): 72.
20. Ibid., 4 (March 1823): 132-33, 158.
21. Ibid., 5 (December 1823): 254.
22. Ibid., 5 (January 1824): 296.
23. Ibid., 7 (January 1825): 219.
24. Ibid., 6 (June 1824): 206.
25. Ibid., 4 (December 1823): 430.
26. Fred Kaplan, *Dickens: A Biography* (New York: William Morrow and Co. Inc., 1988), 27.
27. Ibid., 24.
28. Ibid., 28.
29. Ibid., 28.
30. Ibid., 34-35.
31. "A Christmas Tree," *Household Words*, 2, no. 39 (December 21, 1850): 202.
32. "Getting Up A Pantomime," *Household Words*, 4, no. 91 (December 20, 1851): 426.
33. Mowbray Morris, "Charles Dickens," *Fortnightly Review* (December 1882): 762-69 as quoted in K. J. Fielding and A. W. Brice, "Bleak House and the Graveyard," in Robert B. Partlow, Jr., ed., *Dickens the Craftsman*, (Carbondale, IL: Southern Illinois University Press, 1970), 116.
34. Hudson, *A Quiet Corner in a Library*, 121-22.
35. Robert Garis, *The Dickens Theatre: A Reassessment of the Novels* (London: Oxford University Press, 1965), 40.
36. Ibid., 28.
37. Harry Stone, *Dickens and the Invisible World* (Bloomington; IN: Indiana University Press, 1979), 22.
38. Earle Davis, *The Flint and the Flame: The Artistry of Charles Dickens* (Columbia, MO: University of Missouri Press, 1963)
39. Sylvere Monod, *Dickens the Novelist* (Norman, OK: University of Oklahoma Press, 1968), 40. This was first published as *Dickens romancier* in 1953.
40. Ibid., 41.
41. William Axton, *Circle of Fire: Dickens Vision and Style and the Popular Victorian Theatre* (Lexington, KY: The University of Kentucky Press, 1966), 111.
42. Those books are: J. Hillis Miller, *Charles Dickens: The World of His Novels* (Cambridge, MA: Harvard University Press, 1959) and Steven Marcus, *Dickens: From Pickwick to Dombey* (London: Oxford University Press, 1965).

43. See the annotated bibliography of this whole debate in David Paroissien, ed. *Oliver Twist: An Annotated Bibliography* (New York: Garland Publishing Inc., 1986), 111-24.

44. See Steven Marcus, *Dickens: From Pickwick to Dombey* (London: Oxford UP, 1965), Chapter Three.

45. This devil imagery was first defined by Lauriat Lane Jr., "The Devil in Oliver Twist," *The Dickensian*, 52 (June 1956): 132-36.

46. Axton, *Circle of Fire*, 112.

47. Ibid., 136.

CHAPTER FIVE

1. J. Hillis Miller, *Charles Dickens: The World of His Novels* (Cambridge, MA: Harvard University Press, 1958): 296.

2. Jean-Paul Sartre, *Existentialism and Humanism*, trans. Phillip Mairet (London: Methuen, 1948): 26-27. "If one considers an article of manufacture . . . a paper-knife--one sees that it has been made by an artisan who had a conception of it . . . and [of] the pre-existent technique of production that . . . is, at bottom, a formula . . . Let us say, then, of the paper-knife that its essence--that is to say the sum of the formulae and the qualities which made its production and its definition possible--precedes its existence . . . Here, then, we are viewing the world from a technical standpoint, and we can say that production precedes existence."

3. Then down a green plain, leaping, laughing they run, / And wash in a river and shine in the sun / Then naked & white, all their bags left behind / They rise upon clouds, and sport in the wind / And the Angel told Tom, if he'd be a good boy / He'd have God for his father & never want joy.

4. Steven Marcus, *The Other Victorians* (London: Wiedenfeld and Nicolson, 1966): 105, 136-38.

5. Ibid., 105.

CHAPTER SIX

1. Louis A. Montrose in "Professing the Renaissance: The Poetics and Politics of Culture," *The New Historicism*, ed., H. Aram Veeser (New York: Routledge, 1989): 19, attributes this metaphor of "thick description" as a goal of the New Historicist project to Clifford Geertz.

2. Michel Foucault, *The Order of Things*, 130-32.

3. White, *Metahistory*, x.

4. Ibid., 4.
5. LaCapra, *Rethinking Intellectual History*, 304-5, is quoting Bakhtin, *Rabelais and His World*. tr. Helene Iswolsky (Cambridge, MA: Harvard University Press, 1968), 447.

Selected Bibliography

Altick, Richard. *The English Common Reader*. Chicago: University of Chicago Press, 1957.

Arac, Jonathan. "The Struggle for the Cultural Heritage: Christina Stead Refunctions Charles Dickens and Mark Twain." Reprinted in *The New Historicism*. Edited by H. Aram Visser.

Axton, William. *Circle of Fire: Dickens' Vision and Style and the Popular Victorian Theatre*. Lexington, KY: University of Kentucky Press, 1966.

Bann, Stephen. "The Sense of the Past: Image, Text and Object in the Formation of Historical Consciousness in Nineteenth-Century Britain." Reprinted in *The New Historicism*. Edited by H. Aram Visser.

Beeman, M. M. *Lloyd's of London: An Outline*. Kingswood, UK: Windmill Press, 1937.

Brookbank, Sir Joseph. *History of the Port of London*. London: Daniel O'Connor, 1921.

Camus, Albert. *Lyrical and Critical Essays*. Edited by Philip Thody. Translated by Ellen Conroy Kennedy. New York: Alfred A. Knopf, 1968.

Cazamian, Louis. *Le Roman Social en Angleterre*. Paris: H. Didier, 1934.

Childers, Joseph W. "History, Totality, Opposition: the New Historicism and Little Dorrit." *Dickens Quarterly* 6, no. 4 (December 1989).

Collins, Philip. "Dickens's Reading." *The Dickensian* 60 (1964).

Cooper, Anthony Ashley, Third Earl of Shaftesbury. *Characteristics of Men, Manners, Opinions, Times*. London, 1711.

Daleski, H.M. *Dickens and the Art of Analogy*. New York: Schocken Books, 1970.

Davis, Earle. *The Flint and the Flame*. Columbia, MO: University of Missouri Press, 1963.

DeRose, Peter I. "The Symbolic Sea of David Copperfield." *Proceedings of Conferences of College Teachers of English of Texas* 41 (1976).

Donovan, Robert A. *The Shaping Vision: Imagination in the English Novel from Defoe to Dickens*. Ithaca, NY: Cornell University Press, 1966.

Drama, the, or The Theatrical Pocket Magazine. London, 1821-1825.

Fielding, K. J. and Brice, A. W. "Bleak House and the Graveyard." In *Dickens the Craftsman*. Edited by Robert Partlow.

Ford, George H. *Dickens and His Readers*. Princeton, NJ: Princeton University Press, 1955.

Foucault, Michel. *Discipline and Punish: The Birth of the Prison*. Translated by Alan Sheridan. New York: Pantheon, 1978.

Fowles, John. *Shipwrecks*. Boston: Little, Brown and Co., 1975.

184 Dickens and New Historicism

Garis, Robert. *The Dickens Theatre: A Reassessment of the Novels.* London: Oxford University Press, 1965.

Godwin, William. *Enquiry Concerning Political Justice.* Toronto: University of Toronto Press, 1946.

Gold, Joseph. *Charles Dickens: Radical Moralist.* Minneapolis, MN: University of Minnesota Press, 1972.

Grant, Douglas, ed., *Sterne.* London: Rupert Hart-Davis, 1950.

Horton, Susan R. "Swivillers and Snivillers: Competing Epistemologies in *The Old Curiosity Shop.*" *Dickens Quarterly* 7, no.1 (March 1990).

House, Humphrey. *The Dickens World.* London: Oxford University Press, 1941.

Household Words: A Weekly Journal. 1850-1859. Conducted by Charles Dickens. London: Bradbury and Evans.

Hudson, William Henry. *A Quiet Corner in a Library.* Chicago: Rand, McNally and Co., 1915.

Huntress, Keith, ed., *Narratives of Shipwrecks and Disasters, 1586-1860.* Ames, IO: Iowa State University Press, 1974.

Hyde, Francis E. *Liverpool and the Mersey: The Growth of a Port, 1700-1970.* Newton Abbot, England: David and Charles, 1971

Jackson, T. A. *Charles Dickens: The Progress of a Radical.* London, Lawrence and Wishart, 1937.

Johnson, Edgar. *Charles Dickens: His Tragedy and Triumph.* Boston: Little, Brown and Co., 1951.

Kaplan, Fred. *Dickens: A Biography.* New York: William Morrow and Co. Inc., 1988.

Kennedy, G. W. "The Uses of Solitude: Dickens and *Robinson Crusoe.*" *The Victorian Newsletter* 52 (fall 1971).

Kronik, John W. "The Theory of Literary History." *PMLA: Publications of the Modern Language Association* 107, no. 1 (January 1992).

La Capra, Dominick. *History and Criticism.* Ithaca, NY: Cornell University Press, 1985.

Landow, George P. *Images of Crisis: Literary Iconography.* London: Routledge and Kegan Paul, 1982.

Lane, Lauriat, Jr. "The Devil in *Oliver Twist.*" *The Dickensian* 52 (June 1956).

Larson, Janet. "Apocalyptic Style in *Little Dorrit.*" *Dickens Quarterly* I, no. 2 (1984).

Leinwand, Theodore B. "Negotiation and New Historicism." *PMLA: Publications of the Modern Language Association* 105, no. 3 (May 1996).

Lindsay, Jack. *Charles Dickens: A Biographical and Critical Study.* New York: Philosophical Library, 1950.

Llosa, Mario Vargas. "Updating Karl Popper." *PMLA: Publications of the Modern Language Association* 105, no. 5 (October 1990).

Marcus, Steven. *Dickens: From Pickwick to Dombey.* New York: Basic Books, 1965.

Marcus, Steven. *The Other Victorians.* London: Wiedenfeld and Nicolson, 1966.

McBurney, William H. "Introduction" to *The London Merchant*. In *Regents Restoration Drama Series*. London: E. Arnold Ltd., 1965.

Miller, J. Hillis. *Charles Dickens: The World of His Novels*. Bloomington, IN: Indiana University Press, 1968. Reprint of Harvard University Press edition, 1958.

Miller J. Hillis. "The Geneva School." *The Virginia Quarterly Review* 63 (1967).

Monod, Sylvere. *Dickens the Novelist*. Norman, OK: University of Oklahoma Press, 1968.

Morris, Mowbray. "Charles Dickens." *Fortnightly Review*. December 1882.

Newlin, Claude M. "The Theatre and its Apprentices." *Modern Language Notes* 65 (1930).

Newson, Robert. *Dickens on the Romantic Side of Familiar Things: Bleak House and the Novel Tradition*. New York: Columbia University Press, 1977.

Nicoll, Allardyce. *A History of English Drama, 1660-1900*. Third Edition. Cambridge, UK: Cambridge University Press, 1952.

Palmer, William J. "*Hard Times*: A Dickens Fable of Personal Salvation." *The Dalhousie Review* 52 (1972).

Palmer, William J. *The Films of the Eighties: A Social History*. Carbondale and Edwardsville, IL: Southern Illinois University Press, 1993.

Paris, Barry. "Maximum Expression." *American Film* (October 1989).

Paroissien, David, ed. *Oliver Twist: An Annotated Bibliography*. New York: Garland Publishing Inc., 1986.

Partlow, Robert B. Jr., ed., *Dickens the Craftsman*. Carbondale and Edwardsville, IL: Southern Illinois University Press, 1970.

Pearlman, E. "David Copperfield Dreams of Drowning." *American Imago* 28 (1971).

Postle, Martin. "Dickens and The Fighting Temeraire." *Dickensian* 81 (1985).

Ross, Marlon. "Contingent Predilections: The Newest Historians and the Question of Method." *The Centennial Review* 34, no. 4 (Fall 1990).

Sartre, Jean-Paul. *Existentialism and Humanism*. Translated by Phillip Mairet. London: Methuen, 1948.

Stevenson, Lionel. "Dickens's Dark Novels 1851-1857." *Sewanee Review* 51 (1943).

Stewart, Garrett, "The Secret Life of Death in Dickens." *Dickens Studies Annual* 11 (1983).

Stoehr, Taylor. *The Dreamer's Stance*. Ithaca, NY: Cornell University Press, 1965.

Stone, Harry. *Dickens and the Invisible World*. Bloomington, IN: Indiana University Press, 1979.

Tennenbaum, Leonard, ed., *The Practice of Psychoanalytic Criticism*. Detroit, MI: Wayne State University Press, 1976.

Thornton, R. H. *British Shipping*. Cambridge, UK: Cambridge University Press, 1959.

Visser, H. Aram, ed. *The New Historicism*. New York: Routledge, 1989.

Ward, Sir A. W. "Introduction" to *The London Merchant.* In *The Belles Lettres Series.* London: E. Arnold Ltd., 1967.

Watt, W. W. "Introduction" to *Hard Times.* New York: Holt, 1958.

White, Hayden. *Tropics of Discourse: Essays in Cultural Criticism.* Baltimore: Johns Hopkins University Press, 1978.

Willey, Basil. *The Eighteenth-Century Background.* London: Chatto and Windus, 1946.

Wilson, Edmund. *The Wound and the Bow.* Cambridge, MA: Harvard University Press, 1941.

Wilson, John Harold, ed. *Six Eighteenth-Century Plays.* Boston: Houghton, Mifflin Co., 1963.

Zimmerman, Erich W. *Ocean Shipping.* New York: Prentice-Hall, 1923.

Index